Havens in a Storm

A book in the series

Cornell Studies in Political Economy

EDITED BY PETER J. KATZENSTEIN

A list of titles in this series is available at www.cornellpress.cornell.edu.

Havens in a Storm

THE STRUGGLE FOR GLOBAL TAX REGULATION

J. C. SHARMAN

CORNELL UNIVERSITY PRESS

Ithaca and London

First published 2006 by Cornell University Press

Printed in the United States of America

Library of Congress Cataloging-in-Publication Data

Sharman, J. C. (Jason Campbell).
    Havens in a storm : the struggle for global tax regulation / J. C. Sharman.
      p. cm. — (Cornell studies in political economy)
    Includes bibliographical references and index.
    ISBN-13: 978-0-8014-4504-0 (cloth : alk. paper)
    ISBN-10: 0-8014-4504-3 (cloth : alk. paper)
      1. Tax havens.   2. Taxation—International cooperation.   I. Title.   II. Series.
    K4464.5.S52 2006
    343.05'23—dc22

                                                                    2006019348

Cornell University Press strives to use environmentally responsible suppliers and materials to the fullest extent possible in the publishing of its books. Such materials include vegetable-based, low-VOC inks and acid-free papers that are recycled, totally chlorine-free, or partly composed of nonwood fibers. For further information, visit our website at www.cornellpress.cornell.edu.

Cloth printing   10 9 8 7 6 5 4 3 2 1

To my family and Bilyana

WHERE the remote Bermudas ride
In the ocean's bosom unespied,
From a small boat that row'd along
The listening winds received this song:
"What should we do but sing His praise
That led us through the watery maze
Unto an isle so long unknown,
And yet far kinder than our own?
Where He the huge sea-monsters wracks
That lift the deep upon their backs,
He lands us on a grassy stage
Safe from the storms, and prelate's rage."

—Andrew Marvell (1621–78)
"Bermudas"

CONTENTS

ACKNOWLEDGMENTS

The idea that became this book germinated after I had taught anarchist political philosophy in Bulgaria. With an instinctively realist outlook, students were incredulous that the tiny self-governing political units that anarchists demanded as the price of direct democracy could ever survive without being conquered or colonized. I began to wonder how very small states survive, why they have multiplied, and how they make their way in the international system. After a few abortive starts and a move to Sydney, I randomly happened on a report by the OECD that set up a struggle between the powerful member states of this organization and a group of tiny states and semi-sovereign political units labeled as tax havens. I knew nothing about tax havens, but this issue seemed to provide a good case from which to explore what happens when large and small states come into conflict. Whether small states can get away with annoying big states seems to be a question with a lot of potential for getting at some central issues in the field of International Relations.

The various drafts that became this book took shape over the following four years. During this time I learned much, mainly by seeking out the experts and practitioners in this very specialized field, from academia, government, international organizations, and the financial services industry. Somewhat to my surprise, but also to my infinite benefit, I found that people from each of these backgrounds were generally willing to give up their time to speak with someone with little or no background in the field, who offered nothing in terms of fees, relief from other pressing work, or even favorable publicity. Although I was an anonymous and jet-lagged junior scholar from a distant country, pitching up on some foreign shore, the people I spoke with were extremely patient and generous with their time. It is to these people, the majority of whom may not agree with much of the content of this book, that any contributions it might make are due.

Both outside and inside academia some people have made an especially prominent contribution in helping me along. From those on either side of the polarized politics of the issue, special thanks go to those involved in the cut and thrust: Andreas Antoniou, Richard Murphy, John Christensen, and especially Ben Coleman. The small, energetic and incredibly supportive group of political scientists, lawyers, anthropologists, economists, accountants, and business studies scholars working in and around this area have been consistently welcoming and willing to help, particularly Ronen Palan, Sol Picciotto, and Mark Hampton in the United Kingdom, Michael Webb and Ian Goldman in Canada, Greg Rawlings and Anthony van Fossen in Australia, and Bob Kudrle and David Spencer in the United States.

In Sydney, Graeme Gill, Darryl Jarvis, and John Hobson have provided crucial feedback after being repeatedly lumbered with various portions of this text. Gil Merom and Len Seabrooke provided the idea and encouragement to get in touch with Cornell University Press, and I have been extremely lucky in this match. Several research assistants were invaluable in tracking down a mountain of data on the most obscure topics I could come up with, and I am very grateful to Jesse Dillon Savage, Hugh Wehby, Ryan Thew, Jamie Drysdale, Sharni Chan, Michael Cohen, and especially Abhilash Puljal and Carla Wilshire for their hard work. The Consortium for Qualitative Research Methods workshop at Arizona State University and the European Consortium for Political Research workshop on International Organization and Implementation in Uppsala were both incredibly stimulating and exciting environments for me to reflect on many aspects of the book; the organizers and participants should know how beneficial these events were.

Two anonymous reviewers from Cornell University Press went above and beyond the call of duty in providing very incisive and helpful comments on matters large and small. I am extremely fortunate to have had such expert and generous readers and I am very grateful for all their hard work.

All the travel associated with the book has caused many to wonder if I spend all my time sipping cocktails on the beaches of exotic tropical islands, and others to suspect (I subsequently found out) that I was being bankrolled by one or more intelligence agencies. Unfortunately, the truth is far less glamorous. I would, however, like to thank the University of Sydney for its unstinting financial support and the Australian Research Council for Discovery Grant DP0452269, as well as my travel agent Catherine George for knowing the best way from Road Town to Rarotonga via Vaduz.

Finally, my greatest thanks are to Bilyana for her patience and for holding the fort during my frequent absences.

J. C. Sharman

Sydney, Australia

Havens in a Storm

Introduction

Tax is an area where states are most in need of international cooperation but least able to achieve it. This situation reflects the tension between contemporary economic changes and traditional sovereign prerogatives in a particularly stark form. From the early 1990s, policy makers in the world's richest and most powerful countries worried that changes in the international economy might severely undermine their ability to tax. Discussions about what could and should be done to address this new threat took place within several clubs of rich states: the Group of Seven nations (G7), the European Union (EU), and especially the Organisation for Economic Co-operation and Development (OECD), which was entrusted with formulating a response. The centerpiece of the strategy developed in 1996–98 was targeted at small states, labeled tax havens. These states were accused of fostering "harmful" tax competition at the global level by bidding for mobile investment with fiscal and regulatory concessions. The OECD sought to pressure tax havens to adopt a standard package of tax, financial, and banking regulations in order to tame this competitive dynamic and avert a "race to the bottom" in tax rates. The ensuing struggle between the two sides was above all a rhetorical contest. Both sides tried to garner the support of third parties, and the result of this contest hinged on concerns about losing face in the eyes of various transnational audiences. By 2002 the small state tax havens had prevailed, and the campaign to regulate international tax competition had failed. This book is devoted to explaining the nature and outcome of this struggle.

Why is this particular issue, an attempt to impose global regulations on tax havens, important enough to warrant a book? In economic terms, the sums at stake

1

are huge, amounting to hundreds of billions of dollars of tax revenue and trillions of dollars of investment. The effort to establish global tax standards also sheds light on the problem of implementing international regulation that creates losers as well as winners. If the policy outcome of interest is regulation, then the conceptual goals are to advance our understandings of the use of language for political ends, as well as how actors' concerns about the way they are thought of by others affect their decisions and behavior. In international politics as in everyday life, actors spend a lot of effort and time talking to one another and worrying about what others think of them. These concerns are crucial for explaining the development and outcomes of the tax competition controversy, but also many other disputes in world politics.

Since the 1980s one of the defining issues in the field of International Relations has been the significance of security fears versus utility gains in establishing cooperation between self-interested states in the international arena. Perhaps even more important has been the division between a rationalist approach, imported from economics, and a constructivist approach emphasizing culture, norms, and identity. Overlaying these concerns has been the more popular public discussion of globalization, especially in terms of what growing international economic flows and technological developments mean for the future of the state. The events to be examined are important for each of these controversies. If the transformative effect of economic globalization is to be seen anywhere, it should be in the area of international tax competition. For those scholars interested in solutions to international market failures and collective action problems, the initiative to establish global tax regulation is an important case of the limits of crafting and implementing regulatory solutions. Rather than the proposed regulations creating benefits all around, they threatened to create definite winners (the OECD and its member states) and losers (the tax havens). As such, the conflict is a study in power political economy. The centrality of conflict between state actors thus gives the tax competition controversy a strong affinity with realist concerns. The account of the initiative against harmful tax competition presented in this book aims both to address conceptual criticisms of constructivist explanations in general and to expand the coverage of this approach into international economics. Particular attention is given to several concepts associated with language use for political ends, such as rhetorical action, speech acts, and argument. The second major conceptual focus is on reputation in world politics, that is, on how actors are affected by the opinions others hold of them. These two concepts work together: the way an actor is perceived affects the impact of its rhetoric; the rhetoric of an actor, or of third parties about that actor, in turn affect the way others perceive it.

After examining the political and scholarly significance of the struggle between the OECD and tax havens, I lay out the basic shape of the argument, first as a whole and then in somewhat more detail by previewing the major points to be made in each chapter to follow. I move from sketching out the policy and intellectual background of the struggle (chapter 1), to analyzing the nature of the conflict and surveying the main themes of the rhetorical contest (chapters 2 and 3), and finally providing an explanation of the result centered around the concepts of rhetoric and reputation (chapters 4 and 5).

Globalization, Corporate Power, and Collective Action Problems

Unlike most arcane and abstruse terminology at the center of debates within political science, the term "globalization" has gained wide currency in the media and among politicians. Since the 1990s, many observers became increasingly convinced that "something must be done" to rein in globalization, with the idea of tax competition crystalizing more general fears about global capitalism run wild. The maximalist view of globalization emphasizes the sheer novelty and depth of change associated with the phenomenon. A basic element of this thesis is that economic change, particularly the rise in cross-border trade and financial flows, has far outpaced states' capacities to control it. As a result, governments are said to have less control over economic outcomes and to be losing power to corporations and impersonal market forces. The issue of tax competition is at the heart of disputes and speculation about globalization. International tax competition includes all the main elements of the conventional globalization story. A credible exit option for capital at the domestic level and a severe collective action problem among states at the international level leads to the ascendance of global markets over national polities.

The bare bones of the globalization thesis are that recent advances in communications, information, and transport technology drive and combine with economic deregulation and liberalization to provide the owners of capital with much more mobility than they have had previously ("at the click of a mouse," as the cliché has it). An increasingly large range of goods and services can be produced in more locations, thus fostering competition between countries for scarce investment. In turn, because governments are competing with one another for scarce capital, they must adopt market-friendly or, more narrowly, investor-friendly policies for fear of seeing capital locate in or relocate to other jurisdictions. Capital flight and disinvestment wreck governments' macroeconomic plans, but they also and more directly undermine their capacity by eroding the tax base. Governments that cannot tax effectively cannot do much else, and thus international tax competition for mobile capital—particularly intangible financial assets–threatens to undermine states' power. Taxation is crucial to economic sovereignty. If proponents of globalization as corporate power eclipsing state power are right in the area of tax competition, they can afford to be wrong about a lot of other things and still carry great weight.

At first glance, this version of the globalization thesis seems to provide a good fit with the failure to regulate tax competition. When states are center stage, the result is an upset: small states win out against the interests of core states. Yet if international capitalism as a system, capitalists as a class, or corporations as actors are seen as dominant, then the result becomes much less surprising. Thanks to globalization, corporate interests trump or determine those of even the most powerful states, and the actions of small states become largely irrelevant. This version of events would be an important challenge to our continuing preoccupation with the state as the central actor in world politics.

A different emphasis on the globalization dynamic (closer to that adopted by the OECD) retains states as the prime movers in international standard-setting but sees them as severely constrained by collective action problems. Even if a group, or the majority of the world's states, cooperate to tame the demands of mobile capital, the remaining free-riders will benefit by attracting more capital with the resulting economic benefits. The larger the cooperative group, the larger the benefit accruing to jurisdictions that opt out of such collaborative arrangements. Thus the familiar story: if a group or even all other states cooperate to regulate mobile capital, each state is better off defecting to attract the foreign investment looking for a home. And if other nations are not cooperating, then each nation is once again better off by "giving in" to investors' demands, particularly by cutting taxes. This version of the story is reminiscent of neoliberal institutionalism, a gently obsolescing term for scholars drawing on the conceptual tools of micro and new institutional economics to understand how rational states strive to achieve mutually beneficial cooperation. In line with the globalization thesis, this school is also impressed by the importance of collective action problems facing states looking to regulate the international economy, and again tends to put economic concerns at center stage. How is international tax competition important to this research program? Empirically, investigations of international economic cooperation have tended to concentrate on trade and monetary relations, and only then with finance and investment. Yet although international tax competition may mark an empirical departure from the usual questions considered by neoliberal scholars, the structure of the issue marks it out as conceptually at the core of their agenda. This book takes issue with the idea that the toughest problem in global regulatory solutions is solving collective action problems and deterring cheating. Instead, it argues that in this instance there is a conflict of preferences between high-tax and low-tax states and that the latter stand to lose out under the proposed regime.

Power, Conflict, and Constructivism

The attempt to regulate international tax competition quickly developed as a distributional conflict. Rather than overcome a collective action problem in search of mutual advantage, each coalition tried to impose its preferred solution over the opposition of the other. Given realists' emphasis on latent or actual conflict as the defining feature of international relations, the struggle over tax competition and regulation seems to fit squarely within their bailiwick. A realist explanation of the struggle over global tax regulation would lend further credibility to a view of international political economy built on an underlying competition for survival between states, especially as the outlines of the case confirm realist presuppositions concerning the centrality of conflict and power. Among realists, Stephen Krasner has been particularly influential in arguing that disputes over the distribution of gains resulting from international cooperation are more of an obstacle to this sort of collaboration than the fear of being cheated by free-riders. Finding solutions to a given problem of international coordination is at best only half the battle, because states are not indifferent to alternative solutions that produce different distributions of benefits. Which equilibrium solution is picked depends on states exerting their power over other states to secure a disproportionate share of the benefits. Thus, far from power concerns being distinct from international cooperation, Krasner and others have maintained that they are intimately related.

In fact, the struggle over global tax regulation is connected with an ever more basic realist presumption, one less concerned with the distribution of benefits but that instead emphasizes conflicts that create winners and losers in absolute terms. For tax havens confronted with the OECD initiative, the issue was not a contest over the division of benefits but instead the prospect of absolute losses. This case is relevant to recent realist works that focus on how international collaboration in the economic arena can leave some states worse off than they were at the status quo.[1] There was conflict between two large coalitions of states (for realists the OECD is not an autonomous actor) with opposed preferences over an issue of great importance to each side. These features mean that the struggle over global tax regulation is well within core realist territory. However conceived, the outcome largely hinged on power concerns. But the outcome of the struggle poses a challenge to realist assumptions in that the weak defeated the strong; this is an important anomaly that needs to be explained.

In studying the struggle over tax competition, constructivists have an opportunity to step in and explain an anomalous result: there are good theoretical reasons to believe such a conflict should have been resolved by coercion in favor of large rich states, yet it was not. In this way my book includes a competitive test of alternative explanations. Critics of constructivism have rightly pointed out, however, that this approach has a variety of weaknesses. These include a failure to specify causal mechanisms; the "finding" of a norm to explain every event; an inability to explain deviations from norms; unfalsifiable hypotheses; and the static cast of explanations. For example, structural accounts based on shared conceptions of appropriate behavior for a given actor in a given context (regulative norms) have difficulty with variation and change. However, proponents of norms as resources may abandon the distinctive contributions of constructivist research by reinstating a utilitarian approach to social action. Calls to reconcile both views are by themselves not very helpful without showing how this is to be achieved, conceptually and empirically. Constructivists are, however, rising to this challenge, and the controversy over global tax regulation provides an opportunity to respond to critics with better answers.

If the campaign to impose global standards on tax havens marks a departure from realism's traditional concern with "high politics" and security, this is also the case for constructivism, which has until recently tended to shy away from economic issues.[2] As Benjamin J. Cohen noted in 2002, "Even less has constructivism, as a formal analytical approach, yet begun to enter the mainstream of research on financial issues."[3] A major aim of this work is to show that contests over international economic regulation occur in a social context that is vital for understanding the nature and outcomes of these interactions. The focus is on political events and policy developments, not theoretical clashes. Despite my generally constructivist orientation, I emphasize conflict, interstate power plays, and calculated (rhetorical) strategies. This eclecticism allows for the inclusion of insights provided by other perspectives in the field.[4]

Reputation is central to the argument and is defined as the shared totality of thoughts and associations that actors hold for one another. This is consistent with sociological and dictionary definitions of reputation but broader than the definition common in political science and economics. In this sense, reputation is a quintessentially "social" concept, consistent with the book's broader goal of showing that international economic relations are also social relations. Equally important, rhetoric is defined as the deliberate use of language as a means to political ends. In this sense, rhetoric is not signaling or "cheap talk," but potentially can be persuasive independent of material factors. I aim to build on, but also advance, existing scholarship concerning rhetoric, argument, speech acts, and general political discourse. One contribution is the treatment of blacklisting as a speech act. Another is to show how the irreducible plurality of meanings in language can sometimes enable the weak to use the principles of the strong for their own subversive ends. Rhetoric and reputation are inseparably linked. This connection builds on the simple idea that the impact of speech often depends at least as much on who is speaking as on what is said. Much of the book is devoted to illustrating the recursive links between rhetoric and reputation in the struggle for global tax regulation.

Overall, I suggest that norms are somewhat more "up for grabs" and subject to contestation than is often assumed but that reputation is less susceptible to actors' control than the conventional view would have it. The ambiguity and uncertain fit between norms and rhetorical themes on the one hand and the interests of the powerful on the other leaves room for calculated moves from both the strong and the weak. For example, in chapter 2 I illustrate how particular norms come to be relevant to particular issues; how the same norm may have different effects on different actors; and how the effect of a norm on the same actor may change over time. This discussion also explores why actors comply with norms as shared beliefs about appropriate behavior, why they look at the consequences to reputation when norms are violated, and how these views in turn may generate material costs.

The rhetoric in the struggle over global tax regulation was overwhelmingly, though not exclusively, public, often aimed at third parties as much as the direct interlocutor. More than a thousand texts are part of the public record because the protagonists made and rebutted charges in the media, on their websites, through commissioned papers on the subject, and many other sources. Thus there is a clear trail to follow in studying the rhetorical contest. Equally important is the contemporaneous commentary from more or less neutral third parties. In addition to tracing the various rhetorical gambits, the media coverage, and related material give an indication of the fluctuating reputations of the parties involved. But by itself this public material is not sufficient to substantiate some of the most important points in the argument, in particular, the reconstruction of crucial decisions and the discovery of the intentions and motivations behind particular acts.

To remedy this shortcoming, and to push beyond conventional practice in the field, this book is heavily based on fieldwork and interviews conducted by the author with key participants in Antigua and Barbuda, Aruba, Australia, Austria, Barbados, Belgium, the British Virgin Islands, Canada, the Cayman Islands, the Cook Islands, Fiji, France, the Isle of Man, Jersey, Liechtenstein, Mauritius, Montserrat, Seychelles, St. Kitts and Nevis, the United Kingdom, the United States, and Vanuatu in the period 2002–2005. Those interviewed are from many different backgrounds: the public and private sectors in tax havens and OECD member states; the OECD and international organizations that opposed the OECD; third party international organizations who were publicly neutral, such as the World Bank, International Monetary Fund, Financial Action Task Force, UN Ad Hoc Group of Experts on International Cooperation in Tax Matters, and UN Office on Drugs and Crime; nongovernmental organizations and think tanks like Oxfam and the Center for Freedom and Prosperity; and academia and the media. The strongest degree of confirmation is given when different sources of evidence converge on a common picture or explanation. For instance, public and private (interview) sources from opponents and supporters of the OECD, as well as relatively independent third parties, agree that Bush administration criticism of the OECD in May 2001 was a product of ideologically motivated persuasion rather than corporate pressure. Often (and unsurprisingly) interviewees were more willing to admit errors committed by their own government or international organization than representatives of those same institutions did in public. For example, in public and in private opponents, third parties, and supporters outside the OECD itself agreed that the OECD was losing the rhetorical contest in 2000–2001, and that changes to the initiative around this time marked a major backdown. Private sources inside the OECD also square with this picture, but in public the organization has insisted that there were only "misunderstandings," and that the changes merely served to "refocus" the initiative. In line with the OECD's obvious interest in putting the best face on a bad situation, its public statements need to be heavily discounted in this context.

In engaging with the evidence, the first step is to derive the maximum number of observable implications from each element of the argument. These are than tested against material on the public record and interview evidence, with mutually confirming streams of independent evidence indicating strong support for a particular proposition.[5] The depth of interviews and fieldwork also allows for a detailed investigation of the process of policy implementation rather than just policy formulation.[6] Where appropriate, a competitive test of explanations against available evidence is performed, particularly in chapter 2, with regard to corporate power. Nonetheless, this book is not based on a winner-take-all battle royal between constructivist and rationalist alternatives. In one sense the book is a single case study. But "what is a case?" is more a question of approach than a given. And, as noted above, the book concentrates on maximizing observations for testing rather than simple description.[7]

Argument Summary

The main response to international tax competition has taken the form of a struggle between the OECD, on one hand, and three dozen small tax haven jurisdictions, on the other. I trace the course of this struggle as the large states delegated the conduct of the campaign to the OECD, which attempted to induce tax havens to reform their tax and financial codes in line with an OECD-devised blueprint. The stakes for both sides were high, including hundreds of billions of dollars of tax revenue each year for OECD member states, and a crucial source of economic viability for targeted small states. Despite their power, the large-state coalition failed in its central goal of preventing tax havens from using tax concessions to attract foreign investment.

It is necessary to explain not only the nature of the struggle but also why the contest was rhetorical and not a test of corporate lobbying or of economic or, worse, military strength. My goal is to explain how the striking outcome (small states prevailing over powerful ones) came about as it did, and why the rhetorical struggle went in favor of the tax havens as opposed to the OECD. Reputational issues are central to this story.

Regulative norms, generally shared conceptions of appropriate behavior, limited the scope of the struggle by ruling out certain means as illegitimate or unbecoming for members of the international community. Most prominently this included the use of military force, even though tax havens were essentially defenseless. However, these normative prohibitions also extended to the use of economic coercion. Unlike the clear and unambiguous prohibition of gunboat diplomacy, economic coercion is less strictly regulated by norms. Why did norms rule out economic pressure in this context? This strange reluctance to use materially efficient means, despite the presence of only an uncertain normative restraint, is explained by a determined rhetorical campaign waged by targeted states, the Commonwealth secretariat, and certain

U.S. lobby groups. This campaign persuaded key decision-makers to interpret the issue of economic coercion in terms of the principle of nonintervention, instead of the OECD's preferred parlance of legitimate "defensive measures." Another factor was uncertainty within the OECD secretariat itself over whether sanctioning small, developing nonmember economies really constituted appropriate behavior for a community of experts charged with furthering international prosperity and amity. Regulative norms of varying scope and specificity thus ensured that the conflict did not take the form of a military showdown or a campaign of economic coercion.

An alternative explanation might be that business interests, acting to protect their tax shelters, were crucial in sabotaging the OECD campaign. Although superficially plausible, a close investigation of the evidence fails to support this view. Corporate interests were deliberately shut out in the formative stages of the initiative, when they otherwise might have had most influence. Big business subsequently failed to mount a lobbying campaign along the lines of those conducted in response to other international tax policy issues. Interview evidence from participants on all sides, particularly relating to developments in Washington, also tends to disconfirm the existence of a powerful behind-the-scenes business lobbying effort.

Instead, the contest took the form of a rhetorical battle. Each side tried to associate itself with a few generally accepted principles, while accusing opponents of transgressing these principles. The resulting debate coalesced around several themes. The OECD portrayed the havens as "poaching" taxes rightfully belonging to others and facilitating criminal activities. It further claimed the role of the reasonable, enlightened interlocutor and champion of fair competition or the "level playing field." Conversely, those resisting the initiative characterized it as a coercive and hypocritical exercise in big-power bullying by states and organizations that sought to rewrite the rules of international economic competition in their own favor. Targeted jurisdictions claimed that they were the real guardians of fair competition and accused the OECD of being uninterested in genuine dialogue and reasoned debate. Detailing the course of the debate raises the question of why states or other international actors should care about being seen to be in the wrong, or why they should devote energy to putting their opponents in this position. In both cases the answer is reputation.

Although eschewing the use of economic sanctions, the OECD could exert pressure on targeted jurisdictions by formally blacklisting them. Rather than empty bombast ("mere rhetoric"), this approach threatened tax havens in an extremely sensitive area: their reputation in the eyes of international investors. Tax havens spent (and spend) a great deal of effort trying to project an image of stability, security, and probity to potential foreign investors, and negative judgments by authoritative international actors threatened to wreck these carefully cultivated reputations. Blacklisting is in itself an action that brings about a change in the condition of the referent. Rather than being a description or signal for an action that changes some part of the world, blacklisting *is* an action that changes some part of the world. In this context, once jurisdictions were blacklisted, their reputations were changed. They were left vulnerable to capital flight because third party investors were more likely to either avoid or withdraw from listed states.

Targeted jurisdictions countered with a more indirect strategy. They declared that the OECD was in violation of the very same principles it was created to uphold, particularly the virtues of market competition and the need to bring about change by consensus. Opponents sought to delegitimize the organization, win the sympathy of third parties, and split the coalition of states arrayed against them. By 2002 they had achieved these aims. The OECD had to be sensitive to what others thought of it, as it was dependent on its narrow functional identity and reputation to achieve policy influence in the absence of other means (such as conditional loans), and to convince its members who paid the bills that they were getting value for their money. To the extent that third parties were persuaded by targeted states and other critics that the OECD was being untrue to its own values and was acting inappropriately in the tax competition campaign, the OECD suffered a loss of institutional standing that directly reduced its effectiveness. The authority of the OECD depends on its being perceived as an impartial, expert, rational-legal bureaucracy. The OECD couldn't afford to ignore the verdict of the rhetorical contest. The OECD backed down not only because it feared negative consequences in the future but also because by 2000–2002 there were signs that these consequences already existed. The tide of opinion ran against the initiative, and the previous dominance of the OECD's Committee on Fiscal Affairs in setting international tax standards came under threat from newly created competitors.

The secretariat and member states also faced internal pressures and had to decide on the appropriate, rather than just the instrumentally optimal, course of action. With the unexpectedly tough resistance to the campaign, doubts emerged within the OECD secretariat about whether the organization should be in the business of imposing its recommendations on nonmembers instead of seeking to persuade them. Canada, Australia, and New Zealand came to favor a more consensual solution without blacklisting or sanctions—in part because of Commonwealth links with tax havens. Finally, Caribbean jurisdictions made common cause with conservative think tanks in Washington, such as the Center for Freedom and Prosperity, which convinced congressmen, senators, and new political appointees to the Bush administration Treasury Department to withdraw U.S. support for the campaign in May 2001.

Given the particular restrictions that applied to the OECD and the eventual result, it may be asked why core states did not foresee these problems and choose a different institutional steward. However, the weaknesses of the OECD that eventually stymied the campaign were the same qualities that had initially recommended it: its reputation for technical expertise and impartiality and, most of all, its ability to facilitate consensus among its members on sensitive topics. In 1996 securing a common position on tax regulation that the United States, France, Germany, Britain,

Japan, Switzerland, and the other twenty-two members could agree on looked much harder than convincing tiny island states to sign on.

The OECD suffered a defeat when the central goal of the initiative—the prevention of tax havens from "poaching" geographically mobile investment by means of tax and regulatory concessions—was abandoned. The OECD was also forced to disavow the exclusive, confrontational approach toward nonmember tax havens that had characterized the initiative and revert to its traditional methods of dialogue, peer pressure, and persuasion. Although in 2002 the OECD was thought to have salvaged a consolation prize in the form of commitments from tax havens to exchange financial information, this achievement largely unraveled over the following three years.

Overview

Chapter 1 provides historical background to the issue of tax competition and tax havens, as well as the development of the central dispute. It briefly summarizes economists' theories of tax competition. These range from the analogy that competition between governments promotes efficiency in the same way as competition between firms, to more recent writings on "negative fiscal externalities" and empirical data on the responsiveness of investment decisions to tax differentials. Policies meant to regulate international tax competition have often overlapped with distinct but related campaigns against money laundering and more general efforts to shore up the international financial system. In both instances a closed-membership international organization of core states agreed in advance on a package of regulations relating to tax and trade in financial services and then worked to impose these rules and practices on nonmember small states. Moving to the initiative against "harmful" tax competition, particular attention is given to the initial 1998 report that lays out the OECD's diagnosis of the problem and the rationale for the subsequent campaign. The report defines key terms (harmful tax competition, tax havens) that form the basis for the subsequent dispute, sketches out the acceptable standards, and finally presents the OECD's strategy to bring violating states into compliance. The report has subsequently been amplified in press releases and by sequel reports in 2000, 2001, and 2004.

The general policy and scholarly context of the campaign now established, in chapter 2 I argue that the bounds and nature of the controversy were set by regulative norms. My goal is to show why the struggle was not decided by armed force, economic sanctions, or corporate power. Regulative norms constrained large countries and the OECD by ruling out certain means as inappropriate in the context of this dispute. Military force was obviously ruled out on normative grounds, because the arguments that military solutions would have been "objectively inefficient" are implausible. Economic coercion would have had a devastating effect on small island economies, yet this was not used because of normative prohibitions regulating the use of sanctions and the identity of the OECD, especially its technocratic or epistemic authority. Instead of this prohibition being deeply internalized or taken for granted, small states in the firing line and their supporters managed to persuade third parties and sectors within the OECD to see the issue in terms of the norm of nonintervention, rather than the OECD's gloss of "defensive measures." Key policy-makers and third parties faced with the option of sanctions asked themselves, "What is the appropriate course of action in this context?" Each side aimed to persuade others with distinct norms that legitimated or delegitimated this course of action, with the latter mustering more converts.

A leading alternative explanation rests on the power of corporate interests (spurred into action by OECD efforts to close down tax shelters) to sabotage the initiative through behind-the-scenes lobbying of G7 governments, especially the Bush administration in the United States. This explanation has little empirical support. Corporate power might well be most influential by preventing policy initiatives inimical to business interests ever reaching the agenda, but given the public release of the report in 1998, agenda-setting power was not exercised. There was little overt participation or lobbying from business interests in the way commonly observed in comparable international regulatory exercises, such as the OECD's work on the taxation of e-commerce or the EU Savings Tax Directive. The idea of the "hidden hand of corporate power" fails to find support in the anonymous interviews with key participants from the private and public sector carried out in twenty-two countries. Those interviewed are unanimous that the Bush administration's change of heart concerning the initiative owed more to ideologically motivated think-tankers who won converts across the political spectrum than to money politics or the involvement of business elites. Corporate power was not so much hidden as absent.

Rhetoric, argument, and attempts at moral suasion were the predominant means employed by both the OECD core-state coalition and the tax havens. Each side sought to publicly persuade or shame the other, but even more to win the sympathy and mobilize the disapproval of third parties—states, international organizations, transnational policy communities, the media and domestic political actors. By choice and force of circumstance, the dispute was very public, with a wealth of data on each charge and countercharge. In chapter 3 I examine and classify the main strands of the public campaign and rhetorical contest over tax competition and tax havens. The rhetorical campaign involved the OECD secretariat, member states and targeted countries, other international organizations (EU, Caribbean Community, Pacific Islands Forum), international accountancy and legal firms, domestic political actors, think tanks, academics, and the media. The dominant themes of the rhetorical contest were illegitimate secrecy versus legitimate privacy; the sovereign right to set tax law versus the responsibility to observe other states' sovereignty; consistency and the "level playing field"; and following and violating the norms of debate. Both sides generally agreed on which themes were important, but each cast itself as in compliance and its opponent as in violation.

In chapters 5 and 6 I recast this rhetorical struggle in conceptual terms to explain the outcome, a qualified tax haven victory and a qualified OECD defeat. Above all, it is necessary to show why each side should care about its fortunes in the rhetorical contest. The main (somewhat successful) rhetorical tactic used by the OECD against its opponents was to attack the reputations of tax havens. Public statements charging that listed jurisdictions did not measure up to accepted international regulatory standards were not an implicit *threat* of sanctions; they *were* sanctions, in and of themselves. This notion of "words as deeds" is examined in terms of J. L. Austin's concept of speech acts. It is argued that rather than just describing the world, black-listing as a particular form of speech act was an action that remade the world, specifically by damaging tax havens' reputations. In contrast, third-party perceptions of tax havens as investment destinations constitute the most important determinant of economic success or failure for the small states.

Because the effectiveness of these speech acts was a product both of the havens' and the OECD's dependence on reputation, a large part of the chapter is devoted to explaining this concept. The definition of reputation advanced in this book is broader than and differs from the view currently dominant in the field. First, reputation is argued to be more of a relational concept, the way others think of an actor, than a property or "economic good" that can be owned, spent, and accumulated by that actor.[8] Second, reputation has a fundamentally intersubjective character as a social fact, rather than being only a collection of individual opinions. Finally, reputation is often important in inverse proportion to the amount of information available about an actor, and is based on the totality of associations and feelings about a referent, rather than just inductive calculations from past behavior.

Chapter 5 builds on the conceptual discussions of the previous chapter to look at the effect on the OECD of the rhetorical contest, especially in the light of its back down in 2001–2002. The OECD's policy influence and institutional effectiveness depend on its being perceived as an "apolitical," rational, and expert bureaucracy, but this image proved to be a two-edged sword. On the one hand, it enabled core states to reach consensus on regulatory standards, and it lent authority to criticisms of tax havens. But on the other hand, this reputation also ruled out certain means as inappropriate and made the OECD especially sensitive to reverses in the rhetorical contest. Schimmelfennig's idea of "rhetorical action," the strategic use of norm-based arguments, is crucial in this respect, as is "rhetorical self-entrapment." Powerful actors may be bound by verbal commitments or principles announced earlier on, even after unforeseen changing circumstances make these commitments a liability. The self-interested actions of the weak are often crucial to this process of binding or entrapment, as they highlight any backsliding from earlier positions. As a result, the powerful can only renege at the expense of their standing and influence in the community. For example, tax havens used elements of dominant ideas such as free markets, deregulation, and the virtues of competition, propounded by large countries but especially the OECD itself, to further their own aims and resist the imposition of common regulations. Subordinate actors may be able to turn ambiguity to their advantage, because even when dominant actors use language with the intention of entrenching their position, the meaning is often flexible or contestable enough to be subverted and appropriated by the weak, as happened in the case of the OECD and the tax havens.

The conclusion recapitulates the findings on the course and result of the struggle over "harmful" tax competition and examines the general implications to be drawn for world politics and International Relations theory. The discussion sums up the theoretical significance of the understandings of rhetoric and reputation presented for the field. The conclusion also looks to current and future multilateral initiatives that may once again see a similar conflict with the same dramatis personae. The tax competition campaign was deliberately designed as a prototype for regulating other areas of the international economy using an approach that combined a limited negotiating circle with a global reach. To what extent have these expectations been revised or discarded? To what extent does the fate of the campaign against harmful tax competition cast doubt on the viability of other international organizations' regulatory initiatives?

Chronological Overview

The story of the initiative against harmful tax competition is not presented chronologically in this book, so I include here a summary account of the sequence of events. Formal negotiations within the OECD Committee on Fiscal Affairs were launched in 1996 after consultations with the European Commission and in line with a request from the G7 heads of state summit. This summit in Lyon called on the OECD to respond to the new problem of "harmful tax competition." Co-chaired by the Japanese and French representatives, discussions in the Committee on Fiscal Affairs went on for two years before the results were published as *Harmful Tax Competition—An Emerging Global Issue* in April 1998. The report, discussed extensively in chapter 1, was crucial in laying out the diagnosis of the problem at hand and in recommending a solution. In essence, harmful tax competition referred to the practice whereby a jurisdiction bid for a portion of other countries' tax bases by tailoring its tax code specifically to attract mobile foreign capital. One solution advanced was for OECD member states to draw up a list of "potentially harmful preferential tax regimes" in their own tax codes through self- and peer-assessment. Members would then commit to freeze the introduction of such measures and dismantle those that did exist by 2003 or 2005 at the latest.

Much more radical, however, were the plans to induce nonmember tax havens to join members in adopting a common set of minimal standards. Tax havens were said to be distinguished by a combination of low tax rates, little substantial economic activity, lax regulation, a lack of transparency, and being perceived to be a tax haven. The slate of solutions to tax haven–driven harmful tax competition was centered on the demand that these jurisdictions eschew special concessions to attract foreign investment, especially those that did not generate "substantial economic activity." The 1998 report concluded that the irreducibly global problem of tax competition could only be met with a global response and specified a list of "coordinated defensive measures" that could be applied by members to uncooperative tax havens that refused to adopt the OECD's regulatory demands. Significantly, Switzerland and Luxembourg, two of the biggest competitors in the market for international financial services, publicly dissented from the report and refused to be bound by any of its provisions, a fact that became a constant embarrassment to the OECD.

The release of the report did gain some media coverage, but initially received surprisingly little attention from either the financial services industry or the jurisdictions that later came to be targeted as tax havens. This began to change in 1999, as the OECD's new Forum on Harmful Tax Practices began compiling a list of states to be "named and shamed" as tax havens; this carried the ultimate threat of "coordinated defensive measures" to be applied to those that failed to adopt the OECD's prescriptions. Forty-seven states were reviewed, with forty-one adjudged prima facie to meet the criteria for being a tax haven. Jurisdictions began both to lobby to be left off the list and to criticize the whole project. Ahead of the official release of the blacklist of tax havens in late June 2000, six jurisdictions (Bermuda, Cayman Islands, Cyprus, Malta, Mauritius, and San Marino) committed to reform their laws and regulations in line with the requirements of the 1998 report, specifically by agreeing to abolish special concessions for foreign investors, abstain from attracting investment not engaged in "substantial economic activity," and exchange tax information with OECD member states. In June 2000, a blacklist was released officially labeling the remaining thirty-five jurisdictions as tax havens, and the listed jurisdictions were given one year to comply with the new OECD-mandated regulations or be faced with being listed once again, this time as "uncooperative tax havens," and sanctioned.

Jurisdictions Listed as Tax Havens by the OECD in June 2000

Andorra	Maldives
Anguilla	Marshall Islands
Antigua and Barbuda	Monaco
Aruba	Montserrat
Bahamas	Nauru
Bahrain	Netherlands Antilles
Barbados	Niue
Belize	Panama
British Virgin Islands	Samoa
Cook Islands	Seychelles
Dominica	St. Lucia
Gibraltar	St. Kitts and Nevis

(continued)

Grenada	St. Vincent and the Grenadines
Guernsey	Tonga
Isle of Man	Turks and Caicos
Jersey	U.S. Virgin Islands
Liberia	Vanuatu
Liechtenstein	

However, the tone of the sequel report released in 2000, *Towards Global Tax Co-operation*, was slightly less confrontational than its predecessor, and the term "harmful tax competition" was replaced by "harmful tax practices."

During 2000, and particularly after the blacklist was released, criticism of the campaign and the OECD itself steadily increased. A meeting of Commonwealth Finance Ministers in Malta in September 2000 attacked the initiative as harsh and unfair, and from this point the Commonwealth secretariat became involved on behalf of targeted jurisdictions, as the majority of those listed were former or current British colonial possessions. A few other jurisdictions made commitments to the OECD, either in the form of a press release or by signing an OECD Memorandum of Understanding that set out the slate of reforms to be implemented. In December 2000, the Isle of Man made an independent commitment to the OECD but managed to include the crucial proviso that it would only consider itself bound to introduce reforms if all OECD members did likewise, that is, including Switzerland and Luxembourg.

In late 2000 the Secretary General of the Commonwealth on behalf of the Prime Minister of Barbados invited the OECD to co-chair a meeting on the initiative with affected jurisdictions in Barbados. Small state officials later identified this meeting, which took place in January 2001, as crucial in coordinating their efforts, which had previously been undertaken in isolation or, at best, at a regional level. The OECD agreed to set up a Joint Working Group on harmful tax competition, with equal representation for OECD member and nonmember states. Little came of the Working Group, but it did slow momentum toward sanctions and set a precedent for including tax havens in a deliberative forum on an equal footing with OECD members. After these meetings, with the help of the Commonwealth, the International Tax and Investment Organisation (ITIO) was formed to consolidate linkages between small states and resist OECD demands. In Washington, meanwhile, the Center for Freedom and Prosperity was set up in October 2000 with the explicit aim of derailing the OECD's efforts. In conjunction with influential right-wing think tanks such as the Heritage Foundation and Cato Institute, it immediately began lobbying influential figures on Capitol Hill. Thus between June 2000 (the time of the listing of the thirty-five jurisdictions) and January 2001 strong opposition to the initiative against harmful tax competition had coalesced at the international level and in the United States. The consensus behind the initiative began to further erode within the OECD as Australia, Canada, and New Zealand (members of both the Commonwealth and the OECD) also began privately to signal reservations about the initiative.

The members of the newly elected Bush administration, especially Treasury Secretary Paul O'Neill, were at first unsure whether or not to support the OECD, in contrast to the Clinton-era Lawrence Summers, who had been a driving force behind the "name and shame" approach. While the Joint Working Group ground to a halt after bitterly contested meetings in London and Paris in February–March 2001, the Center for Freedom and Prosperity worked hard to gain more supporters in Congress and among the new administration. This lobbying paid off spectacularly on 10 May 2001 when O'Neill made some very serious public criticisms of the OECD initiative, reproducing the very points earlier made by the tax havens. Other OECD members and the secretariat, who had been given no advance warning of O'Neill's volte-face, were incensed and dismayed. The July 2001 deadline for sanctions was quietly dropped.

The harmful tax competition initiative did not quite die, however. As a consequence of the terrorist attacks of September 11, 2001, new demands for financial transparency were made in the name of combating terrorism. Tax havens could not be complacent. In November 2001 the OECD published a progress report on the newly "refocused" initiative, marking the defeat of the campaign as originally conceived. Gone was the prohibition on tax codes meant to lure foreign investment and the accompanying tax revenue. Protecting tax revenue had been the basic goal of the exercise as spelled out in the 1998 report. Through 2002 the OECD was forced to abandon its exclusive, confrontational approach and include tax havens in consensual decision-making bodies concerning the initiative. I understand this to be the end of the OECD's attempt to regulate international tax competition as such, though it is important to follow the story further. Despite this climb-down, the OECD was dealt further defeats.

From 2002, the much-reduced aim was to secure commitments to exchange information between jurisdictions on civil tax as well as on criminal matters (i.e., distinct from exchanging information on fraud, money laundering, drug trafficking, and so on) by 2006. Even this limited agreement was still too much for Switzerland and Luxembourg, while Austria and Belgium also defected. The deadline for listed states to commit to exchanging information was extended to February 2002, with the deadline for sanctions pushed back to April 2003. Having fought off the most serious threat, the listed jurisdictions rushed to commit to information exchange, with the important rider that no reforms would be undertaken until every single OECD member state and listed state had committed to do the same (the "Isle of Man clause"). Although by May 2002 seven jurisdictions were labeled as "uncooperative tax havens" (Andorra, Liberia, Liechtenstein, Monaco, Nauru, the Marshall Islands, and Vanuatu), the OECD had repudiated its earlier confrontational approach. Tax havens, now referred to as "participating partners," negotiate on an equal basis in a new Global Tax Forum with OECD members, and standards are binding on none until all have agreed to be bound. Even with the much more modest aim of information exchange, the initiative suffered further embarrassment in January 2003 when an internal EU deal on the taxation of nonresident savings excused Austria, Belgium, and Luxembourg from participating in tax-information exchange until at least 2011. Tax havens pointed out that as the OECD had promised that no jurisdiction would be bound by the new standards until every OECD member had made such a commitment, they were in effect not committed to anything. Finally, tax havens won the concession in October 2003 that even if every OECD member agreed to the new standards, they still would not be bound to introduce these regulations until third party competitors such as Singapore and Hong Kong had done likewise. As a result, the OECD abandoned the goal of establishing a uniform standard and timetable for the exchange of civil tax information, freeing "participating partners" from the commitments they had made earlier. Thus the OECD had to give up its ambition to regulate international tax competition. Furthermore, it had abandoned the exclusionary "name and shame" approach and had been forced back on its traditional methods of seeking to raise regulatory standards by dialogue, persuasion, and peer pressure.

A Note on Terms

Given that I emphasize the significance of language and rhetoric, a remark on terminological bias is in order. The term "small states" needs only a technical clarification; the use of "tax haven" and "harmful tax competition" is more complicated. I discuss the jurisdictions listed by the OECD as "states," even though some are dependencies of states and do not have formal juridical sovereignty in their own right. I use this simplification because each jurisdiction has control over its own tax and financial laws and regulations, and because on no occasion could the metropolitan state simply command its dependency to come into line. Aruba and the Netherlands Antilles in the Caribbean are coequal with the Netherlands as part of the Dutch Kingdom. Niue and the Cook Islands in the Pacific are in voluntary "free association" with New Zealand. Although London can in theory use an Order in Council to impose legislation on United Kingdom Overseas Territories—these include Anguilla, the British Virgin Islands, the Cayman Islands, Montserrat, Turks and Caicos in the Caribbean, Bermuda in the Atlantic, Gibraltar in the Mediterranean—or suspend self-government and impose direct rule, this would be unprecedented for fiscal measures and has never been seriously considered. The United Kingdom does not even have these powers over the Crown Dependencies (the Isle of Man, Jersey, and Guernsey), the latter two Channel Islands being the remnants of the Duchy of Normandy, while the Isle of Man was once part of a Norwegian and then a Scottish kingdom. The U.S. Virgin Islands has less autonomy, because it has self-governance under a 1954 act of Congress and has almost exactly the same tax code as the United States but allows tax exemptions for some qualified foreign companies.[9]

Talking about "tax havens" and "harmful tax competition" is an altogether different kind of simplification and in some eyes a much less forgivable one. Very few of the jurisdictions that I call (and, until 2002, the OECD called) tax havens would regard this term as either fair or accurate, and they would most strenuously deny its application. How, then, can a work about rhetoric, reputation, and stigma be so insensitive as to use such a loaded term? Although "tax haven" elicits a pained look and quick correction from officials of such a jurisdiction, it is more immediately meaningful to nonspecialists than more euphemistic terms like "offshore financial center" (OFC) or "small state international financial center" (IFC), which, in any case, are well on their way to being stigmatized too. Tax havens, or OFCs and IFCs, would like to be considered the same sort of entities as financial centers like London and New York. Although this claim has some merit, I believe the line between them is too strongly drawn in the thoughts of both specialists and nonspecialists, so much so that it cannot be erased. As I discuss in chapter 5, to a certain extent individuals can change the discourse, but to a much larger extent we must work with the conventions as they are (biased as they may be) if we want to communicate, and this logic leads to us accepting the term "tax haven."

Also, the routine use of a term like "harmful tax competition" could also be attacked for bias in reproducing a tendentious and contested term coined by the OECD. Many deny that there is such a thing (is tax competition really harmful? If so, when and for whom?). As a result of such criticism, the OECD itself thought better of the term, looking to relabel its campaign retroactively as the initiative against harmful tax *practices*. This later rendition tends to obscure what was new and most significant about the OECD campaign and marks the first stage of the OECD's retreat. Although I discuss in chapter 1 why the term, harmful tax competition, is contentious, I won't place the term in scare quotes, which quickly become tiresome. Their lack, however, should not be interpreted as an endorsement of the term.

CHAPTER ONE

Death, Taxes, and Tax Havens

The struggle between rulers and ruled over the collection of taxes, whether for the maintenance of the city-state, the feudal domain, the empire, or the modern state, has been one of the longest and most keenly fought contests in world history. The efforts of subordinate populations to escape taxation have taken on a vast array of forms; they stand as an enduring testament to human ingenuity. From great revolutions that overthrew ancient dynasties and recurrent peasant rebellions to countless daily evasions, dissimulations, and adaptations, conflict over tax has been a prime motive of political change throughout the centuries. Charles Tilly has taken the lead in investigating the interaction of war, taxes, and the development of the state across a millennium of history.[1] The vast majority of attempts to conceal taxable revenue from the ruler's agents have taken place within the borders of a given polity. Yet despite the comparatively recent pedigree of many of the tax havens and the even more contemporary notion of international tax competition, neither is without precedent, perhaps even in ancient times.[2]

This chapter is devoted to four main tasks. The first is to give a brief account of the rise of tax havens and the sorts of services they provide. The second is to put the OECD's initiative against harmful tax competition in the broad policy context of other European- and U.S.-sponsored multilateral initiatives that either had similar goals of restraining international tax competition or adopted similarly confrontational tactics in trying to secure the compliance of small states. Relevant are the efforts of the EU in relation to tax competition and the Financial Action Task Force's efforts to pressure tax havens to adopt new regulations against money laundering. The third task is to review the prevailing debate over the positive or negative aspects of tax competition among economists, a debate that has been strangely underutilized by the OECD and its opponents. Finally, in this chapter I set out the OECD's case against "unfair" or "harmful" tax practices: how they can be recognized, why they are harmful, and what should be done about them.

In a 1998 report that provided the rationale and road map for the campaign to date, the OECD Committee on Fiscal Affairs presented its diagnosis of harmful tax competition. It proposed a set of minimal standards, together with a strategy for bringing countries inside and outside the organization into line. This confrontational "top-down" strategy marked a crucial departure for the OECD. It also tested a new strategy of global regulation by international organizations in general. In contrast to the usual methods of inclusive rule-making, consensus-seeking, peer review, and issuing models of best practice, the campaign against tax havens sought to secure the unwilling compliance of nonmember states that had no say in designing or evaluating the standards against which they were to be judged. My final section is a link to the argument about how regulative norms defined the scope of the conflict and the means available (chapter 2) and the content and significance of the public exchange of claims and counterclaims (chapters 3, 4, and 5).

The Birth and Proliferation of Tax Havens

The term "tax haven" lacks a clear definition, and its application is often controversial and contested. The term has increasingly become pejorative. As discussed in chapter 4, what is counted as a tax haven has much less to do with objective features of the tax regime or financial regulations than a country's reputation and the motives of the observer. This caveat to one side, the development of tax havens, from the late nineteenth century up until the last few decades, cannot be adequately explained by any single variable. Historically, tax haven status has often resulted from the unintended consequences of quirks of the legal or tax codes or through the interaction of changing economic circumstances with static rules and regulations. By the 1980s at the latest, however, small island states in particular began to copy established tax haven jurisdictions as a deliberate development strategy. It was easy to pass a suite of legislation adapted from the state of the art in the field.[3] Often this development strategy was adopted by small states on the advice of former colonial powers and development agencies.

No two lists of tax havens look quite the same; the number of entries ranges anywhere from around twenty to almost one hundred jurisdictions.[4] Nevertheless, there is usually a good deal of overlap in the lists of places included. Featuring prominently on these lists is a cluster of small island states in the Caribbean and the South Pacific. Many others are European microstates and dependencies that escaped the pull of centralizing states in the modern era. In Central America, Belize and Panama are often included; in Africa, Liberia; in the Indian Ocean, the Seychelles and Mauritius; in the Persian Gulf, Dubai and Bahrain; and in Asia, the Malaysian island of Labuan, Brunei, and perhaps such prominent financial centers as Singapore and Hong Kong, although left off the OECD list, might qualify. Crucially for the OECD campaign, two of its own members, Luxembourg (also a member of the EU) and Switzerland, are often classified as tax havens.

The oldest present-day tax havens are in Europe; they are holdovers from a previous era and exist in association with a larger neighbor. The Isle of Man, Gibraltar, and the Channel Islands are affiliated with Great Britain; Monaco is affiliated with France; Andorra is affiliated with France and Spain; San Marino is affiliated with Italy; and Liechtenstein with Switzerland.[5] Palan notes that

> The distinguishing feature of European tax havens . . . is that they tend to be small anachronistic formations. Originally, these jurisdictions did not set themselves purposefully to establish laws that would attract tax evaders; rather, it was the other way around: the world around them launched on a course that has led to an unprecedented rise in taxation and regulation. These small and conservative states refused to follow suit.[6]

Specifically, European tax havens such as Andorra and Monaco declined to follow the example of larger states that introduced personal and corporate income taxes, or they have combined low taxes with the Swiss model of banking secrecy laws, like Liechtenstein.

Switzerland has in many instances been the standard-bearer for European tax havens. Immediately after World War I, investors responded to rising taxes elsewhere in Europe by transferring their savings to Swiss accounts, though as far back as the French Revolution exiled aristocrats had sought to safeguard their wealth in Geneva's banks. The security of Swiss bank accounts was enhanced when in 1934 the federal government passed strict banking secrecy laws that made it a criminal offense to pass on any details relating to accounts and account-holders to either foreign or domestic government agencies. Switzerland differs from most countries in adopting a particularly narrow definition of tax evasion, which sharply limits its obligations to exchange information with foreign authorities on tax matters.[7]

Outside of Europe, a large variety of countries have evolved into or have deliberately chosen to become tax havens by copying existing models. The diversity of this list notwithstanding, the conventional picture of a tax haven is a small "island in the sun," recently independent and (apart from financial services) relying on a handful of commodities and tourism for economic viability. This stereotype has a good deal of truth to it. Naylor points to the importance of organized crime networks displaced from Cuba by the revolution of 1959 in explaining the rise of Caribbean havens. However, even though laundering drug money was a crucial fillip for some havens, this is an overly simplistic account.[8] The regional leaders were the Bahamas, Bermuda, and the Cayman Islands. The latter two British dependencies, with their long tradition of self-rule and fiscal autonomy, have successfully attained first world standards of living, thanks to financial services. Rather than competitively cutting taxes, these islands merely maintained traditional low or zero rates. Successive battles with foreign (mainly U.S.) tax authorities meant that firms gradually expanded on their initial "brass plate" or letterbox presences to shift employees and operations to the islands in order to beat the accusation of having "no substantial economic activity" in the low-tax jurisdiction. Ironically, but in some ways typically, the sequence of pressure from the U.S. tax authorities and corporate responses meant that successively greater layers of substance were added to the fiction of island-based companies until, for example, Bermuda and the Cayman Islands became world leaders in some aspects of the insurance and hedge fund industries.[9]

The tide of drug money that washed over the region in the 1970s and 1980s compounded the U.S. government's worries about tax evasion by American individuals and corporations. Together with fears of Communist subversion after the 1983 invasion of Grenada, the Reagan administration responded to these concerns with the Caribbean Basin Initiative. The initiative comprised a package (designed in Washington with little if any input from the Caribbean countries) of concessions on import duties for commodities like bananas, rum, and sugar.[10] Whatever it might have done to contain Communist forces, the initiative did not persuade islands to abolish their banking secrecy laws. Through the 1980s and 1990s, other countries in the region were also entering the market for offshore financial services, including Turks and Caicos (1981), Antigua and Barbuda (1982), British Virgin Islands (1984), Nevis (1984), Grenada (1990), Anguilla (1991), St. Kitts (1996), St. Vincent and the Grenadines (1996), Dominica (1996), and St. Lucia (1997), such that of the thirty-five tax havens listed by the OECD in 2000, seventeen were in the Caribbean Basin (including Belize and Panama). Pacific islands face the challenges of small size and remoteness to an extreme degree. Since Norfolk Island set the precedent in 1966, Vanuatu (1970–71), Nauru (1972), the Cook Islands (1981), Tonga (1984), Samoa (1988), the Marshall Islands (1990), and Niue (1994) have increasingly taken the standard route of copying legislation from the current leaders in the field and then engaging in fierce competition for business that has often generated only the thinnest of margins.[11]

Several pressures in the 1990s pushed small island states toward offshore finance as a solution to development problems. Bilateral aid from major countries was in decline. Commodity prices for agricultural goods were volatile in the short term and stagnant or declining in the long term, with trade preference concessions under the EU's African Caribbean Pacific program under threat. High birthrates coupled with the emigration of those with education and skills marketable in North America, Europe, and Australasia meant that these countries faced stiff challenges with chronically limited resources. Compounding these difficulties are inherent geographical limitations that made diversification difficult and left the islands vulnerable to devastating natural disasters.[12]

In these circumstances, it is not surprising that financial deregulation in the world's major economies and technological innovation prompted some small countries to set themselves up as tax havens. The proliferation of tax havens was also a product of low barriers to entry, combined with the example of earlier success stories in the field. Other forms of the "commercialization" of small state sovereignty[13] have included offering shipping flags of convenience, selling citizenship, selling internet country codes,[14] hosting on-line casinos, acting as routing centers for telephone or on-line pornography, and the older expedient of bargaining for recognition of either the Republic of China on Taiwan or the People's Republic of China on the mainland.

Small states did not come to the tax haven option unaided, however, as both former imperial powers and the international development community suggested that they try to build a financial services industry based in large part on the lure of a low-tax regime.[15] Vanuatu, the former Anglo–French condominium of the New Hebrides in the Pacific, made its first bid for financial services while still under colonial administration and with strong encouragement from London.[16] Strapped for other alternatives aside from tourism, British administrators followed the reasoning that

> If you have a largely subsistence agricultural sector and virtually all your revenue is raised by indirect taxes or resource rents, you do not need income taxes, capital gains taxes, withholding taxes or death duties. If you do not have these taxes, there is no need to enter into tax treaties. Vanuatu is thus a natural tax haven.[17]

In recommending financial services to small developing economies, the World Bank pointed out that for small jurisdictions to attract mobile capital, they had to offer a tax rate at or very near zero.[18]

What sort of financial services do tax havens offer their individual and corporate customers? Individuals and firms invest in tax havens for an enormous variety of reasons. Aside from a host of "do it yourself" guides to tax evasion, perhaps the authoritative source is made up of the various editions of Caroline Doggart's *Tax Havens and Their Uses*, produced for the Economist Intelligence Unit from the 1970s until 2002.[19] Most simply, tax havens allow rich individuals, often celebrities like Sean Connery (Barbados) or Luciano Pavarotti (Monaco) a place of residence free of income tax. But much more commonly than physical relocation, tax haven products create a legal separation or, better still, layers of separation between an owner and an asset or income. In this sense, talk of "borderless finance" is highly misleading, in that tax havens' legal separation from other regulatory spaces is the foundation of their activities.[20] The aim is to enjoy the benefits of ownership while simultaneously erasing the legal link to an asset or revenue stream as it concerns tax collectors, creditors, and other claimants. To be sure, such a separation is at the heart of nearly all modern business and corporate law, with the idea of limited liability, legal personality, and so on, but tax havens allow for this concept to be used in more radical and complex ways.

As mentioned earlier, one of the chief attractions of putting money in tax havens is privacy. Many havens have copied the famous Swiss numbered bank accounts where the identity of the account holder is known to only one or two bank officials (or in some cases none at all). Heavy prison terms are often mandatory for bankers and other financial professionals for releasing information about their clients. Furthermore, as tax evasion cannot be a crime where there are no direct taxes to evade, authorities in such jurisdictions are commonly not under any legal obligation to cooperate with investigations by foreign tax authorities. Individuals may engage in estate planning in tax havens or protect their assets in the event of divorce or in order to ensure that disinherited parties cannot dispute wills. Trusts can be set up and structured in such a way as to escape creditors, or to distance the owners of assets from the income derived, which thus no longer counts as a tax liability in their home jurisdiction. Companies may be composed of "bearer shares," whereby there is no central share register and thus individuals holding share certificates are the only ones able to disclose this asset. Such companies may also be relieved of the duty of conducting audits and filing accounts. Tax havens often make special deals for foreign investors, so-called ring-fencing, meaning that certain entities like International Business Companies (IBCs) or international trusts are barred to residents of the jurisdiction in which they are incorporated and must carry on all activities outside that jurisdiction (though similar special tax deals and sweeteners for foreign investors are also widely employed in OECD countries as well).

One example of a popular product that epitomizes the principle of establishing a legal separation between individuals and their assets is the Asset Protection Trust. Such trusts were first created in the Cook Islands in 1984 and widely copied by other jurisdictions thereafter, including Alaska. Trusts, a common law concept, usually comprise a person transferring ownership of money or property to the trust, with these assets managed by a separate party in line with a document drawn up by the original owner of the assets, for the benefit of another third party. A trust is thus a relationship among three parties: the person transferring the assets is the settlor or grantor, the person (or company) managing the trust's assets is the trustee, and the eventual recipient is the beneficiary. The document formalizing the terms of this relationship is the trust deed. Commonly, the settlor might be a parent, the trustee an investment adviser, and the beneficiary a child of the settlor. The trust deed would lay out the conditions of inheritance. Conventionally, once the trust has been created, neither the settlor, trustee, nor beneficiary actually owns the assets.

Asset Protection Trusts use this separation of ownership so that the settlor's assets are protected from lawsuits, creditors, and divorce proceedings, while allowing the settlor some measure of control over these same assets. Thus under such an arrangement the settlor may also be the beneficiary. Furthermore, the settlor may be a co-trustee exercising joint control of the assets and any resulting income stream. The goal is to leave the settlor with as much practical control of the assets as possible, while simultaneously being able to demonstrate in court that, because the assets no longer legally belong to the settlor, they cannot be claimed by creditors, litigants, or ex-spouses. This arrangement is commonly marketed to those in the medical profession facing a high risk of litigation where insurance is very expensive or unavailable. These trusts are formed offshore to take advantage of the special legislation that allows for their existence. But equally important, locating the trust offshore limits the ability of courts in the settlor's home jurisdiction to declare the trust invalid, and thus dissolve the separation between settlor and assets. Because of this legal separation those with Asset Protection Trusts can enjoy the benefits of wealth while being legally poor.[21]

For corporations, tax havens present a further range of options. As the prominent tax planner Milton Grundy explains, "There is often the possibility of reducing the tax cost by basing the business elsewhere, or by routing it through other jurisdictions, or otherwise modifying the form of the transaction. It is these possibilities which constitute the world of international tax planning."[22] This basic principle creates room for a huge variety of corporate activities involving tax havens. It bears noting at the outset, that many of these same tax-related inducements are also offered by individual OECD economies on a "ring-fenced" basis (i.e., available only to foreign investors). Corporations may move their headquarters to low-tax jurisdictions or reincorporate in such locations to minimize their corporate tax bills. This practice, recently known as "corporate inversion," was the subject of controversy in the United States in 2001–2002 with companies reincorporating in Bermuda and shifting their corporate headquarters to Barbados. By this ploy, U.S. companies could avoid paying tax on profits earned outside the United States and possibly relabel domestic American profit tax-deductible interest. The same result can be achieved when a tax haven–based company merges with another, and the resulting merged company then adopts the tax haven as its legal address.[23]

Tax haven subsidiaries of a company based in Europe or North America can be used to manipulate transfer pricing to undermine the "arm's length" principle which specifies that international intrafirm trade must be counted for tax purposes as if the different parts of the firm were conducting business as independent entities in an open market. In this way corporations may try to attribute as much of their worldwide profit to subsidiaries in low-tax countries and losses to high-tax countries so as to minimize their overall tax bill. Employers may choose to set up employee stock option and health and pension plans offshore, and investment companies can set up collective investment schemes like mutual and hedge funds. A network of tax treaties means that holding companies in some tax havens play a "turntable" or "conduit" role. This allows for dividends and royalty payments to avoid withholding taxes by taking an indirect route home in situations where income taking the direct route would be subject to such a tax. Leasing assets through tax havens may permit depreciation allowances to be collected in more than one jurisdiction and tax on leasing payments to be minimized. Risk can be transferred offshore by forming captive insurance companies. More recently, Special Purpose Vehicles (provided both on- and offshore) have allowed companies to flatter their balance sheets by either hiding poorly performing assets or transferring liability from the parent company to the Special Purpose Vehicle.[24] Another recent innovation is the Protected Cell Company pioneered by Guernsey in 1998 and widely copied elsewhere, for example, in Delaware and Nevada. Protected Cell Companies "provide a single corporate vehicle that has multiple separate identities for bankruptcy purposes."[25] The Protected Cell Company has a core of share capital for the company as a whole but it also has individually capitalized cells, akin to subcompanies. Individual cells are liable only for claims against them up to the limit of their own assets; the assets of other cells and the company as a whole are legally distinct. Protected Cell Companies are generally used for insuring different classes of risk or for collective investment schemes incorporating different types of funds. Such an arrangement provides both the low transaction fees associated with moving assets within a single company (when transferring assets between cells) with the legal protection of a multicompany structure (limiting the risk to the whole entity if one cell goes bust or is sued).

Although these examples only scratch the surface of activities performed in tax havens, a few important general conclusions can be drawn. The idea of tax havens is not particularly new, and the proliferation of such locations cannot be reduced to any one recent factor, whether it be international crime, rising regulatory or tax burdens in Europe, North America and Japan, or recent advances in communication technology.[26] Almost every country in the world can be used to avoid or evade another country's taxation. Many countries now identified as tax havens historically came into this status by accident as much as by design, sometimes as an unintended consequence of legal changes in another jurisdiction. More recently, however, a much larger number of jurisdictions have deliberately designed their tax and banking codes to attract nonresident capital and savings. In doing so, small states that often lack other options have been following an established model provided by early leaders in the field.

Tax Competition and the European Union

The European Union and the United States came to settle on the OECD initiative against tax havens from different perspectives. The continental European countries (and Japan) were worried about tax competition as such. At least some EU members were keen to establish an upward convergence in the taxation of capital, if not outright harmonization of tax rates (i.e., a single uniform rate).[27] Many Western European economies performed sluggishly during the 1990s. Politicians became anxious that the combination of relatively high tax rates, extensive welfare benefits, and underfunded public pension schemes to cover a rapidly graying population might leave them particularly vulnerable to tax competition. The strict budget-deficit criteria for monetary union in the run-up to the Euro also meant that European governments were especially sensitive to the prospect of eroding tax bases. In contrast, the U.S. support for the initiative had more to do with law enforcement and information exchange, in part bending to the overriding priority of the "war on drugs," in part reflecting an emphasis on tax evasion.

I will now examine how these actors came by their differing concerns and how each used multilateral international institutions in response before partially submerging their differences later and opting for the OECD campaign in 1996. While the United States pushed for the founding of the Financial Action Task Force (FATF) to combat money laundering, the EU pushed the issue of tax competition and tax harmonization to the forefront after early leads from the European Commission and several pivotal member states.

The 1957 Treaty of Rome, which founded what was then the European Economic Community, has little if anything to say about the taxation of corporate and personal income. The European Commission has, however, sporadically tried to assert itself on tax matters, only to be rebuffed by members jealous of their sovereign prerogatives in this area. The 1963 Neumark Report, the Van den Tempel Report in 1971, and the 1992 Ruding Report all urged members toward harmonization by proposing fiscal rules setting some taxes on capital within a common band, but these proposals were buried.[28] After a long period of neglect, tax was put back on the agenda in 1989.

> Essentially, the Commission withdrew ambitious proposals and attacked specific domestic taxes—such as cross-border withholding taxes on the operations of multinationals—hampering free trade and investment in the single market. European tax policy . . . would be limited to the elimination of distortionary domestic taxes, to be assessed on a case-by-case basis, thus providing a level playing field.[29]

Even this more modest approach made little headway, however, until in 1995 the Commissioner for Competition Mario Monti began to link wide differentials in corporate tax rates and tax competition with the idea of a "race to the bottom." This idea represented a destructive and ultimately futile bidding war to attract capital that could severely undermine members' tax bases and even endanger the "European social model" itself. What the "race to the bottom" scenario lacked in theoretical underpinnings and strong supporting evidence (as is discussed below for theories of tax competition), it made up in political impact and utility. As Radaelli details, this "doomsday" picture made for a compelling story, given its simple causal account and some supporting circumstantial evidence. It epitomized broader concerns with some of the effects of globalization current at the time.[30] An informal discussion paper from the March 1996 European Council of Finance Ministers (Ecofin) referred to the problem as "fiscal degradation," a phrase coined in the OECD several years earlier. In terms that are strikingly similar to those of the 1998 OECD report, fiscal degradation was said to threaten member states' overall tax revenues, to contribute to unemployment as the tax burden shifted from mobile capital to relatively immobile labor, and to undermine the goals of the single European market.[31] From 1996, the French and German governments had swung behind the Commission. The "problem" of tax competition within the Union, together with its possible solutions, was firmly on the agenda of the negotiations over the European Constitutional Treaty 2002–2004. From here it was only a short step to try to regulate tax competition outside the (then) fifteen member states. This extra step was consistent with the global nature of the issue; as a result, intra-EU deals were made conditional on extra-EU outcomes.

Two of the most important tax controversies within the EU since 1996 concern the specter of harmonizing corporate tax rates and taxation of nonresident savings. Both have been important in shaping European views on tax competition in general and in convincing EU governments that a global approach was needed to regulate trends that, if left to themselves, could undermine the European social model. The EU has long agreed to a rough harmonization of value-added taxes based on a minimum level. Apart from the Commission's persistent interest in regulating tax, Germany, France, Italy, and Belgium rallied to the cry of stamping out "unfair" or "harmful" tax competition after the 1996 Verona meeting of Ecofin. They argued that such competition had been (or would be) responsible for shifting the tax burden from capital to labor, exacerbating already high unemployment rates, and eroding tax bases. France was most concerned with special tax breaks to entice foreign firms and with low, across-the-board corporate tax rates in Ireland and elsewhere. From 1997, the French government was active in calling for a legally enforceable code against the former and an upward harmonization of the latter.

Germany, with the highest corporate tax rate of the fifteen, shared France's concerns about firms relocating for tax reasons, but was perhaps even more exercised about the taxation of its nationals' savings held elsewhere in Europe. By placing their savings in jurisdictions that had strict bank secrecy, such as Luxembourg and Austria, account holders could evade tax at home by failing to declare income earned; Germany was reckoned to lose in the range of $12 billion annually in tax revenues in the mid-1990s.[32] Indeed, the majority of EU governments have now been forced to levy less tax on interest than wage income on account of massive tax evasion by savers. This example is the sort of development that those worried about the "race to the bottom" adduce as evidence for their case.[33] European Union tax wrangles have not proceeded in isolation from broader concerns about global tax competition and tax havens. As early as April 1996, Commissioner Monti approached the head of the OECD to discuss a "common concern for tax competition."[34]

A basic difference has run through EU debates over corporate tax rates, both between member states and inside the Commission. The same division has also impacted on the OECD. Are tax practices only unfair when they discriminate between foreign and domestic investors (ring-fencing), or do some states' low across-the-board rates also constitute unfair tax practices? Many in the French and German governments have wanted to scrap the national veto in tax matters and thus facilitate an upward harmonization of rates. Meanwhile, the Commission itself was (and is) similarly divided over whether "harmful tax competition" refers to a low level of corporate taxation in some member states or only to special tax deals used to attract big international investors. The former were decried on the grounds of eroding national tax bases and shifting the tax burden on to labor. The latter were argued to create distortions in the single market and constitute an illegitimate form of state aid. The issue of harmonization flared up during the negotiations over the Constitutional Treaty 2002–2004, and in relation to the very low corporate tax rates of new, formerly Communist EU members.[35]

In 1997, an Ecofin Code of Conduct was adopted to prevent ring-fencing, tax advantages for brass plate operations, departure from the arm's length principle of transfer pricing, and secret tax deals with particular investors. The resulting 1999 Primarolo Report, which studied the incidence of these practices, found that all EU members, except Sweden, practiced some form of "harmful tax competition" according to this definition. The most prominent target of criticism from within the EU in general was Ireland. A traditional laggard among the European economies, in the 1990s Ireland catapulted itself into the top half of the table, thanks to a range of social and economic reforms, and generous transfers from Brussels. But the policy innovation that caught the most attention was the concessionary 10 percent tax on the profits of foreign manufacturing and financial companies that relocated to Ireland. Ireland managed to escape further criticism of special concessions for foreign investors by lowering its standard corporation tax to 12.5 percent (from 32 percent) and announcing that the separate rate for overseas firms would be dropped by 2010. This response answered the charge of distorting the single market with de facto state subsidies, but exacerbated the basic Franco-German contention that Irish corporate tax rates in general were simply too low and should be harmonized upward.

While further harmonizing tax rates is an issue that looks likely to stay on the agenda without a solution for some time to come, more progress has been made in the area of the taxation of nonresident savings within the EU. This issue has had a long history, but much of the controversy has been centered on which of two solutions to adopt. The first option, initially proposed by the Commission in 1989, is a uniform withholding tax to be applied by all members on interest earned within their borders, whether the account holders were domestic or foreign. The second is that banks should automatically provide information to all member state tax authorities on their clients' interest earnings. Britain opposed the idea of a withholding tax on the grounds that this could wreak havoc with the huge and profitable bond market in London. The British government (supported by the OECD) insisted on information exchange, even to the point of vetoing a 1998 "coexistence model" that would have allowed countries to choose either a withholding tax or information exchange. On the other hand, Luxembourg and Austria (since joining the EU in 1995) have been very reluctant to water down their banking secrecy laws, fearing that foreign investors would withdraw their funds (back to Germany or elsewhere). Because each country wields a veto on tax matters, this deadlock prevented any progress for over a decade. Exacerbating this stand-off was the broader concern about simply displacing the problem, in that whichever solution was adopted might simply lead to the flight of savings from the EU to nonmember jurisdictions in Europe and beyond without member governments capturing any compensatory benefits.[36] This concern with preventing displacement through regulatory arbitrage and the resulting need for a "level playing field" between jurisdictions has been a recurring theme in international tax regulation, especially with respect to the OECD initiative.

The first obstacle, agreement within the EU, was surmounted in 2000 with a deal that fudged the underlying conflict. In principle, all members committed to information exchange. But in practice Austria, Belgium, and Luxembourg were allowed a seven-year transition period during which time these three were to collect a withholding tax on interest payments to EU citizens. Even beyond this compromise, the deal was also carefully hedged, as member governments were only bound if the United States, Switzerland, Andorra, Liechtenstein, Monaco, and San Marino, plus member state dependencies like the Channel Islands and the British and Dutch Caribbean territories, also signed up. The logic for including non-EU jurisdictions was that abolishing banking secrecy within the EU or levying a withholding tax does not stop EU nationals transferring their money to a third country and continuing to evade tax. As these third country jurisdictions were at best unenthusiastic about the Savings Tax Directive, the Commission had its work cut out from 2001 in terms of convincing them to make a commitment. A combination of strong-arm pressure against the dependencies, a withholding tax deal with Switzerland and the four small European tax havens, and the tactic of interpreting an American "no" to mean "yes" saw the Commission claiming victory in 2003.[37] The Directive came into force in July 2005, sixteen years after negotiations began and six years after the original deadline. The Savings Tax Directive had mixed effects on the OECD initiative. On the one hand, it put a premium on a global solution to tax competition in order to avoid the EU package being out-flanked by investors moving their funds to Singapore, Hong Kong, or independent Caribbean states not covered by the deal. On the other hand, the deal caused severe embarrassment for the OECD, with the OECD's insistence on universal information exchange and the level playing field being undermined by the special opt-out arrangement made for Switzerland, Austria, and the others.

The United States, Money Laundering, and "Top-Down" Multilateral Regulation

If the European Union came to the OECD *Harmful Tax Competition* report worried about the integrity of the single market and the corrosive effect of tax competition on the welfare state, across the other side of the Atlantic the United States was more concerned with information exchange and anti-money laundering efforts aimed at the drug trade. Continuing with the policy background to the OECD tax competition initiative, this section looks at U.S.-led multilateral efforts to tackle money laundering, particularly the Financial Action Task Force (FATF), as well as unilateral attempts from Washington to address tax haven–assisted tax evasion. Particularly significant is the decision under the Clinton administration to adopt a confrontational "top-down" approach to multilateral standard-setting in tax and financial services, a decision that was strongly manifested in the OECD initiative. Whereas the Europeans took the lead in defining the ends of the 1998 OECD report, the United States did most to determine the means by which the initiative progressed.

Following mixed success at best after passing the 1986 Money Laundering Control Act and attempts to unilaterally open up Caribbean tax havens in the 1980s, the United States opted for a multilateral approach with the creation of the FATF in 1989, pursued under the auspices of the G7. The small secretariat is housed in the Paris headquarters (and web pages) of the OECD, and it shares almost perfectly overlapping membership with its host. From the 1990s, there were pronounced similarities between the FATF drive against money laundering and the OECD project against harmful tax competition. Procedurally, there was a common "top-down" or exclusionary approach, in that both bodies came to settle on blacklisting as a means to pressure small nonmember tax havens to comply with new international standards they had had no say in designing. This method is in contrast with the traditional inclusive "bottom-up" approach of consensus and compromise. Substantively, after its efforts fell apart in preventing tax havens from attracting foreign investment with tax concessions, the OECD attempted to salvage an information exchange agreement that mostly overlapped with FATF demands. The similarities between the OECD and FATF are so pronounced that they have been repeatedly represented in the media and elsewhere as being one and the same, the FATF's practice of issuing press releases on OECD stationery and using OECD business cards hardly helping to resolve the confusion.

The FATF was conceived as a group of experts charged with drawing up a list of recommendations on legislative and regulatory measures to combat money laundering. In 1990 "The Forty Recommendations" were released, and have subsequently been revised on several occasions. As the name suggests, these are not legally binding on members (let alone nonmembers), but have been widely endorsed and are very influential. The recommendations included such items as criminalizing money laundering and making it an extraditable offense, coordinating international searches and account freezes, establishing national guidelines for banks, instituting a suspicious transaction reporting regime, specifying due diligence requirements for banks and other financial institutions, and modifying financial secrecy laws to aid the investigation and prosecution of money laundering crimes. As part of its mission of generating and disseminating knowledge on the subject, the FATF has encouraged the improvement of members' laws against money laundering through peer review, conferences, and meetings with private firms in the financial industry and nonmember states. Later, it fostered the creation of eight regional anti-money laundering bodies, such as the Caribbean Financial Action Task Force and Asia-Pacific Group on Money Laundering,[38] each committed to diffusing the Forty Recommendations. Annual reports were produced to measure progress in enforcement and to respond to changing trends in criminal activity. After some debate in the early 1990s, until 1999, "The global [FATF] strategy has been to build, from the G7, a wider epistemic community of money laundering compliance based on peer review from within the whitelist of participating states."[39]

Led by the United States, the FATF began to run out of patience with its consensual lead-by-example approach,[40] and in 1999 began work on a blacklist (the Non-Co-operative Countries and Territories or NCCT list) of jurisdictions accused of failing to meet minimum standards. The switch to more confrontational tactics by the FATF and the OECD was explicitly contrasted with the traditional consensus-based style of standard-setting by international organizations, as evidenced by the very revealing statement of the former Special Adviser to the Secretary of the U.S. Treasury:

[The] new problem lies in clamping down on underregulated jurisdictions and the new threats they pose to U.S. interests—and that requires a new strategy. . . . The Clinton administration realized that any new approach had to focus on stemming the proliferation of underregulated jurisdictions and tackling those jurisdictions that were already established. The strategy also had to recognize the limits of traditional law-enforcement and regulatory channels as well as the relative ineffectiveness of previous diplomatic efforts. Furthermore, any strategy had to be global and multilateral, since unilateral actions would only drive dirty money to the world's other major financial centers. Yet Washington could not afford to take the "bottom-up" approach of seeking a global consensus before taking action; if the debate were brought to the UN General Assembly, for example, nations with underregulated financial regimes would easily outvote those with a commitment to strong international standards.[41]

The switch to a more confrontational style of operations came despite the fact that many of the FATF members themselves were well short of having introduced all of the Forty Recommendations.[42]

Undeterred by uneven compliance with standards against money laundering within its own ranks, however, the FATF published the first round of the NCCT list in June 2000. Subsequently, countries said to have "serious systemic problems"[43] in their approach to dealing with money laundering were added until November 2002, when new listings were suspended. Being removed from the list has been conditional on jurisdictions demonstrating to the FATF that they have introduced and are implementing the specified package of legislation and regulations.[44] Sanctions were set out for those listed countries and territories that failed to take action after being blacklisted. These were largely devoted to further increasing scrutiny applied to transactions with these jurisdictions (already enhanced after the initial listing), but also included restrictions on banks from noncompliant jurisdictions being able to open subsidiaries or branches elsewhere.[45] This shift away from whitelisting and capacity building toward blacklisting nonmember countries marked a crucial turn toward the use of "naming and shaming" (see chapter 4) that mirrored the OECD's approach to bringing tax havens into line. They have also overshadowed, but not prevented, the voluntary and consensus-based efforts of the UN Office on Drugs and Crime (formerly the UN Drugs Control and Crime Prevention office) and the regional anti–money laundering bodies to raise standards in this area. These bodies have operated by providing policy models, peer review, and technical assistance.[46] Additionally, since 2002 the World Bank and International Monetary Fund have become more involved in helping countries combat money laundering and terrorist financing.[47]

The converging tactics of the FATF and OECD tax competition initiatives (using blacklisting to ensure nonmembers' adherence to a common slate of standards) were complemented by a growing overlap in substantive interests. The 1998 meeting of the G7 called for better coordination between authorities investigating money laundering and tax evasion, and for information gathered in the pursuit of money laundering to be freely available to tax authorities, both domestically and internationally. In January 1999 the FATF and OECD Committee on Fiscal Affairs met to respond to this call. The former agreed to work toward closing the "fiscal loophole" that excused countries from lodging suspicious transaction reports when the crime in question was tax evasion. The OECD committed to encouraging members to pass information collected to fight money laundering to their tax authorities.[48] An OECD report published in 2000, *Improving Access to Bank Information for Tax Purposes*, drew links between bank secrecy, money laundering, and tax evasion. The report attributed the same adverse consequences to banking secrecy as the 1998 report did to harmful tax competition.[49] This report reiterated "the 8 May 1998 Conclusion of G7 Finance Ministers that they had agreed to enhance the capacity of anti-money laundering systems to deal effectively with tax related crimes."[50] Thanks to stubborn opposition to weakening bank secrecy by Austria, Belgium, Luxembourg, and Switzerland, perhaps motivated by their experience with the initiative against harmful tax competition, this project has remained deadlocked.[51]

Again relating to the nexus between financial crime and tax issues, in 2001 the OECD Steering Group on Corporate Governance published *Behind the Corporate Veil: Using Corporate Entities for Illicit Purposes* in line with a request from the Financial Stability Forum the previous year. Jeffrey Owens, a senior OECD official responsible for implementing the *Harmful Tax Competition* report, wrote that

The international community has recognized this linkage between money laundering, tax evasion and other international criminal activities. . . . The Financial Action Task

Force . . . has issued a clarification that claims that a transaction is merely just a tax of-
fence should not alleviate the obligation to report a suspicious transaction (removing
the tax excuse).[52]

Currently the OECD is still working toward convincing members to allow financial
information collected on the grounds of ending money laundering to be made available to tax authorities.[53] Thus as the OECD's tax haven campaign became more and
more concerned with issues of transparency and information exchange between tax
authorities, the differences between this campaign and the FATF continued to narrow. From the late 1990s, both represented a novel and potentially powerful form of
regulating the global economy, with various clubs of larger, developed states setting
standards and then working to impose them on those countries outside the club by
blacklisting.

Yet another multilateral institution adding to the alphabet soup of existing intergovernmental financial regulators is the Financial Stability Forum (FSF). Set up
following the Asian financial crisis in 1997–98, the FSF was created to flesh out
vague pronouncements concerning a "new international financial architecture"
aimed at preventing another crisis. William Wechsler, the U.S. Treasury Special Adviser quoted above, identified the FSF as part of the "three-pronged strategy" together with the FATF and OECD for tackling problems related to tax havens.[54]
Although the FSF's brief did not directly relate to tax havens, and though it distanced itself from the OECD's initiative against harmful tax competition, it did produce a report on offshore financial centers. This included a three-part classification
of most to least likely centers to promote the stability of the global financial system.
Released on 26 May 2000, the rankings were based on "their perceived quality of
supervision and perceived degree of cooperation [with FSF member states]."[55] The
FSF thus resembled the other multilateral initiatives for governing the financial system. Aside from endorsing broadly similar principles of transparency and good governance, it is also a select group of predominantly large, rich countries that set down
universal standards and rated how nonmember jurisdictions measured up. The FSF
has yet to achieve the same impact or profile as the FATF and OECD initiatives, and
has not released a second ranking of offshore financial centers. In October 2000, this
institution's work on offshore centers was largely taken over by the IMF, reflecting
some uncertainty as to the most suitable institutions to carry out this function.[56]

That the United States has pushed for multilateral rather than solely unilateral
solutions to money laundering and tax evasion does not mean that it has eschewed
unilateral measures in these areas. The attempts of the Treasury to combat firms'
and citizens' efforts to escape tax obligations by way of Caribbean tax havens have
been a model to others, yet they also serve to illustrate the serious limitations of unilateral approaches to the problem. After decades of innovation in methods to stop
those who avoided or evaded paying taxes, the Treasury not only failed to halt or even
slow the use of tax havens but instead has often contributed to their rise. Indeed,
such regulation may have led to higher administration and compliance costs, greater

distortions in the economy, and a vastly complicated tax code.[57] The United States pioneered the use of Controlled Foreign Corporation laws, designed to levy taxes on offshore companies owned or controlled by resident taxpayers, and Foreign Investment Funds laws, to facilitate taxation of residents' passive income from foreign mutual funds and similar entities, as well as tightening up transfer pricing for intrafirm international trade.[58] Recent changes in Qualified Jurisdiction and Qualified Intermediary regulations force non-U.S. financial institutions with investment in America to meet complex Internal Revenue Service (IRS) reporting requirements and provide information on nonresident foreign clients, or face prohibitive withholding taxes on U.S. income.[59] But in its unilateral responses, the United States has confronted the same problem of displacement that has plagued EU tax regulatory efforts. The limitations of unilateral countermeasures were recognized by the IRS as far back as 1981.

> The United States alone cannot deal with tax havens. . . . The United States should take the lead in encouraging tax havens to provide information to enable other countries to enforce their laws. . . . However, such steps taken unilaterally would place United States business at a competitive disadvantage as against businesses based in other OECD countries. Accordingly, a multilateral approach to deal with tax havens is needed.[60]

Thus in terms of approach the U.S. Treasury, particularly under the Clinton administration's Lawrence Summers, has been the strongest proponent of the FATF and OECD blacklists.[61] Substantively, since the terrorist attacks of 2001, the fixation on the "war on drugs" has been superseded by the "war on terror," in particular in the form of the Patriot Act. Yet the Patriot Act has largely reemphasized the measures contained in the FATF's Forty Recommendations, and reaffirmed the power of the Treasury Secretary to prohibit transactions with jurisdictions "of primary money laundering concern" first established under the Kerry Amendment to 1988 legislation.[62] Despite the unilateral cast of much U.S. diplomacy, the Patriot Act specifies that jurisdictions of concern are to be identified as such based on "the extent to which that jurisdiction is characterized as an offshore banking or secrecy haven by credible international organizations or multilateral expert groups."[63] The United States looks unlikely to abandon its robust unilateral efforts to breach banking secrecy in tax havens, but equally seems dependent on multilateral initiatives to achieve its aims. The OECD and FATF initiatives from 1999 were thus novel attempts to achieve the broad coverage of a multilateral initiative without the perceived limitations of a conventional inclusive and consensual approach to standard-setting and implementation.[64]

Harmful and Beneficial Tax Competition: Theory and Evidence

Central to the difficulty the OECD and others have had in tackling the "problem" of tax competition (or at least the "harmful" or "unfair" varieties) has been establishing whether it is a problem at all. A brief survey of the economic literature below reveals that there is remarkably little expert consensus on the issue. Crucially, this discussion sketches out the fundamental disagreements among the experts in order to support the point that the debate between the tax havens and the OECD was decided on normative rather than technical grounds.

Many economists and commentators in the financial services industry have argued that, far from being harmful, tax competition helps to keep governments honest and is a boon for general economic welfare. Notwithstanding the power of the "race to the bottom" metaphor, which has exercised such a powerful grip on the imagination of politicians and publics alike, the question has to be asked as to how much support there is to back up the proposition that tax competition is in fact harmful. Deductive conclusions are highly sensitive to initial assumptions. Although simple models may yield clear answers for or against tax competition, those that reflect even a small portion of real-world complexity do not. Empirically the situation is little better in providing conclusive results, though there is an emerging consensus that investment decisions by companies are sensitive to tax differentials between countries. However, there are many qualifications to this finding. It is important to provide a summary of the available findings that were selectively appropriated by both sides in the rhetorical contest laid out in chapter 3, especially as professional economists are obviously an important component of the transnational tax policy community. Perhaps most surprising, however, is how little either side has engaged with the academic literature on the subject.

Economists first came to the issue of tax competition at the local or substate level, not the international one. Most of the deductive work on international tax competition is derived from this local work. Substate tax competition studies were designed to handle the effect of tax differentials between municipalities or units of a federal state on mobile factors, either labor, capital, or both. The pioneer in the field was Charles Tiebout,[65] whose work has been used to support the disarmingly simple conclusion that competition between governments is good (promotes efficiency) in the same way as competition between firms in the marketplace—subsequently referred to as the "Tiebout Hypothesis." The hypothesis has often been presented in a highly simplified form without the caveats the author originally included. Following this stylized rendering, localities (firms) are competing for mobile residents (customers) with bundles of public goods (products) funded by a particular tax regime (the price of the products). The competitive process will result in citizens voting with their feet and living in jurisdictions that offer them an optimal combination of public goods and tax rates. From the 1970s, the Tiebout Hypothesis was applied to mobile firms instead of mobile households, and later to regulatory burdens imposed on firms rather than tax rates as such. It is important to note that Tiebout employs a variety of unrealistic assumptions in arguing for the welfare-enhancing effects of interjurisdictional competition (local rather than international). Different localities are assumed to be identical aside from tax rates and public goods offered, and there is only one perfectly mobile factor (residents) which is in fixed supply.

Tiebout's optimistic view of the benefits of tax competition came to be questioned by those studying federal systems in the 1970s and 1980s.[66] These critics held that in federal systems, one locality's decisions on tax created interjurisdictional "fiscal externalities." The most important of these, the tax base externality, refers to "a situation in which the tax rate set by one of the jurisdictions affects the tax revenues of the other jurisdiction."[67] These fiscal externalities can be either vertical or horizontal, positive or negative. Vertical externalities occur between national and subnational governments, and in the absence of a world government are not relevant to international tax competition. Horizontal externalities occur among governments at the same level and thus are very relevant to the international system. A positive fiscal externality occurs when a change in jurisdiction A's tax policies result in a tax revenue gain for jurisdiction B. From the 1990s, OECD members were particularly worried about negative fiscal externalities, produced, for example, if state A becomes a tax haven and lowers rates, reducing the tax revenue for state B. Apart from the discomfort caused to state B when faced with an eroding tax base, there are also reasons why such competition may be economically inefficient. Governments, whether local or national, may be deterred from raising government spending to the point at which marginal benefits equal marginal costs because of the prospect of mobile factors, and thus their share of the tax base, fleeing to lower tax locations. The mobile factors (usually taken to be capital) may be misallocated across jurisdictions. High-tax localities may have too much land and labor relative to capital, and low-tax localities too much capital for too little labor and land. From here the theoretical conclusion is that the resulting international collective action problem leads to an inefficient outcome in terms of global welfare, as individual states cut taxes to attract and retain mobile capital.[68]

The pendulum swung back in favor of tax competition as public choice economists criticized the assumption, common to Tiebout and his critics alike, that governments act as selfless, benevolent dictators immune to the charms of rent-seeking coalitions and the temptation to "interfere" in the economy for political gain. Brennan and Buchanan instead took the government to be a "Leviathan" interested maximizing tax revenue no matter what the cost to public welfare.[69] Taking political motivations (such as rent-seeking and office-seeking by politicians and bureaucrats) into account means that tax competition may impose a necessary discipline on governments that would otherwise inexorably ratchet up tax rates. It is more likely, however, that instead of tax competition generating only negative fiscal externalities, or only serving as a valuable restraint on entirely greedy governments, in practice it exerts different effects simultaneously. Such a situation means that the net benefit or harm caused by tax competition is almost impossible to predict. Indeed, even leaving the political complications to one side, the economic models of harmful tax competition are still very far from reality in their abstraction. "In the basic model, the only potential source of inefficiency is tax competition, making it relatively easy for this competition to turn out to be a bad thing."[70] Deductive models thus are inconclusive as to whether tax competition promotes or retards economic efficiency, and their findings tend to be highly sensitive to a number of highly unrealistic simplifying assumptions.

How much help are inductive studies of tax competition? Aggregate tax data gives little support to the notion of tax competition driving down government revenue, or even redistributing the incidence away from corporations and capital.[71] Perhaps surprisingly, many economists have been skeptical that low rates make much difference in inducing a firm to invest in one country over another. Not only is a high proportion of economic activity fixed to a particular physical and legal location, but taxes are argued to be only a relatively minor ingredient in the mix of factors that make a place an attractive destination for foreign investment. States with high tax rates can compensate firms with more public goods (an educated work force, well-maintained transport and communications infrastructure, an efficient and transparent legal system, etc.).[72] Furthermore, accountants have become so skilled at helping firms to avoid taxes at home, there may be little point in going to the extra effort and expense of moving offshore. In the 1990s, the climate of opinion began to change, however, as large-N quantitative studies of foreign direct investment decisions by United States multinational corporations suggested that firms were indeed sensitive to tax differentials between countries, and were making greater use of tax havens, particularly in the Caribbean.[73] In an influential 1994 article, Hines and Rice reported indications that U.S. firms had dramatically increased their use of tax havens in the early 1980s and that "tax havens account for over one-quarter ($359 billion) of the $1.35 trillion of corporate activity conducted worldwide by overseas affiliates of American firms," more than all of continental Europe.[74] In a study of five hundred U.S. multinationals, Grubert and Mutti found that "A lower tax rate that increases the after-tax returns to capital by 1 percent is associated with about 3 percent more real capital invested if the country has an open trade regime."[75]

The importance of such findings is that firms' sensitivity to tax differentials when choosing where to invest is a crucial element of the "race to the bottom" story. Yet once more there are ambiguities and limitations that muddy the overall picture. First of all, these studies only cover a narrow range of economic activity relating to tax competition, foreign direct investment by U.S. multinational corporations. Hines explains this bias not only on the grounds that the United States is by far the world's largest economy but also because it releases much more and better data than any other country.[76] A complementary explanation might rest on the fact that a large majority of the world's economists are based in the United States. Even with respect to the U.S. Internal Revenue Service, however, Hines and Rice found that the implications for a greater U.S. presence in tax havens may actually result in more, not less, tax revenue. U.S. firms that pay tax on their profits in foreign jurisdictions may credit this amount toward reducing their U.S. tax bill. The more firms invest in high-tax countries, the more tax credits they bring home to reduce their tax bill. Conversely, firms that earn profits in tax havens, pay little if any tax (by definition), and thus generate very few credits with which to reduce their overall tax liability. Once again, the question is not amenable to clear-cut conclusions, and both sides on the benefits or costs of tax competition can gain some support for their position. Equally puzzling, Stewart and Webb have found that although there is greater evidence of corporations using tax shelters, this does not show up as a decline in the aggregate corporate tax take.[77]

In summarizing the state of the field regarding tax competition, the aim has been to sketch out some prominent features of the intellectual background that informed the design of the OECD initiative. But more important is to show why the public debate between the OECD's critics and supporters was not just, or even primarily, a technical, aseptic matter open to definitive resolution by an epistemic community of experts. Both sides could muster partial, highly stylized, yet compelling stories of why tax competition was beneficial (the Tiebout Hypothesis) or harmful ("race to the bottom"), together with some evidence and expert support for their case. Because of this lack of consensus, strands from the expert debates were woven in with, but also subordinated to, broader appeals to principles, norms, and justice in a broader public discursive struggle, as discussed in chapter 3.

The OECD's 1998 Manifesto on Harmful Tax Competition

At about the same time as tax matters reappeared on the European Commission's agenda in May 1996, the Lyon G7 summit requested that the OECD investigate a new issue: harmful tax competition. The summit communiqué concluded:

> Globalization is creating new challenges in the field of tax policy. Tax schemes aimed at attracting financial and other geographically mobile activities can create harmful tax competition between States, carrying risks of distorting trade and investment and could lead to the erosion of national tax bases.[78]

The OECD was requested to "develop measures to counter the distorting effects of harmful tax competition on investment and financing decisions and the consequences for national tax bases, and report back in 1998." The 1997 G7 heads of state summit again endorsed these goals. Members of the European Commission had also met with the Secretary General of the OECD to raise this issue in April 1996, and the same European politicians that were worried about the prospect of tax competition within the Union were no less apprehensive about the prospect of tax competition at the global level. Japan, mired in a slump since the bursting of the property price bubble in 1990, with a huge public debt and a population graying faster than any other of the G7, needed little convincing, and from 1996 it co-chaired the production of the report with France.

Since the beginning of the decade the concerns expressed by politicians and bureaucrats within national tax authorities intersected with broader currents circulating within the OECD, especially the Committee on Fiscal Affairs (CFA). These concerns centered on what basic changes (among them, financial deregulation, the growing influence of international financial markets, and technological change) would mean for the way governments raised taxes and conducted fiscal policy in general. Marcussen's work on the OECD's role in disseminating a discourse on "structural globalization" is relevant in that this discourse held that fundamental changes in the global economy threatened states' traditional capabilities for economic management, hence making governmental reform an imperative.[79] According to Marcussen, various parts of the OECD secretariat have been able to "sell" governments a problem (declining state capacity in the face of globalization), but also the solution in terms of OECD advice and models.[80] This move was successful to the extent that it corresponded with governments' need to explain policy failures, like high unemployment, or unpopular measures, like spending discipline, and present solutions.[81] The CFA secretariat had actually produced a report after work along very similar lines to the initiative against harmful tax competition in the period 1993–96, looking at the problem then labeled by the OECD and the EU as "fiscal degradation."[82] Much like the earlier efforts of the European Commission to influence tax policy, this work had been ignored by member states; the OECD Ministerial Council had failed to endorse the report, which was thus shelved. As the 1996 Ecofin discussion paper noted, "Important work has already been carried out within the framework of the OECD paying particular attention to special tax regimes which give rise to opportunities for tax avoidance and evasion. . . . These useful discussions have not yet produced concrete results." It went on to recommend that "a coordinated approach by member states within the OECD would be highly beneficial."[83] By 1996, the concerns of member states had converged with the groundwork laid earlier by the secretariat.

The process of drawing up the 1998 report and its subsequent development among member states proved to be an extremely delicate task, because of the novelty of close multilateral cooperation in an area so intimately connected with states' sovereign prerogatives. Unusually, the OECD did not consult private business interests in drawing up the report, and even excluded its own "in-house" business peak body, the Business Industry Advisory Committee (BIAC). OECD members believed that for there to be any chance of a successful conclusion in such a sensitive area, the number of participants had to be kept as small as possible, and also guessed that business groups would be unenthusiastic about an initiative to shore up corporate taxation.[84] Because of the uncertain fit between the different priorities of OECD members, and the consensual and deliberative style fostered by the need to generate unanimity (or at least avoid provoking a veto), drafting the report took much skill. Conflicting perspectives were handled by either settling on a "lowest common denominator" solution, or by emphasizing different priorities in different parts of the report. Thus Webb convincingly argues that the continental Europeans, particularly France and Germany, much more worried about differential tax rates as such, were suspicious of any kind of tax competition, and would have liked to encourage some measure of tax harmonization. The United States and Britain on the other hand were more concerned with special nontransparent tax breaks and saw some kinds of tax competition as legitimate and positive. Different parts of the report could be seen to endorse both views.

The report published in April 1998, *Harmful Tax Competition: An Emerging Global Issue,* sought to do three things: to define what harmful tax competition was, to make an argument for just why it was harmful, and to set out a response to the problem. As could be expected for a document written by a committee whose members had different priorities, the report did not always speak with one voice. Under public scrutiny many of these underlying differences came to the fore. There was, however, a rough core of agreed principles concerning the nature of the problem and the appropriate remedial actions to be taken. Unlike the EU Code of Conduct on harmful tax practices, the report confined itself to financial services and intangibles, partly because these were the most mobile and thus most likely to contribute to bidding wars between governments to attract such capital, but also partly as a pragmatic decision to avoid offending manufacturing interests in OECD countries. It portrayed financial liberalization and the increasing mobility of capital and economic globalization in general as positive developments that helped to enhance welfare and economic efficiency throughout the world. But the report also noted that these largely beneficial forces had the potential to produce serious problems ("the dark side of globalization"), such as harmful tax competition.

Harmful tax competition was said to spring from two main sources: tax havens and "potentially harmful preferential tax regimes." The implication was that while tax havens were outside the OECD, many OECD members were themselves guilty of the second kind of harmful tax competition. This was akin to the Commission's worries about EU member countries offering special deals on tax that were equivalent to subsidies to particular foreign investors. Likewise, the fear was that investment would be driven by tax concessions rather than broader economic factors. The four hallmarks of these harmful preferential deals are: a low or zero rate of tax on the relevant income, ring-fencing (the regime is only available to foreigners), no public availability of a regime's details, and lack of information exchange by tax authorities with other countries.[85] There were good conceptual and policy reasons to tackle harmful preferential tax regimes. But those in charge of drawing up the report already anticipated, even at this early stage, that the OECD could expect considerable criticism if it foisted all the burden of taming tax competition on small tax haven states without members being seen to take some tough decisions themselves. Despite the difficulty of getting member states to own up to even potentially harmful features of their tax codes 1996–2001, it was seen to be impossible to drop this aspect of the initiative while still demanding reforms from tax havens.[86]

Moving to tax havens, the report acknowledged the difficulty of coming up with a generally-agreed-on definition. Nevertheless, the OECD maintained that an important distinction could be made between tax haven and non-tax haven jurisdictions, with the former being "countries that are able to finance their public services with no or nominal income taxes and that offer themselves as places to be used by nonresidents to escape tax in their country of residence."[87] In contrast to the potentially harmful nature of preferential tax regimes, tax havens are said to cause actual harm and do so deliberately. Aside from offering a zero or low rate of tax, a necessary condition, a tax haven is a jurisdiction that "offers itself, or is perceived to offer itself, as a place to be used by nonresidents to escape tax in their country of residence."[88] This subjective "reputation test" (or "smell test"), whereby tax havens are identified on the basis of how others perceive them, is vital in making explicit the intersubjective nature of the whole exercise; if enough of the right sort of people think a country is a tax haven, it is a tax haven. The report specified several other "key factors" that also serve to distinguish tax havens. These jurisdictions do not participate in information exchange with foreign tax authorities regarding tax matters, even if they may cooperate with investigations into fraud and money laundering. Their tax and banking codes and practices are opaque. Consistent with "brass plate" or "booking center" operations, a "no substantial activity" clause was included: tax havens attract investment solely on the grounds of the tax advantages conferred rather than for "real" economic reasons. Additionally, OECD officials have held that many tax havens also practice ring-fencing and tend to have a very large financial sector relative to the rest of their economy.

After identifying the characteristics of potentially harmful preferential tax regimes and tax havens, it remained to explain just what sort of harm could be brought about by tax competition. The primary consequence identified was that one country could tempt capital away from home jurisdictions with tax incentives, thereby also diverting the accompanying share of the home countries' tax base, causing overall tax revenues to be eroded.

> Here the effect is for one country to redirect capital and financial flows and the corresponding revenue from other jurisdictions by bidding aggressively for the tax base of other countries. Some have described this effect as "poaching" as the tax base "rightly" belongs to the other country. Practices of this sort can appropriately be labeled harmful tax competition since they do not reflect different judgments about the appropriate level of taxes and public outlays or the appropriate mix of taxes in a particular economy, which are aspects of every country's sovereignty in fiscal matters, but are, in effect, tailored to attract investment or savings originating elsewhere or to facilitate the avoidance of other countries' taxes.[89]

The report claimed that tax competition could frustrate the attempts of elected governments to achieve desired levels of tax and public spending, and that the tax burden could be skewed toward cutting taxes on mobile capital while increasing taxes on relatively fixed labor and consumption. Tax competition could also raise the cost of administering tax systems and enforcing the law, as well as increasing the resources that other companies and citizens have to devote to understanding and negotiating more complicated tax codes. If some corporations like Enron as well as wealthy individuals can escape their tax obligations through the use of tax havens, whereas the majority of taxpayers cannot, this has a corrosive effect on the perceived legitimacy of the whole tax regime, ultimately diminishing spontaneous compliance and undermining "tax morale."[90] Finally, tax competition may be harmful in that it distorts investment flows as firms pay more attention to tax shopping and bargaining between different jurisdictions than deciding on these locations' inherent economic qualities.

The OECD was keen to stress that the problem of harmful tax competition was an inherently global one, which could only be solved by coordinated action.[91] Some unilateral measures were recommended, such as introducing Controlled Foreign Corporation laws designed to prevent "re-flagging" a company to avoid tax at home. It was also recommended that bilateral tax treaties concluded by OECD members should include information exchange provisions. However, the report emphasized the need for a collective response because of the tendency for individual remedial actions to displace rather than fix the problem, akin to a Prisoner's Dilemma situation generating a race to the bottom. This section of the report thus closely followed the concerns about displacement earlier expressed both by the EU and the United States, as covered previously. A state that cracked down on the problem by strengthening tax enforcement would put its companies at a comparative disadvantage against foreign competitors in the world market place. In turn, such a crack down would provide greater incentives for corporations to relocate and invest elsewhere, and further undermine the state's tax base (or, in other words, create a positive fiscal externality for tax havens). On the other hand, doing nothing may condemn states to successive rounds of tax cuts to avoid capital flight: "Governments cannot stand back while their tax bases are eroded through the actions of countries which offer taxpayers ways to exploit tax havens and preferential regimes to reduce the tax that would otherwise be payable to them."[92] Inaction may be preferable to unilateral action, but both are inferior to a coordinated global response.

The OECD thus set itself an important goal that broke with long-established tradition: the global regulation of tax policy. It then moved on to specify an equally novel method for achieving this goal. Having defined and operationalized the concept of harmful tax competition in the report, and specified why it was a problem, it remained to fulfill the last part of the G7 mandate: to design a response to address the issue. Two tracks to dealing with harmful tax competition were outlined. The first countered potentially harmful preferential tax regimes, and this was very much in line with standard OECD practice: collectively writing a model of best practice and then encouraging member states to come on board through technocratic and normative suasion. Member states would collaborate on a code of conduct, self-assess and report on how they measured up, submit themselves for peer review, and commit to freezing and then removing any elements of their tax codes adjudged as harmful by 2003, or 2005 in a few cases. The tone as much as the substance of these recommendations was important, with members very reluctant to step on toes, become engaged in any public disagreements, or employ confrontational rhetoric or accusations.

The distance between the traditional inclusive and consensual approach toward member states and the novelty of the exclusionary and confrontational stance toward nonmember tax havens is fully developed in chapters 3 and 6, but it is important to stress just how much of a break this new approach was. The OECD is not an arena for member state bargaining like the World Trade Organization, still less an institution designed to deliver the grudging compliance of nonmembers. Instead, it seeks to instill its pro-market economic liberal policy solutions among national bureaucrats through a process of disseminating models of best practice, discussion, and problem-solving debate, peer review, and peer pressure. The last two are particularly important, the OECD being more closely associated with these techniques than any other institution. The requirements for peer review and peer pressure were carefully followed in identifying member states' potentially harmful preferential tax regimes, but conspicuously missing in dealing with nonmember small states. Peer review saw the secretariat and fellow members evaluate each member against standards designed and consented to by all. Not only do members have to give their consent to be evaluated in the first place, those evaluated then discussed the results with their examiners, having the right to excise points they disagree with, suppress publication or veto the review as a whole. Peer pressure is "nonadversarial," "relies heavily on mutual trust among States involved in the review, as well as their shared confidence in the process . . . and never implies a punitive decision of sanctions."[93] The treatment of tax havens lacked every single one of these elements. Indeed, it "presented the strongest and most specific collective attack ever made on 'tax havens.'"[94] The second track of the report, responding to the challenge of tax havens, thus marked a clear break from past OECD practice in looking to bring about changes in the national policies of specific nonmember states by means of coordinated multilateral pressure.

The report itself was intended as the first shot in the campaign against tax havens. It was aimed at sending "a clear political message that the OECD member countries are prepared to intensify their cooperation to counter harmful tax practices."[95] In order to maintain a continuing institutional focus on the issue, conduct dialogue with nonmember states and organizations, and monitor progress, a Forum on Harmful Tax Practices was set up under the Committee on Fiscal Affairs. Crucially, the new Forum was also given the responsibility of compiling a list of tax havens, using the guidelines described above. Members whose dependent territories were tax havens were asked to use their influence to encourage these jurisdictions to adopt the OECD guidelines for reform, or at the very least refrain from introducing measures that would accentuate existing harmful tax practices. Countries that had tax treaties with havens were asked to consider abrogating them. While there were as yet few details about the multilateral sanctions (or in OECD parlance "defensive measures") to be coordinated by the OECD secretariat, the message was indeed clear that it would not be business as usual for tax havens.

The sequel to the 1998 report, *Towards Global Tax Co-operation* (2000), building on the deliberations of the Forum on Harmful Tax Practices, made the strategy for bringing tax havens into line much more explicit. First, after scrutinizing forty-seven jurisdictions, it included a list of thirty-five tax havens. Second, it specified that jurisdictions on this list had one year to make a "scheduled commitment" to the OECD to eliminate their harmful tax practices by the end of 2005, specifically on such matters as sharing information with foreign tax authorities in both criminal and civil cases, and making their tax regimes transparent. This list was compiled both by national delegates and members of the secretariat. It drew on members' past experiences and impressions of jurisdictions, surveys of existing public literature on the field, questionnaires sent out to the jurisdictions, and some brief on-site visits. Six of the forty-seven jurisdictions examined were found to have "no case to answer," in that they did not meet the tax haven criteria. Six more (Bermuda, the Cayman Islands, Cyprus, Malta, Mauritius and San Marino), somewhat to the surprise of the OECD, were interested in making a commitment to undertake the specified reforms in order to stay off the June 2000 list.

The specifics on how these commitments were to be made varied slightly over time. Those listed as tax havens were initially asked to make an official commitment by publishing an OECD text on their official government letterhead and publicly releasing the letter (though the details of the reforms were kept secret). In November 2000, the OECD included the main points of this text in a Memorandum of Understanding which tax havens were expected to sign. This proved unpopular, however, and from January 2001 it was sufficient to issue a press release endorsing the general points of the initiative. Any of the thirty-five jurisdictions that failed to make such a commitment, or committed and then failed to follow through with the necessary reforms as adjudged by the OECD, would be included on a further list of "uncooperative tax havens." The 2000 report also included a long list of measures to be employed against uncooperative tax havens, in addition to options already suggested in 1998. These included placing transactions with uncooperative tax havens under special scrutiny by tightening up reporting requirements for firms and individuals dealing with these jurisdictions. Another group of measures threatened to disallow tax deductions or credits earned in listed havens, or to impose special charges on transactions with them, or to apply a withholding tax on payments to residents of listed countries. Finally, OECD countries were urged to reconsider any "nonessential" aid granted to targeted jurisdictions that refused to make scheduled commitments.[96] These multilateral sanctions would not be imposed by the OECD as such, but by individual member states using the secretariat as a coordinating framework.

Although the OECD initiative garnered consistent endorsements from the various G7 heads of state and finance ministers' meetings, and benefited from the complementary work of the FATF and FSF, this did not mean that it could rely on a united front. A particularly damaging split within the OECD was the decision of Luxembourg and Switzerland to abstain from endorsing the report. Both countries announced that they would not be bound by its recommendations, and appended summaries of their criticism of the OECD's whole approach to tax competition in the 1998 report. The Swiss emphasized that they had considered vetoing the whole report (given that the OECD must operate by unanimity), but had presumably decided that the degree of ill-feeling this would arouse among other members, particularly the G7 members, ruled out this course of action. Both countries are commonly classified as tax havens, indeed many small, island tax havens have copied Swiss and Luxembourg models of banking secrecy and other financial regulations. The critical stance of these countries toward the campaign was a persistent embarrassment to the OECD, leaving it vulnerable to charges of hypocrisy and double-standards as detailed in chapter 3. The dissenting statements in the 1998 report were critical of the decision to restrict its scope to financial and other geographically mobile services while leaving out manufacturing, which made it "partial and unbalanced." They further took issue with the implication that either tax competition or low tax rates were inherently bad, defended bank secrecy, and condemned the procedures and tone as one-sided and coercive.[97] Neither country has since changed its position or moderated its criticism of the project.

Although tax havens are certainly nothing new, financial deregulation, advances in communication technology, and especially a growing public concern about globalization (broadly and variously conceived), have helped to increase the awareness of tax havens both in small poor states and in large rich ones. The former have seen entry into the financial services industry as one of their only options for diversifying their economies and responding to declining commodity prices and aid budgets. Over the last decade or two the G7 and OECD states have become increasingly sensitive to the fiscal consequences of the mismatch between national taxation authority and the global economy, particularly with regard to the potential for tax competition and tax avoidance/evasion to undermine government revenues. Political concerns about tax competition were sharpened by the availability of economic theories that emphasized negative fiscal externalities, the potential for international collective action problems, and empirical literature suggesting that corporations were becoming more sensitive to tax differentials. From the mid-1990s, Western governments responded with several multilateral regulatory initiatives. These initiatives included the EU Code of Conduct and Savings Tax Directive, the FATF, the FSF, and most directly the G7-mandated OECD report on tackling "unfair" tax competition.

The tax haven track of the OECD initiative broke new ground for the organization with regard to substance and approach. For the first time there was an attempt to regulate tax policies, formerly the quintessential sovereign prerogative of states, at the global level. And for the first time the OECD sought to pressure unwilling non-member states to adopt laws not of their choosing or design.

CHAPTER TWO

Regulative Norms and
Inappropriate Means

In their efforts to impose or fend off global tax regulation, both the OECD and targeted small states resorted to rhetorical strategies to advance their interests. With the huge power disparities between the two sides, small states listed as tax havens had few other options than a rhetorical strategy. For OECD member states, however, a range of other options was available and potentially more efficacious. Thus before surveying the main themes of the rhetorical contest in chapter 3, and analyzing the results in chapters 4, 5, and 6, it is important to establish why the dominant powers ruled out military and economic coercion. The absence of such coercion is puzzling because, as we will see, any one of these tactics would have had a very good chance of forcing small states to comply with the OECD's demands. The other major goal of the chapter is to investigate an alternative hypothesis consistent with the OECD's retreat from its main goals in 2001. This alternative account holds that corporations sabotaged or defeated the OECD's regulatory ambitions in order to protect their tax shelters. As opposed to focusing on states and intergovernmental organizations, this view privileges capitalist or corporate interest. Rather than assuming the small states won a victory, this view maintains that big business beat the tax collectors.

We will see how potential approaches to coercing the compliance of the smaller states were normatively ruled out, and thus how the OECD came to depend upon a rhetorical strategy. This choice, which was relatively favorable to the small states, given their minuscule military and economic resources, was shaped primarily by regulative norms that ruled out military force and economic coercion. I argue that there are good reasons for believing that these coercive tactics would have been effective, but that they were not used because they were inappropriate in normative terms, as opposed to inefficient in instrumental terms. My demonstration will be based on the rather familiar "three-cornered contest," between the norm-based hypothesis advanced in this chapter, the leading alternative explanation, and the available evidence.[1] The sections that consider these issues are prefaced by a discussion of the definition and nature of regulative norms in general. The regulative norms in question were a mixture of generalized principles governing relations between states that sharply limit the use of force and more specific norms relevant on account of the technocratic identity of the OECD as an international organization comprised of "apolitical" experts.

Given that the G7 countries have the vast majority of the world's naval power at their disposal, and their opponents have only token armed forces or none at all, gunboat diplomacy would seem to offer a quick, easy, and effective means to enforce compliance with regulatory demands. Such interventions by larger states against small and / or non-Western polities over economic and financial disputes have a long history.[2] There are no reasons to think that changes in the technology of modern naval warfare have made these tactics obsolete. Instead, what has changed and made this option almost unthinkable is the evolution of regulative norms which rule military action out of consideration. Objections that this option is so far-fetched as to not be worth discussing miss the point: gunboat diplomacy was so common in the recent past that its current illegitimacy is remarkable in and of itself. The prohibition against military force in this context illustrates an instance of an almost universally shared and deeply internalized norm acting to remove one possible avenue of action from the calculations of states. Because the use of armed force against tax havens was so obviously inappropriate, because the relevant norm was taken for granted, this part of the explanation has a strong structural cast. In contrast, actors and agency had a prominent role in deciding whether or not economic coercion was an appropriate response to the resistance of small states.

Proponents of economic sanctions and economic coercion more generally have fallen upon hard times of late. Critics have noted the low success rate of sanctions, success defined as effecting the desired policy change in the target state, and the long list of accompanying conditions that tends to be associated with the rare successes that are recorded. Yet despite this disillusionment, most of the small states running afoul of the OECD tax competition initiative are extremely vulnerable to economic coercion, broadly defined. They are characterized by tiny economies generally dependent on only tourism and a few commodities, which means they have to import almost everything. Most advantageous for opponents, targeted small states are often dependent on aid from the very same core countries whose tax bases they are accused of eroding. Furthermore, rather than needing to coordinate the efforts of thirty different countries, only a small subgroup of the OECD's larger states would have needed to participate in order to make sanctions effective. In the 2000 report, *Towards Global Tax Co-operation*, the OECD went so far as to develop a range of "defensive measures" to pressure recalcitrant small states into compliance under eleven different headings, from abrogating tax treaties, to imposing special fees on transactions with noncompliant jurisdictions, to cutting aid payments.

Despite advantageous factors, economic measures have never been employed. This chapter argues that the reluctance to use economic coercion can again be traced to regulative norms. In contrast to the clear-cut force and relevance of the prohibition against military action, however, the question of whether or not economic coercion was an appropriate means for actors in this context was far less certain. Within the international organizations, national governments and the transnational audience, people asked, "does the use of economic coercion constitute appropriate behavior in this context?" In 2001, crucial actors resolved that overt coercion was inappropriate, and thus, after repeated delays, the threat of "defensive measures" was discredited.

Finally, and moving away from the predominant focus on states, it is important to consider business interests. Aside from the targeted states themselves, the biggest losers from an OECD success would be those wealthy individuals and corporations who use tax havens to escape their domestic tax obligations. In turn, these actors had a strong incentive to mobilize and defeat the OECD initiative. Such a result would leave tax havens as impotent and incidental beneficiaries. Despite the close fit of this view with deeply entrenched preconceptions in some parts of the field, there is little evidence that corporate interests played the most important, or even *an* important, role in the defeat of the OECD campaign. Private sector interests were deliberately shut out of the agenda-setting stage, the time at which such interests could have had most influence. They had no role in defining "harmful tax competition" or designing the strategy to respond to it. Once the campaign was under way, a united business front was unlikely, as some firms and industries in high tax countries stood to benefit from the removal of tax haven–based competitors. Two of the OECD's most important opponents, the predominantly Caribbean intergovernmental International Tax and Investment Organisation and the Washington-based Center for Freedom and Prosperity, cannot be reduced to fronts for business interests. Both were poor and depended on a media-based rhetorical strategy. Interviews with those across the spectrum confirm that when the Bush administration defected from the OECD initiative in 2001 this was a product of ideologically motivated persuasion and not narrow money politics. More generally, the closeness of links with the corporate sector often proved to be an unreliable gauge of support or opposition for the OECD's efforts.

Regulative Norms

Some actions are motivated by rational calculations of self-interest, some by adherence to norms governing appropriate behavior, and some by a mixture of both.

Rationality stipulates "Do X to get Y," whereas norms stipulate simply "Do X" or "Don't do X."[3] Rational action is instrumental: means are chosen (and considered of value) as part of a strategy to achieve an end, whereas norm-based behavior is noninstrumental. Norms influence behavior through external and internal sanctions. External sanctions are social and imposed on norm-breakers by a community or peer group by means of disapproval and ostracism. Internal sanctions refer to feelings of shame, guilt, and conflict with respect to beliefs and self-conceptions.[4] The coincidence of norms with self-interested rational behavior is problematic in that people often subscribe to norms that they interpret in a way that advances their own selfish interests (as in the case of rhetorical action considered in chapter 5).

"Regulative norms" delimit socially acceptable rather than selfishly optimizing behavior. A "logic of appropriateness" accounts for the behavior of actors in contrast to an instrumental "logic of consequences."[5] Regulative norms "shape the instruments or means that states find available and appropriate. . . . Even when actors are aware of a wide array of means to accomplish their policy objectives, they may nevertheless reject some means as inappropriate because of normative constraints."[6] This chapter is focused on regulative norms in discussing options that were materially open to the OECD countries (military force), and to the OECD as an institution (invoking economic coercion), options that were normatively closed off to the OECD and its member states.[7]

In dealing with regulative norms it is possible to draw on the rich vein of work on this subject developed over the last two decades. Sometimes regulative norms clearly delimit appropriate from inappropriate behavior, such as the prohibition against gunboat diplomacy. But in everyday life as well as international politics, norms are often vague, their application to a specific circumstance may be uncertain, and there may be conflicting norms at play.[8] This was particularly the case with the potential application of economic pressure against defiant tax havens, either at the behest of the OECD or by an ad hoc coalition of its member states. In dealing with these situations of ethical uncertainty, I follow the conventional view that actors engage in a process of reasoning to determine the appropriate course of action in the given context.[9] This reasoning process may be internal, but it also may involve debate and persuasive efforts by others to clarify which norm is applicable in the circumstances.[10] Deeply internalized norms that are taken for granted may produce unreflective compliance. However because of the scope for ambiguity and debate, more often which norm affects behavior is to some degree contested and "up for grabs." The play of norms thus has a strong component of agency, as recognized by those who introduced this concept to International Relations.[11]

It has been a common criticism from those skeptical of norms, but also by more sympathetic observers, that scholars have not devoted sufficient attention to the mechanisms by which norms take effect. It is argued that there is a need for more careful use of evidence in tracing their impact.[12] To avoid this pitfall, the chapter provides a detailed investigation of the reasoning behind key actors' decisions using public sources and confidential interviews. Rather than merely showing that actors' behavior was consistent with prevailing norms, the aim is to demonstrate that a norm-based argument better accounts for political developments than leading alternatives. In line with conventional practice, a "three-cornered contest" is set up between the norm-based explanation, alternative explanations, and available evidence.[13]

Aside from looking at norms trumping rational self-interested courses of action like gunboat diplomacy, the book also examines instances where both norms and rational considerations interact and jointly shape decisions and behavior.[14] It is hard to maintain that actions may be a product of either the desire to conform to shared social standards or calculating self-interest, but never some combination of the two. Although this chapter sees regulative norms as providing the main reasons why plausible and compelling alternative means of bringing targeted jurisdictions into line with the OECD's preferred standards were eschewed, it does not aim to show that rational self-interest had no role in this result.

The Military Non-Option

When asked about Jersey's options in the face of pressure to reform its financial system, the relevant minister replied: "What are they going to do, send in the gunboats?"[15] Likewise, in talking about compliance issues associated with the initiative, an official from the secretariat prefaced his remarks: "The OECD doesn't have any aircraft carriers."[16] No one has ever seriously raised the prospect of using force in settling the dispute over tax competition. Realists and those convinced that norms are little more than "organized hypocrisy"[17] would probably maintain that the decision to rely on nonmilitary means was the product of cost-benefit calculations by policy makers—in this case, due to the inefficiency of military solutions and cost relative to other options. In response, this section argues that military coercion would have been eminently efficacious and almost cost-free in material terms, and the fact that such coercion was not employed reflects the power of regulative norms. In a sense, it is correct to assert that military action would have been "too costly." But this is true only if the costs are counted in normative terms that run directly against the realist view of the world, in particular, because of their contention of historical continuity and the perpetual centrality of military rivalry.[18] A discussion of military means in relation to an issue of this nature seems to belong to a bygone era, not because these means would be so inefficient, but rather vice versa; they would be highly costly because the standards of legitimate conduct toward small states have changed so much.[19]

Several of the nations on the OECD June 2000 list have been subject to military action in the last couple of decades. Grenada and Panama were invaded by the United States in 1983 and 1989 respectively. Such operations were not necessarily low cost, with the best part of three divisions committed to Panama and even tiny Grenada costing nineteen U.S. dead, but in each case the goal was to force a regime change and completely occupy the country rather than change a policy. Much less demanding were the type of limited naval actions previously used by imperial powers to compel loan repayments, open ports to trade, and capture customs houses. Now merely a term of abuse for other people's foreign policy, gunboat diplomacy was a common and effective tool of statecraft in commercial disputes until somewhere around the interwar period.[20] In 1923, for example, warships from Britain, France, Japan, Italy, and Portugal ensured foreign control of Canton's customs houses against Chinese efforts to regain them and the accompanying flow of tax revenue.[21] For decades, naval demonstrations and gunboats were also standard operating procedure in extracting loan repayments from delinquent Latin American and Eastern Mediterranean governments. Methods included visibly patrolling the littoral area, blockades, seizing shipping, bombardment, and landing marines.

There are two possible material reasons, compatible with a realist account, as to why the practice of gunboat diplomacy has fallen into disuse and thus was not entertained as an option against tax havens. The first would be that during the nineteenth century seaborne trade became less important relative to domestic production. As a result, countries have moved away from being dependent on customs duties and tariffs for government revenue. The relevance is that previously, by imposing a blockade or capturing port facilities, relatively small naval forces could not only deny tax revenue to the local government, but also could take the revenue for themselves. With the rise of direct taxes, this is no longer the case.[22] The exceptions to both these trends, however, are small island states, overwhelmingly dependent on seaborne trade for almost all the goods they consume and generally relying on customs and import duties for a very large part of their tax revenue.

A second explanation for the decline of the peacetime use of naval coercion against small states, eminently in line with realist logic, would be advances in the technology of war. Potentially, such technological changes might mean that hostile ships have become much more vulnerable to a range of relatively cheap weapons that can inflict catastrophic damage, including torpedo boats, anti-ship guided missiles, and, above all, mines. Mines, in some cases of World War I vintage and capable of being dropped over the side of civilian ships, have successfully crippled a U.S. frigate in 1988, and a cruiser and helicopter carrier in 1991.[23] But these technological advances have hardly made naval power obsolete in such roles as seizing disputed islands and enforcing claims to territorial waters. In any case, nearly all of the states listed by the OECD have no armed forces to speak of nor any of the capabilities listed above.

What has changed is the legitimacy of using naval power in resolving economic differences between states. The term "gunboat diplomacy" is inextricably associated with imperialism, the oppression of the weak by the strong, and the absence of international law. As such, the unacceptability of naval coercion in these circumstances is linked to much broader changes relating to when it is acceptable for large states to use force against smaller ones, and indeed when it is acceptable to use force at all. Handel notes that great powers have become increasingly sensitive to "a loss of prestige resulting from the appearance of 'bullying' a weak state."[24] Speaking of weak post-colonial states, Jackson argues that they are the beneficiaries of a kind of "sovereignty-plus" that grants them protection from military predation by the major powers.[25]

The normative restrictions on the use of force against small states are incisively examined by Alexander Wendt, using an apt hypothetical case.

> Consider the question of why the U.S. does not invade the Bahamas. Coercion does not seem to be the answer, since probably no state could prevent the U.S. from taking them. . . . The self-interest argument initially seems to do better: U.S. policymakers might calculate that conquest would not pay because of the damage it would do to U.S. reputation as a law-abiding citizen, and because the U.S. can achieve most of the benefits of conquest through economic dominance anyway [more on this later]. Both of these assumptions about the cost-benefit ratio are probably true, but there are two reasons to doubt that they explain U.S. inaction. First, it is doubtful that U.S. policymakers are making or even ever did make such calculations. It may be that respecting Bahamian sovereignty is in the self-interest of the U.S., but if this does not figure in its thinking then in what sense does it "explain" its behavior? Second, the definition of what counts as "paying" is shot through with cultural context.[26]

Using military force against tax havens would be "too costly" precisely because of the damage done in violating such an important regulative norm. But more than this, historical changes redefining what constitutes legitimate international behavior "have removed that option from our decision tree."[27]

Economic Coercion

Against small and developing states, freezing overseas assets, blocking multilateral loans, imposing antidumping measures on a few key commodities, issuing tourist advisories, cutting air links or imposing visa restrictions on target country nationals could all inflict a great deal of damage. As discussed previously, the 2000 report *Towards Global Tax Co-operation* provided a list of options for "defensive measures" to be taken against "uncooperative tax havens" by OECD member countries, with these measures to be invoked and coordinated by the secretariat. Such measures included imposing extra fees on financial transactions with listed jurisdictions, abrogating existing tax treaties, and suspending "nonessential" bilateral aid.[28] The measures suggested by the OECD never amounted to the kind of economic sanctions in the narrow legal sense that have had many well-publicized failures (Iraq 1990–2003, Cuba) and a few ambiguous successes (South Africa).[29] But in a broader sense the measures clearly constitute sanctions or economic coercion. Their aim was to bring targeted states into compliance with the wishes of those applying these measures by way of the threat or actuality of economic pain.

A wide range of measures could potentially be applied to force tax havens into line, including but not limited to the "defensive measures" specified by the OECD. But despite the excellent prospects for success, there has been a strange reluctance to use this kind of instrument. A series of "final" deadlines notwithstanding, no such measures were ever called for by the OECD. Indeed, by 2003 the OECD press spokesperson was happy to state on the record that there was effectively no chance of "defensive measures" ever being invoked, even against jurisdictions that still refused to commit to the initiative or had reneged on their earlier commitments.[30] Sure enough, in 2003 the last deadline for "uncooperative tax havens" to comply with OECD demands passed without any mention of sanctions.

Some observers have speculated that the OECD could face legal difficulties or conflicts with the World Trade Organization (which counts ten of the listed jurisdictions among its members) if it applied sanctions aimed at pressuring listed states into tax and banking reforms. Conceivably, this possibility might have inhibited the OECD from following up on its threats. The OECD may have been particularly sensitive to these concerns after its proposed Multilateral Agreement on Investment had to be abandoned late in the peace after concerns were raised about its compatibility with WTO agreements. (Protests from developing countries and NGOs and divisions within the OECD itself were also major contributing factors to this failure.) Two papers written on this question by officials associated with the Commonwealth (one of very few international organizations to support the listed states as discussed below) have raised potential problems with the "defensive measures" suggested by the OECD.[31] The first set of potential challenges to OECD sanctions could be based on a violation of market access, according to Article XVII of the General Agreement on Trade in Services (GATS). Another might relate to a potential violation of the Most Favored Nation principle that "if an OECD service consumer . . . purchasing banking services in a listed tax haven which is deemed to be an uncooperative jurisdiction has a discriminatory withholding tax imposed on their financial transactions inside an OECD country."[32] A possible case could be made before the WTO Dispute Resolution Mechanism that OECD countries were practicing "unjustifiable discrimination" and "arbitrary discrimination," given that Switzerland and Luxembourg have very similar features in their tax and banking codes and are not sanctioned.[33]

Gilmore notes that the OECD seems to have been short on legal expertise in compiling its reports.

> Neither the 1998 nor the 2000 Reports seem to have been written with a legal audience in mind. . . . By way of illustration, while the 2000 Report talks of "coordinated defensive measures" the 1998 text uses a range of terms ("countermeasures," "enforcement

measures," "counteracting measures," and "defensive measures") seemingly inter-
changeably. A similar tendency is evident in the News Releases of and public statements
made on behalf of the OECD in this context. While such terms may be capable of use
as general synonyms in political or economic discourse this is not the case within the
context of general international law where certain of the above have broadly settled technical meaning.[34]

He further observes that the OECD could conceivably be in violation of the principle of nonintervention according to commitments made by its members in the UN
General Assembly (Resolution 2625 XXV) or in the case of the United States,
Canada, and Mexico, the Charter of the Organization of American States (Articles
19 and 24).

However, for all these speculations there has been little movement on behalf of
the targeted tax havens to mount a legal challenge. The GATT and GATS were explicitly designed not to cover tax matters. Other observers are skeptical that jurisdictions subject to OECD countermeasures would in fact have any legal recourse.[35]
At best, such a move would direct OECD countries toward unambiguously legal
measures, such as terminating aid flows, and direct them away from others, such as
generalized withholding taxes that would be vulnerable to transactions routed
through third parties. Concerns about international legal complications have thus
played at best a very secondary role in explaining the OECD's reluctance to employ
sanctions to bring listed jurisdictions into line.

Despite the probable effectiveness of economic coercion, and the OECD's public threats to impose "coordinated defensive measures," general but ambiguous regulative norms ruling out sanctions as inappropriate behavior in this context became
fixed in transnational and domestic political discourse through debate and persuasion. In particular, key decision-makers within the OECD secretariat, Commonwealth OECD member states, and the United States became convinced that
sanctions were not appropriate behavior in the context. These decision makers asked
themselves "what is the appropriate course of action given the situation?" This
prompted a second-order question: "What kind of situation am I in?"[36] Although
the coverage of the themes and content of the debate is left to the following chapter,
the specific pathways in which these abstract norms came to affect particular policy
decisions is traced here. These routes comprised two generally parallel efforts on the
international level and within the United States to convince decision makers to define the situation and the appropriate course of action in such a way as to rule out
imposing sanctions. These efforts got under way in earnest in September–October
2000 and had born fruit by 2002, with the de facto abandonment of sanctions, and
the most important substantive elements of the initiative. Working from interview
data, supplemented with press coverage and secondary sources, it is possible to follow the processes through with which policy makers classified and characterized
their situation and what in turn they felt to be appropriate courses of action.

Debating the Inappropriateness of Sanctions

Although targeted states were always hostile to the initiative, coordinated opposition was slow to get going. In part this was a result of uncertainty by the OECD and affected states about where the initiative would end up; the campaign to enforce global tax regulations was new territory for all concerned.[37] Many outside the OECD by their own admission did not understand the novelty and ambition of the 1998 report until confronted with the June 2000 list. Additionally, almost all of the jurisdictions contained in this list had very severe resource constraints because of their small size. Individuals within their governments often had an improbably wide range of responsibilities, and the OECD was not a priority. In some cases the correspondence from the OECD sat around in in-trays for months without being opened.[38] Commercial and political rivalries within and between regions also hindered coordination. Small states later came to regard this slow response as an important mistake, one they are determined not to repeat.[39]

The release of the OECD's list of tax havens in June 2000 made countries sit up and take notice. Opposition first coalesced within the Caribbean, given the large number of jurisdictions targeted from the region. Possible reactions were discussed at the Caribbean Community (CARICOM) summit in St. Vincent and the Grenadines in July 2000, also attended by the Commonwealth Secretary General, with the Prime Minister of Barbados taking a leading role. In turn, a special CARICOM heads of government committee was formed to consider possible responses; it met later that month in St. Kitts and Nevis. The committee decided on a number of measures: a promise not to sign up to the OECD initiative, publicly challenging the OECD in international fora, bilaterally lobbying more sympathetic OECD member states, coordinating opposition with listed jurisdictions in other regions, inviting the Commonwealth to become involved in the issue, and canvassing legal options. A Caribbean Association of Regulators of International Business was formed involving representatives from central banks, insurance firms, and stock exchanges to enhance regional coordination on the issue.

Further momentum was generated when the OECD initiative was put on the agenda of the September 2000 Commonwealth Finance Ministers' Meeting in Malta at the behest of Canada and Caribbean countries. Because twenty-five of the thirty-five countries to appear on the June 2000 list, and five of six jurisdictions that had made advance commitments just before the list, were former or current British colonies, the Commonwealth became closely involved with the tax competition issue.[40] The subsequent annual meetings in 2002 and 2003 (the 2001 meeting was canceled in the wake of terrorist attacks that September) reaffirmed this support for listed states. Although bound to represent the interests of the Commonwealth's membership as a whole (including OECD members Britain, Canada, Australia, and New Zealand), the secretariat was particularly sympathetic to the small, developing members targeted by the initiative. It became a crucial source of financial and organizational support, sometimes to the annoyance of larger members, particularly Britain.[41]

Despite the fact that the Commonwealth includes four OECD members, the Finance Ministers' Meeting was generally critical of the OECD, and it provided a rare opportunity for the majority of the affected jurisdictions in Europe, the Caribbean, and the Pacific to meet, compare notes, and take the first steps toward a coordinated defense.[42] Delegates concluded that the OECD had misrepresented the views of some targeted jurisdictions to the others, which had so far reacted in isolation.[43] The Barbadian Prime Minister asked Secretary General McKinnon to set up a joint meeting between targeted jurisdictions and the OECD in Barbados.

The OECD was initially unsure how to respond, but agreed to co-host the meeting in January 2001.[44] While the OECD regarded this meeting as a chance to clear up "misunderstandings," affected jurisdictions that attended came to regard the meeting as a vital turning point in forming a united front. As such, they also saw the meeting as a crucial mistake by the OECD.[45] At the conclusion of the two-day event, it was hurriedly agreed to form a Joint Working Group. In large part this decision reflected the feeling among delegates that an achievement of the meeting had to be announced to the media. Co-chaired by Australia and Barbados, and including representatives of five other OECD members and six other non-OECD states, the Working Group was charged with continuing the discussions that had begun in Barbados in order to attempt a mutually agreed solution to the impasse. The Joint Working Group was abandoned after follow-up meetings in London and Paris made little progress, as the OECD delegates felt they did not have the authority to change the shape of the initiative. However, this was far from wasted effort for small states, whose representatives, assisted by the Commonwealth secretariat, formed the International Tax and Investment Organisation (ITIO, later to become the International Trade and Investment Organisation) in March 2001 to institutionalize their efforts to counter the tax competition initiative.

Led by Barbados, the British Virgin Islands, the Cayman Islands, and the Bahamas, the new organization included ten other members (Anguilla, Antigua and Barbuda, Belize, Cook Islands, Malaysia, St. Kitts and Nevis, St. Lucia, St. Vincent and the Grenadines, Turks and Caicos, and Vanuatu; later Samoa, Panama, and the Isle of Man joined). The Caribbean Community secretariat, the Pacific Islands Forum secretariat, the Eastern Caribbean Central Bank, and the Commonwealth secretariat participated as observers. The ITIO allowed for a far more effective platform from which to publicize critiques of the OECD initiative than it had done previously in terms of its uncoordinated responses; it hired a press spokesperson to run a highly effective media campaign. The ITIO had a chair that rotated on a half-year basis and relied on member state government ministries rather than a dedicated secretariat, holding meetings in advance of important Commonwealth and OECD summits.

The organization's small budget is provided by a modest $3,000 annual membership fee (which not all members manage to pay), supplemented by extra contributions from the more established Caribbean centers and the Commonwealth secretariat.

The Commonwealth-mediated connections began to pay dividends as small state representatives repeatedly put their case to Australia and New Zealand, which became reluctant to impose sanctions on targeted jurisdictions. This change was also reflected in, and accentuated by, the Pacific Islands Forum's (PIF) communiqués that were critical of the OECD's confrontational tactics.[46] The Prime Minster of New Zealand and the Australian Department of Foreign Affairs and Trade came to regard the application of economic coercion against small, fragile economies as an unseemly overreaction to policy differences.[47] More important, Caribbean jurisdictions, and particularly Barbados, had the opportunity to bring Canadian officials over to their side in various Commonwealth and hemispheric forums. Further close links existed as the Canadian executive directors in the Bretton Woods institutions represented the Caribbean. In turn, Canadian officials reproduced complaints by targeted states of the OECD initiative almost word for word in a presentation to U.S. government officials at a meeting in Quebec in April 2001; this echoed the presentation of the Antiguan Prime Minister to the newly elected President Bush at the same gathering.[48]

After the Barbados and Joint Working Group meetings, many in the OECD secretariat felt that sanctions should at least be delayed to allow more time for a consensual solution to be reached, one senior OECD official reporting that it would be "aggressive and confrontational" to go ahead with sanctions as originally planned.[49] Symptomatic of the OECD's discomfort with the notion of sanctions is the lengths it had gone to in order to avoid the term from the beginning. When asked by an interviewer about when sanctions would be imposed, Jeffrey Owens, head of the OECD Centre for Tax Policy and Administration, replied: "I do not like the term sanctions. What has been anticipated right from the inception of this work is that there will be defensive measures—measures which national governments, not the OECD, can take, if it is in their interest, to effectively enforce their tax rules and protect their tax bases."[50] Owens reiterated the same point two years later when asked what the OECD would do to compel uncooperative tax havens to come on board, replying: "I don't like the word 'compel.' The OECD as an organization has no powers by which to compel anyone to do anything."[51] Speaking on the same topic, Gabriel Makhlouf, Chair of the Committee on Fiscal Affairs, "characterized these not as counter-measures but rather as defensive measures that OECD and non-OECD countries have the right to take to protect their revenue base."[52] Writing on the 1998 report, an official from the New Zealand tax authority argued that "The OECD report does not propose sanctions. It lists possible measures that OECD members might consider employing against uncooperative tax havens."[53]

These denials were an uneasy fit with the fact that it was the OECD as an institution, led by the secretariat, that had compiled the list of possible measures to be applied, and would again draw up the list of jurisdictions to be targeted. And as outside critics pointed out, deliberately wrecking small, poor economies hardly fitted within the OECD's defining mission of promoting economic cooperation and development.[54] General and diffuse norms against sanctions were especially relevant because of the OECD's particular institutional identity and role expectations. Doubts in the secretariat about the wisdom and appropriateness of economic coercion thus intersected with increasing reservations within the Canadian, Australian, and New Zealand governments (the UK, with an eye to intra-EU negotiations over the Savings Tax Directive, was much less sympathetic). The second, sometimes intersecting, effort against the OECD initiative played out in the United States.

The campaign against the OECD initiative began in the United States with the formation of the Center for Freedom and Prosperity (CFP) in October 2000, comprised of Andrew Quinlan, Daniel Mitchell (also of the Heritage Foundation), and Véronique de Rugy (also of the Cato Institute and American Enterprise Institute). What the CFP lacked in numbers it quickly made up for in influence, as even OECD and European Commission officials grudgingly admit.[55] Critics and supporters alike characterize the CFP trio as genuine ideologues rather than actors providing a façade for hidden corporate interests. Representative of growing suspicions in Congress and elsewhere, these lobbyists were incensed by the thought of a "global tax police" operating on behalf of high-taxing European "socialist" governments, directed by a supranational bureaucracy based in France.

These lobbyists were vital in fixing the issue as one of protecting fiscal sovereignty and defending the principle of nonintervention among key sectors of the U.S. government, leading to Washington's defection from the campaign in May 2001. This change of heart in large part reflected the domestic political resonance of international norms. Initially the CFP had assumed that the Democrats would win the 2000 presidential election, and thus they opted to try to block U.S. participation in the initiative through the Congress,[56] quickly gaining the support of Dick Armey, then-Republican majority leader in the House. They established an extensive website (www.freedomandprosperity.org), a regular email bulletin, and set to work lobbying various Washington insiders. Mitchell and Quinlan were invited to the January 2001 Barbados meeting by Sir Ronald Sanders, High Commissioner and foreign policy representative of Antigua and Barbuda. There they coached Caribbean delegates, sparred with Jeffrey Owens and OECD press spokesman Nicholas Bray, and traded threats and insults with U.S. Treasury officials, who accused them of being "traitors." Although briefly part of the Antiguan delegation, they were excluded from the official sessions after OECD delegates threatened to withdraw.[57] Their sweeping and vitriolic attacks on the OECD helped to restore listed states' morale.[58] Furthermore, the CFP brought along Armey's main tax adviser Elizabeth Tobias to strengthen links between the opposition to the OECD in Washington and the Caribbean.[59]

The Bush administration came into office uncertain about the initiative against harmful tax competition and, for several months, gave conflicting signals on whether it would continue to support the OECD. The CFP lobbyists and their allies were by no means kicking against an open door in seeking to persuade the new administration to abandon the OECD campaign. As a result of the disputed election results and the slow transition, Washington paid little attention to the Barbados meeting or the subsequent Joint Working Group. Secretary of Treasury O'Neill endorsed a G7 finance ministers' communiqué in February 2001, praising the OECD's work in combating harmful tax competition. Career Treasury officials were also consistently committed to the initiative. However, thanks to the CFP's extensive connections and barrage of emails, articles began appearing about the OECD campaign under the headline "Global Tax Police."[60] Powerful Congressmen and Senators such as Tom DeLay, Jesse Helms, and eighty-four others wrote to O'Neill, arguing that "Sovereign nations should be free to determine their own tax policies."[61] The CFP also successfully lobbied such key officials as Mark Weinberger (the Assistant Treasury Secretary for Tax Policy), Lawrence Lindsey (presidential economics adviser), Cesar Conda (domestic policy adviser to Vice President Cheney), and Glenn Hubbard (Chairman of the White House Council of Economic Advisers) in February–March 2001. Nobel prize–winning economists Milton Friedman and James Buchanan came out in support of the CFP and against the OECD campaign. Finally, by working through Washington-based Caribbean representatives, the CFP also gained the endorsement of all twenty-six members of the Congressional Black Caucus whose members, like the Commonwealth, were offended by the prospect of applying sanctions against small developing states.[62] The diversity of the coalition that the CFP managed to build in opposition to OECD sanctions, together with the initial indecision of the Bush administration, indicate that this success was premised on persuasion rather than unthinking ideological reactions. In parallel to their domestic activities, Quinlan and Mitchell were in close contact with Caribbean governments. And in this way, when O'Neill announced in the media on 10 May 2001 that he was withdrawing U.S. support for the initiative in its present form, the main points of the tax havens' critique as developed in the previous two years (discussed extensively in the following chapter) were reproduced in his statement, particularly regarding the illegitimacy of using economic coercion to effect change in the tax policies of sovereign states.[63]

Thus although the OECD had threatened various forms of economic coercion against noncompliant small states in 1998 and 2000, from 2001 it was forced to back down. Jurisdictions listed in June 2000 did not comply with the conditions set out by the OECD 1998–2000, while the OECD's "defensive measures" turned out to be bluff. The OECD has refrained from calling for sanctions to be applied against uncooperative tax havens and publicly admits it has no plans to do so in the future. This climb-down was part of the more general process by which the initiative as a whole was discredited, as is covered in detail in chapters 4 and 6. The retreat was not caused by any change in the distribution of capabilities between the two sides or by changing judgments about the effectiveness of economic coercion against targeted states. Instead, key actors in OECD member governments and the secretariat itself, who had initially supported sanctions or were undecided as to their use, changed their minds and came to the conclusion that such pressures were an inappropriate way to resolve this dispute. These actors reached this conclusion after being persuaded by officials from targeted states, the Commonwealth secretariat, and Washington lobbyists, that their behavior should be governed by generalized though ambiguous norms of nonintervention and pacific dispute settlement which ruled out this kind of economic pressure. Rather than "floating freely," these primarily normative appeals, developed at the international level, became fixed in U.S. domestic politics as links formed between Caribbean states, sympathetic third countries, and Washington lobbyists.[64]

The OECD's disavowal of sanctions was one facet of the more general difficulties increasingly faced by the initiative. Critics' success in de-legitimating sanctions was part of their more general success in mobilizing opinion against the initiative as a whole. Similarly, the sensitivity of the OECD in relation to the rhetorical contest over sanctions reflected tenets of its reputation and identity, which will be analyzed in detail in chapter 5. It is appropriate, however, to briefly foreshadow this discussion to complete the explanation of why sanctions were not imposed. Harking back to the general treatment of norms at the beginning of the chapter, there were both external and internal pressures on the OECD relating to the question of sanctions. In neither case were these pressures inevitable or irresistible; instead, they flowed from the development of the rhetorical contest to persuade participants and observers of the relative merits and legitimacy of the opposing perspectives. Although the OECD made the public threat of sanctions a central feature of its strategy to bring listed states into line with new global regulations, there were early signs of discomfort within the institution about this approach.

Taking the external factors first, the OECD's influence and effectiveness depend on a type of reputation and authority that would be eroded if the institution started twisting governments' arms to adopt its preferred policy solutions.[65] To this extent, staying "in character," or in line with institutional role expectations, is not only a matter of conscience or etiquette, it is also crucially linked with continued influence. Thus social sanctions and an enlightened self-interest in maintaining reputation pushed the OECD away from economic coercion. Additionally, regulative norms had also become internalized at an institutional and even individual level. To this extent, norm compliant actions have been noninstrumental as well as instrumental. As such, OECD norm-compliance represents a halfway point or hybrid case between the deep normative structures preventing the use of force against tax havens, and the damage to reputation by blacklisting tax havens. Institutional culture and professional socialization limit options for decision makers, who then search within a set of choices restricted by conceptions of appropriateness:

> Political actors associate specific actions with specific situations by rules of appropri-
> ateness. What is appropriate for a particular person in a particular situation is defined
> by political and social institutions and transmitted through socialization. . . . The ac-
> countant asks: What does an accountant do in a situation like this?[66]

When officials asked themselves, "What does a member of the OECD secretariat
do in a situation like this?" the answer did not involve threatening or inflicting economic pain. The OECD sees itself, and is seen by others, as a community of experts,
technocrats, or scientists. Individuals within the institution reflect this identity both
by selection and socialization, the latter facilitated by the slow turnover of person-
nel, meaning that even by the standards of other international organizations like the
IMF, the OECD has particularly homogenous staff.[67] Molded by this professional
background and in an institution devoted to the accumulation of scientific knowledge, disseminated by a process of reasoned persuasion, the idea of coercing others
to adopt recommended policy solutions goes very much against the grain: "The prototypic expert engages in research; the prototypic politician engages in logrolling."[68]
The biases against "untoward" or inappropriate behavior thus operated at the individual and the institutional level through both internal and external mechanisms.
Regulative norms that may exert a relatively weak influence on states applied much
more strongly to the OECD.

The Hidden Hand of Corporate Power?

If sanctions fizzled, can this be ascribed to pressure from domestic and transnational capital? Aside from targeted states, nonresident investors threatened by the
closure of their offshore tax shelters had the most to lose by any successful effort to
regulate international tax competition. Here I address the possibility of a hidden
corporate hand, first, by arguing that there was little in the way of corporate lobbying, either to keep the issue of regulating tax competition off the agenda, or to oppose it once it got going. Second, in the United States and elsewhere, having a
material stake in the defeat of the OECD initiative was, for domestic and transnational actors, neither a necessary nor sufficient condition for opposing it. Finally,
neither supporters nor opponents of the initiative have credited corporate actors
with much influence over the result. Empirically, my account involves a return to
parts of the story told earlier, in particular, the crucial period of the first few months
of the Bush administration up until Secretary O'Neill's public criticisms of the
OECD in the media on 10 May 2001. Ultimately, though, it is impossible to prove
a negative like the nonexistence of a powerful corporate lobby, and to this extent the
evidence presented is suggestive rather than conclusive.

Corporate lobbies or dominant classes may best protect their interests through
agenda control, ensuring that unwanted proposals and projects never see the light

of day. This might even extend to the point where decision makers are captured by class interests to such an extent that they cannot even conceive of policies disfavored by elites.[69] Of course, as the OECD initiative did see the light of day, these more extreme forms of elite control can be discounted in this instance. There was little involvement on the part of the business sector or financial services industry in the preparatory work of the OECD on tax competition from the early 1990s to 1996, and none in the design of the tax competition initiative 1996–98. In part this reflects a deliberate choice by the OECD. Those drafting the report realized that, because of the sensitivity of the issue, to include corporate representatives could make an already difficult task impossible.[70] A comparison with the OECD's work on the taxation of e-commerce indicates what a departure the exclusionary approach was from standard procedure in not soliciting the input and opinion of business.

The Committee on Fiscal Affairs' work on e-commerce has been much more typical of the OECD's general working methods and shows a prominent level of business involvement that is entirely lacking in the tax competition area. In addition to governmental representatives, the Technical Assistance Groups designing standards in this area include formal representation from such firms as Microsoft, KPMG, Hewlett Packard, eBay, Deloitte and Touche, British Telecom, and the Confederation of Swedish Enterprise.[71] In this context, private sector groups have been active both inside these formal groups, and in releasing and responding to public discussion drafts and critiques as standards in the area of e-commerce are hammered out. In contrast, the unusual lack of consultation with corporate interests from drafting the 1998 tax competition report led the OECD's own in-house Business Industry Advisory Council to issue a public condemnation of the initiative in June 1999. Corporate interests were thus excluded from the process of designing the initiative, the stage at which they could have probably had the most impact. Instead, like tax havens, they were presented with the definitions, aims, and strategies of the initiative as a fait accompli.

After the 1998 report was published, the corporate response was fairly muted, though there was some isolated criticism from industry publications.[72] The most common reaction from the corporate sector to the OECD's tax competition initiative was to sit on the sidelines. Writing three years after the publication of the 1998 report, one of the best-informed business commentators on the topic, and a critic of the OECD, bemoaned the passivity of business interests in the face of the initiative.

> The financial services industry has generally taken a watchful wait-and-see approach.
> . . . [T]he business community in general and the financial services industry in particular have not taken a proactive role. . . . [I]n the OECD countries the financial services industry has not actively expressed a concern about the harmful tax competition initiative. The financial services industry has both the financial and political clout to persuade the decision makers (i.e., politicians) to reconsider. As the train moves farther from the station, the opportunities for the financial services industry to persuade decision makers become increasingly infrequent.[73]

Richard Hay, one of the few private sector practitioners to devote substantial amounts of time and effort to opposing the OECD, made a similar criticism concerning the inactivity of global financial institutions:

> To the extent that such institutions have followed developments, they have tended to passively monitor and then simply reduce activities in, or move off, struggling platforms. In a strictly commercial sense this limited contribution is irrational, considering the costs of winding down infrastructure in one jurisdiction and then rebuilding it in another.[74]

There was certainly no lobbying campaign by potentially affected business on the scale of that related to the taxation of e-commerce (either in U.S. or OECD forums), or with the EU Savings Tax Directive. With reference to Europe, the UK was resolutely against a withholding tax solution because of the fear that this would severely damage the London bond market. Luxembourg, and to a lesser extent Austria and Belgium, openly linked their opposition to the option of information exchange to the damage it would do to their banking industries. In these other important tax policy debates, taxing e-commerce and nonresident EU savings, corporate interests have played a very important, or even determinant interest, but neither private firms nor governments acting at their behest have felt any great need to hide these links, which are readily observable from the public record.

It would be a mistake to assume that the corporate sector had a uniform attitude toward the OECD initiative or was automatically in favor of tax havens. As outlined in the previous chapters, tax havens are used by a very wide range of firms and individuals for very different purposes. The potential losers, those corporations and individuals making tax savings, not only were largely unknown to each other, but were extremely publicity shy in a way that has prevented effective political campaigning on the issue.[75] In an important paper devoted to analyzing the corporate responses to international tax competition and regulatory measures to counter it, Bernauer and Styrsky show that firms are just as likely to be *in favor* of greater regulation and *against* tax competition as the other way around.[76] Onshore firms have lobbied governments and international organizations to prevent competitors gaining advantage through their offshore position. Critics in small states often charged that it was precisely because the OECD countries were so solicitous of their domestic financial services industries that they had decided to crack down against tax haven-based competitors, acting in a mercantilist fashion to protect them from foreign competition. Nor was the attitude of the financial services industry in listed states toward the initiative monolithic. Predictably, some were violently opposed to the initiative and strongly lobbied their governments to stand fast against the OECD, such as in Vanuatu, the Cook Islands, and Liechtenstein. In Barbados, however, the financial services industry urged the government to give in to OECD demands, to no avail. In the Cayman Islands and Bermuda, the private sector was supportive of the decision to make an advance commitment to the OECD in June 2000.[77]

The failure to exercise agenda setting control and a lack of evidence for an open campaign of lobbying still leaves open the possibility of a decisive role for corporate interests behind the scenes or via proxies. Returning to the problem of proving a negative, such a hypothesis is very hard to disconfirm. But again, reconstructing key elements of the struggle using interview data fails to dig up much evidence in favor of a powerful but hidden corporate role. One candidate for a "front organization" might be the ITIO, the organization formed by a group of Commonwealth states from the Caribbean and the Pacific. Yet the ITIO until 2006 had not a single paid employee, and has subsisted on less than $200,000 a year; as a result, it has led a fairly intermittent and precarious institutional life.

The most likely candidate, however, is the Center for Freedom and Prosperity, especially because of the crucial role it played in the Bush administration's defection. The CFP does not provide information on its funding, but in the period 2000–2005 it has had one salaried employee, the president Andrew Quinlan, while Véronique de Rugy was supported by the Cato Institute and then American Enterprise Institute, and Daniel Mitchell, perhaps the most active of the three, was at the Heritage Foundation. In the period 2000–2005, it is unlikely to have spent much more than $600,000. Like many other lobby groups, the CFP tends to exaggerate its size and importance, and it has a very extensive website and excellent contacts in the Republican party. But as even critics point out, it is a highly ideological group, rather than a manifestation of money politics. Its members and supporters achieve influence over the policy process through their persuasive efforts rather than promising campaign funding or delivering large blocks of electoral support. In this way, it is similar to the Heritage Foundation (which has worked closely with the CFP), referred to by Newt Gingrich as "the most far-reaching conservative organization in the country in the war of ideas, and one which had a tremendous impact not just in Washington, but literally across the planet."[78] The Heritage Backgrounder (written by Mitchell) against the OECD project conformed to specifications pioneered by the Foundation for maximum impact.[79]

Returning to some of the evidence presented in the earlier section on sanctions, the Bush administration, collectively and individually, came into office genuinely undecided as to the tax competition initiative, as even Congressional Republicans admitted.[80] But key political appointees in the Treasury were persuaded by the CFP and their allies that the OECD campaign was not in the national interest. Some on the political left were also open to suggestion as to where their interests lay in relation to this issue. Two months ahead of Paul O'Neill's public criticism, the Congressional Black Caucus published a letter on 14 March 2001 at the behest of the CFP condemning the OECD campaign in the following terms:

> The primary concern that we wish to address in this letter . . . is that the initiative will impose serious economic harm on developing nations. . . . The free flow of capital plays a critical role in improving economic conditions in poorer nations. Workers benefit from

increased job opportunities and higher wages. Governments also benefit because, even at low rates of tax, there are both direct and indirect increases in revenue. These are funds that are critically needed to provide education, health care, and other social services.[81]

The same right-wing American activist that reproduced the letter commented in response: "Even in my wildest dreams I never imagined that I would be on the same side of any issue as Maxine Waters, Sheila Jackson-Lee and Charles Rangel. But, in this case, I will take help where I can get it." To right wing audiences the CFP was more prone to stress the threat of high-taxing "socialist" European governments and international bureaucracies. They emphasized that tax competition was part of the reason why the United States had been so successful in attracting capital, something that "even Karl Marx and the Communists" had understood as essential to economic success.[82]

On the other hand, supporters of tax havens fumed about the encouragement given to the OECD by the *Financial Times*, accused of acting as the informal arm of the British Treasury by publishing carefully leaked stories to put pressure on tax havens.[83] This judgment is supported by an industry report stating that the *Financial Times* (surely the epitome of the corporate media outlet) "seems to regard itself as a flag-carrier for the FATF and OECD."[84] The "failure" of the *Financial Times*, and the Congressional Black Caucus, to adopt a position in line with their "objective" interests illustrates that favoring corporate interests in general was neither a sufficient nor necessary reason for opposing the OECD on this issue. The Bush administration arrived in office supporting the initiative, and only swung around to oppose it after several months of indecision. Those involved from all sides agree that the subsequent U.S. decision to withdraw was driven by the resonance of anti-OECD rhetoric with key Republican legislators and appointees within the executive, rather than decisions taken with an eye to straightforward corporate support.[85] None of this is to argue that material interests were unimportant. Quite the contrary, they have been central in defining the fundamental opposition between tax havens and core states. But the struggle, and even more the result, cannot be simply reduced to material factors, any more than the phenomenon of offshore finance as a whole can be attributed to corporate power or class interests.[86] Conceptually, this finding supports Finnemore's point that actors' interests cannot be simply assumed by judging from their material circumstances.[87]

Once OECD states decided that "something must be done" about certain forms of tax competition, the means available to them were limited by regulative norms. Conceptually, norms promote a different logic of behavior than instrumental means-ends calculations, but in practice a combination of both logics may apply. Norm compliance is fostered by internal mechanisms as actors are socialized to habitually follow rules of behavior, but also by external social sanctions.

Most obviously, military force was ruled out on normative grounds, even though gunboat diplomacy against small tax haven states would have been an efficient choice in materialist terms and has had a long history of success. Economic coercion used against the tiny and fragile economies of targeted small states would have been similarly effective from an instrumental point of view. When actors deliberated about the appropriateness of economic sanctions, however, the presence of vague and conflicting norms created uncertainty. Actors asked themselves "what sort of situation am I in and what is the appropriate course of action?" This questioning and uncertainty created room for agents to debate and attempt to persuade. Officials from targeted states, the Commonwealth, and U.S. pressure groups convinced key decision-makers in OECD member states and elsewhere that economic coercion was not a legitimate way of resolving the dispute. Critiques that originated among Commonwealth tax havens were transferred to Washington via the CFP, winning support from previously undecided figures on the left and right of Congress, and in the new Bush administration. These efforts were reinforced by doubts concerning this approach in the OECD secretariat. Regulative norms against the use of economic sanctions in these circumstances have exercised a particularly strong hold because of the OECD's identity; in taking measures that conflicted with this identity, the OECD would diminish the very currency of its influence.

The success of the opposition to the OECD initiative against harmful tax competition cannot be put down to overt or covert corporate pressure. Business interests were deliberately shut out of the design phase of the project 1996–98 when they otherwise might have had the most influence. There was no public lobbying campaign against the OECD initiative on the scale as has been seen in several other multilateral regulatory initiatives. Although it is impossible to rule out a hidden lobbying campaign, anonymous interviews with participants on both sides and among third parties does not provide support for an important role for corporate interests.

Finally, the OECD opted for what amounted to a rhetorical campaign, aiming to secure compliance from tax havens by reasoned and moral suasion. Having discussed the roads not taken by the OECD and the key states behind the tax competition initiative, the task remains to trace the course of the rhetorical struggle that ensued in the next chapter before analyzing the results in chapters 4 and 5.

CHAPTER THREE

Hearts and Minds in the Global Arena

Regulative norms exercised a crucial influence on the OECD campaign against what it defined as "harmful tax competition" by ruling out a number of options that would have been eminently practical and efficient. Instead, in delegating the campaign to the OECD, its member states opted for a rhetorical strategy, relying on moral and reasoned suasion and speech acts. This course of action involved public appeals based on generally accepted principles for targeted tax haven jurisdictions to comply with the OECD's specified slate of reforms. It also was based on speech acts that served to impugn the reputation of those countries that failed to cooperate, covered in the following chapter. The OECD was able to set the terms of the rhetorical contest. But it was also exposed to the dangers inherent in a public debate, in particular having to make its case for the sympathies of third party observers. If the OECD came to a rhetorical strategy through a choice constrained primarily by regulative norms, targeted states had little choice but to respond in kind, given their tiny military and economic resources. Thus if not playing to the strength of its opponents, the OECD at least opted to engage listed states on the terrain where they were least weak.

The OECD set the initial terms of the campaign, not only by choosing a rhetorical strategy, but also by appealing to widely shared principles and norms around which the debate subsequently developed.[1] The aim of this rhetorical strategy was to persuade states accused of engaging in harmful tax competition to mend their ways, but even more so to mobilize the support of third parties (states, intergovernmental organizations, and other transnational actors) by convincing them of the rightfulness of the OECD's cause. The OECD case rested on four principles: law enforcement, sovereignty, consistency, and equality in argument.

First, the OECD tried to label the small states as "tax poachers" and associate them with criminal activities such as tax evasion, money laundering, and terrorist finance (the law enforcement principle). Second, it argued that tax haven-driven tax competition undermined others' fiscal sovereignty by creating a race to the bottom (sovereignty). Third, the OECD reasoned that its hostility to "harmful" tax competition did not detract from its strong support of competition overall, nor was the exclusionary conduct of the campaign in conflict with its developmental and cooperative mission (consistency). And fourth, the OECD presented itself as an ideal interlocutor, fully seized of the need for reasoned discussion, dialogue, and listening to alternative points of view (equality in argument).

In response, targeted states insisted on the legitimacy of their behavior and their willingness to fight crime (law enforcement). Furthermore, targeted tax havens seized on OECD claims in order to argue that the OECD itself was violating their sovereignty by seeking to dictate and impose foreign tax laws upon them (sovereignty). They held that the OECD was hypocritical in selecting its targets, given that many of its own members indulged in similar practices (consistency). Finally, it was alleged that the OECD violated the basic norms of a debate between equals by trying to set the agenda unilaterally (equality in argument). States accused of being tax havens thus sought to turn the tables on the OECD, responding with counterarguments based on the same norms, but reversing them in each case in order to claim that they and not the OECD were acting in line with these norms. Both sides worked from the same script, but cast the other in the role of villain. By 2002, not only had the OECD failed to convince tax havens of the error of their ways, but it had also failed to convince key sectors of the international audience of the wisdom and justice of its arguments relative to those of its opponents. In the process, it also had suffered crippling defections from its own ranks. Targeted states put up a successful rhetorical defense.

The OECD was trapped by the very same rhetorical stratagems it had introduced. In committing to the power of reasoned debate and invoking the value of certain norms from the outset, the OECD could not then ignore the result of the argument and declare these same norms unimportant. Having lost the argument it lost the battle. Given that the OECD was an organization founded on the basis of technocratic expertise that seeks to influence members and nonmembers by reasoned dialogue, it would be in danger of doing itself out of a job by belittling the value and power of argument and persuasion. Because rhetoric inevitably puts a variety of meanings into play, even the principles of the powerful can be used by the weak for their own subversive ends.[2]

Chronology, 1998–2002

Rather than following the development of the contest in a step-by-step manner, coverage of the rhetoric employed by the protagonists will be examined thematically, based on the four key norms around which the debate coalesced (international law enforcement, sovereignty and nonintervention, consistency, and equality in argument). In order not to lose sight of the chronology of the controversy, however, I give an overview of events in a more sequential historical fashion, amplifying the brief summary given in the introduction. The coverage of the rhetorical contest is largely restricted to the period from the release of the 1998 report until 2002, when the OECD was forced to abandon the most innovative and ambitious aspects of the project in terms of substance and process.[3] Relatedly, the OECD initiative had a much higher public profile in this period than subsequently.

Although *Harmful Tax Competition: An Emerging Global Issue* had been foreshadowed by G7 communiqués from 1996 and 1997, its release in April 1998 marked the beginning of the campaign and the accompanying discursive struggle. Despite receiving reasonable media coverage in the general and specialized press, the initial response to the report was surprisingly muted in light of later controversy, the exception being the Luxembourg and Swiss dissents in the report itself. Only a minority of jurisdictions later listed as tax havens made public responses, though Caribbean governments did begin some informal internal consultations. Those in the tax planning business were also quiet while the OECD went about holding a series of regional conferences on the subject of tax competition. In October 1998, in an early sign of coordinated opposition to the OECD's aims, a World Association of International Financial Centres was set up in Vancouver and held an inaugural conference in London during April the following year. This body publicly decried the campaign against tax havens and called for interested jurisdictions to join forces to defend themselves. Despite attracting some interest from Barbados, Bermuda, the Cayman Islands, Gibraltar, and Malaysia, the World Association largely fizzled as other centers held aloof.

More telling criticism of the OECD's whole approach to "unfair tax competition" came from the Business Industry Advisory Committee (BIAC), a business peak body brought together by the OECD specifically to provide private sector input but not consulted on the tax question. BIAC published a harshly critical response in June 1999. This defection from within the OECD itself and the sweeping nature of the condemnation were seen as a bad start to the initiative, while comments subsequently in specialist journals (e.g., *International Enforcement Law Reporter, Offshore Investment, Tax Haven Reporter, International Money Marketing, International Tax Review, Intertax, Tax Notes International,* Tax news.com) generally followed the BIAC line, being skeptical at best and scathing at worst. The Committee on Fiscal Affairs reacted with alacrity in opening talks with the BIAC to assuage their fears and "clarify" points that had provoked particular ire. Jeffrey Owens and Richard

Hammer, BIAC's head, eventually published a joint statement in 2001 to demonstrate that the rift between them had been but a temporary difference. Most of the financial services sector adopted a "wait and see" approach, however, with the OECD secretariat keen to emphasize the benefits of a "level playing field" to big legal and accountancy firms in Europe and North America, while playing down the costs of increased regulatory requirements.[4] By November 1999, the OECD had settled on calling for public commitments from low-tax jurisdictions to undertake reforms in line with the problems identified in the 1998 report. Through 1999 the response from small states began to build, particularly in the Caribbean, with increasing criticism of the OECD in the press as well as in various United Nations fora. The Commonwealth also entered the fray, with the secretariat commissioning several reports on the OECD's campaign, all more or less critical, while various meetings of finance ministers and heads of state also issued communiqués defending members' fiscal sovereignty in general terms and calling for modifications in the way the Committee on Fiscal Affairs was driving the initiative.

The planned deadline of June 2000 for jurisdictions to commit was pushed back to July 2001 when a new "uncooperative tax havens" list was to be published. The Committee on Fiscal Affairs had been gathering information on forty-seven jurisdictions by a series of questionnaires and visits from members of the secretariat, later reviewed by teams against the criteria for harmful tax competition.[5] The information that was gathered related to both formal legal provisions and how these features worked in practice in the low-tax jurisdictions. Discussion was then transferred to the Forum on Harmful Tax Practices, the institutional continuation of the 1998 report within the OECD Committee on Fiscal Affairs responsible for finalizing the list of tax haven jurisdictions released in 2000. The forum was also tasked with designing, soliciting, and managing commitments from listed states. June 2000 marked a crescendo of pressure against targeted countries as the OECD, FATF, and the newly created Financial Stability Forum all released reports rating and labeling tax havens. The OECD listed thirty-five jurisdictions, giving them a year to sign up to the specified reforms or face "coordinated defensive measures." Six other countries had preemptively volunteered to adopt the OECD's reforms (the Cayman Islands, Bermuda, Mauritius, San Marino, Cyprus, and Malta).

Public opposition to the tax competition initiative from affected states really began to mount from 2000, with a series of meetings in the Caribbean Community and the Pacific Islands Forum (PIF). These moves gathered steam with growing Commonwealth involvement from September 2000 and the formation of the Center for Freedom and Prosperity the following month. The OECD–Commonwealth cosponsored meeting in Barbados in January 2001 was also critical in terms of launching interregional cooperation and solidarity among targeted states. In turn, the Barbados meeting gave rise to the Joint Working Group and the International Tax and Investment Organisation (ITIO). Increasing doubts about the current structure of the initiative within the OECD secretariat, its Commonwealth member states, and in

Washington came to a head with U.S. Treasury Secretary's public criticisms of the initiative on 10 May 2001. Only a little more than a month ahead of the deadline for compliance, these comments threw the other G7 and OECD members into confusion and provoked considerable dismay. Frantic negotiations ensued to try to put the campaign back on track. To make matters worse, Spain chose to conduct another round of its long-running feud with Britain over Gibraltar, threatening to veto any measure that implied Britain's sovereignty over the territory. As a result of these disputes, the 30 June deadline passed without a list of uncooperative tax havens or even a public comment from the OECD secretariat. The shock and disruption of the terrorist attacks on September 11 also slowed matters down.

Recognizing the determination of the United States to enhance its national security, even if this meant bending or breaking international law, some jurisdictions in the Caribbean looked to make a separate deal on information exchange with the United States. The hope was that these Caribbean countries might well then be shielded from the OECD initiative. Thus in late 2001 and early 2002 the Bahamas, the Netherlands Antilles, the Cayman Islands, and Panama all agreed to Tax Information Exchange Agreements with the U.S. Internal Revenue Service. These agreements all contained the significant rider that "triangular" exchanges were forbidden, i.e., information passed on to the IRS could not then be passed on to third parties inside or outside the OECD. Additionally, Barbados, the loudest and most effective critic of the OECD's tax competition project, made a "separate peace" in reaching an agreement with the OECD whereby it was struck off the list of tax havens without having to make a public commitment or subject itself to ongoing monitoring. From the OECD's point of view this took Prime Minister Owen Arthur, its most formidable opponent, out of the fight. The Maldives and Tonga, having no offshore financial sector, were also belatedly struck off the list of tax havens without having to make a commitment.

By early 2002, the outlines of the scaled-back OECD initiative became clear. The new and much less ambitious project marked a defeat for the OECD in a number of vital substantive and procedural areas. Chapter 4 discusses these changes in detail, but the most important features can be laid out briefly. The initiative had originally been conceived with the primary goal of stopping tax havens from "poaching" mobile capital and the accompanying tax revenue from OECD states by "ring-fenced" special concessions extended to foreign investors who did not engage in substantial economic activity. In November 2001 the crucial ring-fencing and "no substantial activity" clauses, conceptually separate but generally linked in practice, were dropped. This key concession removed much of the fiscal logic of the initiative for OECD countries, giving free rein to "harmful" tax competition for geographically mobile investment. It also removed the existential threat to small states' financial sectors that these two clauses had posed. As a result of these concessions, but also partly as a result of pressure from the OECD's blacklists, a majority of targeted states committed to information exchange, with crucial provisos. Perhaps even more important than the concessions on the content of the initiative were the concessions relating to the way it was conducted.

As originally conceived, the initiative was "exclusionary" or "top-down." The initiative was aimed primarily against nonmember states that had no say in drawing up the new international standards that were to govern them. These new standards did not bind all OECD states (e.g., Luxembourg and Switzerland) to abide by the regulations demanded of nonmembers. Finally, the initiative was coercive; it was based on blacklisting and the threat of economic coercion. Under the new Global Tax Forum as it evolved from 2002, however, small states were represented in standard-setting and procedural questions on an equal basis with OECD members. Decisions were made only by consensus, and threats of sanctions for noncompliance were dropped. Under the "level playing field" condition, the introduction of any new standards now depended on their implementation in all OECD states, and from October 2003 in eight other jurisdictions as well, including Singapore, Dubai, and Hong Kong.[6] Follow-up meetings in the Cayman Islands, Ottawa, Berlin, and Melbourne confirmed the participation of listed states, even those like Andorra and Monaco which had failed to make a commitment. The need for consensus among all parties was also stressed. The exclusionary and coercive approach that had set the project to regulate harmful tax competition apart from the standard procedures of international organizations, intended as a prototype for future regulatory campaigns, had failed and had been repudiated.[7]

The Structure and Significance of the Debate

In setting the nature of the dispute, the OECD made the struggle with tax havens a rhetorical contest, that is, one centered on the public use of language to achieve political ends. This strategy was partly a matter of choice, but also the product of the prevailing norms of appropriate international conduct and the OECD's technocratic rational-legal identity that together ruled out other courses of action. Because the theoretical and empirical material produced by economists on international tax competition is ambiguous and provided uncertain support for the OECD's case, the main themes of the contest tended to crystallize around widely held international norms of appropriate behavior and fairness. The targeted countries, lacking the means to make it anything other than a discursive struggle, even if they had had the inclination, tended to use the very same issues introduced by the OECD, reversing the accusations in each case to paint themselves as upholding these norms and the OECD as transgressor. There has been a great deal of agreement on which norms are valuable and important, but very little agreement about which side actually has been adhering to these norms. The jurisdictions labeled as tax havens worked within the terms set by the OECD in an attempt to rhetorically turn the tables and mobilize international sympathy while dividing and defeating the coalition arrayed against them.

The remainder of this chapter surveys this rhetorical contest under four recurring themes (law enforcement, sovereignty, consistency and equity in argument), which were generally bundled and spliced, rather than adhering to any strict separation. There are obvious overlaps between each, and some participants emphasized one or two norms while ignoring the others. Taking each theme one by one is thus a matter of analytical convenience rather than a claim that the OECD, listed countries, or third parties organized their arguments around this four-part schema. Others have classified the main lines of debate along slightly different lines.[8] Nevertheless, from reading over a thousand articles in the general and specialist press dealing with the initiative (a majority identified by using key word searches on databases LexisNexis, Factiva, and Dow Jones News), as well as numerous reports from professional bodies, think tanks, governments, and international organizations, the repetition of the same claims and counterclaims is unmistakable. The coverage below extends largely until the OECD defeat on the ring-fencing and "no substantial activity" criteria in the second half of 2001, and the abandonment of the exclusionary strategy in 2002.

During this period, listed countries sought to exploit the flexibility of the principles brought into play by the OECD in order to force it to acknowledge how the logic and spirit of these very same principles worked against its campaign. The aim was thereby to damage or threaten the OECD's reputation in the eyes of third parties, hence making the OECD abandon the campaign. Although the conflict was never referred to third-party arbitration, both sides were intent not just on convincing or shaming each other, but of garnering the support of those on the side lines. These other parties ranged from uncommitted states, to other international organizations, to transnational policy communities. Kratochwil thus notes how two-sided bargaining processes can become "triadic" with a commonly accepted body of rules and norms allowing the emergence of a distinct and impartial "moral point of view."[9] The fact that the struggle was played out publicly, in front of an audience, meant that the arguments and rhetoric presented by each side were effective only to the degree they were seen to be consistent and compatible with internationally shared norms.

Who was the audience for the rhetorical contest? Apart from those directly involved, who were the third parties to be potentially swayed by reasoned arguments and emotive appeals? Typically, the OECD's dry, esoteric tax work is hardly headline making material or the stuff of mass politics. But in aiming for a prominent public profile, the initiative against harmful tax competition was a deliberately atypical project. In the period 1998–2002, the struggle between the OECD and those jurisdictions featured on the June 2000 list was covered in mainstream publications like the *Economist, New York Times, Guardian, Le Monde,* and the *Financial Times.* In addition, the contest was closely followed in the specialized tax and financial services journals referred to earlier, as well as the mainstream press in targeted small states. The audience was disproportionately elite, centering on politicians, national and international bureaucrats within the transnational tax policy community, the financial services industry, academics, and think tanks, but only rarely NGOs, and still less the mass public. Although many and probably most third parties came to the issue with preconceptions and established sympathies for one side or the other, critics of the OECD managed to change enough minds to ultimately carry the day.

Because of the way the OECD had initially framed the issue of tax competition, the way the rhetorical justification had been developed, its opponents were able to hoist the OECD with its own petard. The OECD was forced into the position of either admitting errors and giving ground, or bulldozing the campaign through at the cost of the organization's reputation, identity, and *raison d'être*. In the end, the OECD found itself rhetorically entrapped, and opted for admitting errors and giving ground.

Outlaws and Tax Poachers

It is a basic norm that countries should abstain from deliberately harming other states and that states should not tolerate criminal activity within their territory. Both in the 1998 and 2000 reports, and even more so in subsequent press releases and interviews with the media, the OECD and its supporters often sought to characterize opponents as deliberately free-riding on the generosity of the international community. In doing so, it was argued that these free-riders thereby endangered many of the benefits they selfishly consumed, and, even worse, indirectly aided and abetted serious criminal activity. In return, those subject to these accusations tried to establish a clear distinction between legal practices (tax planning and tax avoidance) and illegal ones (tax evasion, money laundering and terrorist financing). Small states repeatedly proclaimed their readiness to join the fight against the latter type of activity. There has thus been considerable agreement on both sides about the need for cooperation in tackling international financial crime, especially money laundering, and to avoid attracting flows of illegal money.

When asked whether the campaign against "harmful tax competition" amounted to "bullying" small developing countries, Jeffery Owens responded:

> Let's be clear. For decades some of these states have been eroding the tax base of not just OECD countries but those of developing countries as well (as confirmed in a recent report by Oxfam). They have been assisting dishonest taxpayers to avoid paying their fair share of taxes in their countries of residence. And who has borne the burden of these activities? Honest taxpayers.[10]

The reserve with which the term "tax poaching" was used in the 1998 report was subsequently cast aside in articles by Frances Horner, head of the OECD Tax Competition Unit.[11] The negative fiscal externalities (capital flight and erosion of the tax base) that tax havens impose on others were said to be deliberately and intentionally harmful, rather than reflecting impersonal market mechanisms.[12] Owens wrote that the listed countries set up their tax regimes "not so much to attract real foreign direct investment, but as predatory policies whose main purpose is to siphon off part of another country's tax base."[13]

One particularly effective rhetorical linkage for the supporters of global tax regulation was to play up the connection between tax havens, on the one hand, and money laundering, criminal tax evasion (in contrast to legal tax avoidance), and even terrorist finance, on the other hand. Fighting international crime certainly provides a more clear-cut and compelling policy narrative than the much more contentious issues of "harmful" versus "beneficial" tax competition and state sovereignty over tax matters. OECD countries repeatedly accused listed states of fostering and facilitating criminal activities through the provision of strict banking secrecy, investment vehicles making it very difficult to identify the true owner, and in failing to exchange information with other countries. Targeted countries thus had to strive to dissociate themselves from money laundering involving Colombian drug dealers, Russian Mafiosi, and Islamic terrorists. To the extent that the OECD could establish a close association between tax havens and such criminal activities, a particularly damning form of guilt by association, they were well on their way to landing a rhetorical knock-out punch.

Some politicians who are against tax havens have tended to blur the difference between tax avoidance (minimizing taxes within the law) and tax evasion (false reporting or other practices outside the law). Initially action against tax havens was to deal with both, and thus a 1998 G7 summit declared: "Our agreement today represents a major breakthrough in tackling the growing problems caused by harmful tax competition, and the tax evasion and avoidance it generates."[14] Tax havens worked strenuously to keep these terms distinct, while their detractors tended to bundle them together as different facets of the same basic problem. When asked how tax avoidance was different from evasion, Owens replied: "It means different things to different people, partly as a result of language and partly because of culture. Some of my colleagues at the OECD use the word "avoidance" when they mean "evasion," because they do not see the distinction."[15] A meeting of Commonwealth small state law ministers and attorneys general protested "the blurring of the distinction between tax evasion and tax avoidance . . . thereby facilitating 'fishing expeditions' which would seek the disclosure of information in cases where there was no evidence of criminality."[16]

Although tax havens have insisted that bank secrecy is a legitimate form of protecting one's privacy (especially Andorra, Liechtenstein, Monaco, Austria, Luxembourg, and Switzerland), Owens summed up a common attitude with a quote from Samuel Johnston: "Where secrecy lies, roguery is not far behind."[17] The 1998 United Nations report *Financial Havens, Banking Secrecy and Money Laundering* and the OECD reports *Improving Access to Bank Information for Tax Purposes* (and the subsequent progress report), *Access for Tax Authorities to Information Gathered by Anti-Money Laundering Authorities,* and *Behind the Corporate Veil: Using Corporate Entities for Illicit Purposes* emphasize these links, while further OECD work on combating bribery is also relevant.[18]

Following this theme, shortly after the release of the 1998 report, Gordon Brown, of the UK, commented at a meeting of G7 finance ministers:

> This initiative paves the way for coordinated international action to allow information to be passed to tax authorities so that honest citizens and businesses do not have to pay the price of the activities of tax fraudsters. . . . We are determined to put in place strong and practical measures to tackle the growing threat of international tax crime and evasion through tax havens and preferential tax regimes.[19]

The British Treasury explained the tax competition initiative as "partly motivated by growing evidence that criminals can evade anti–money laundering systems by presenting their affairs as tax related to reassure their bankers, brokers and professional advisers."[20] This link between tax havens and criminals found some resonance in the media. A *New Republic* article describes tax haven customers as follows: "Some are criminals laundering ill-gotten treasure; others are wealthy individuals or corporate moguls hiding their riches from taxation, often illegally. The common parlance for such people is 'tax cheats.'"[21] *Le Monde* called "harmful tax competition" a "euphemism" for "countries taking part in tax evasion on a large scale, in some cases in laundering money from the worst sorts of trafficking as well."[22] Even more damaging for the cause of listed jurisdictions have been headlines describing them as "drug and terror havens."[23] Jeffrey Owens has expanded on these links:

> Individuals and corporations that engage in money laundering, bribery and other corrupt practices are also likely to engage in tax evasion and an acceptance that in some way tax evasion is morally defensible because it merely involves refusing to give your money to the government is likely not only to undermine the ethical basis of tax systems but also to encourage other international criminal activities. Similarly, the jurisdictions which tolerate or facilitate international tax evasion are in some cases, although not all, the same jurisdictions which facilitate money laundering and bribery.[24]

A UN report noted that with some features of targeted states' tax regimes "it is difficult not to get the impression that the real purpose is to give a competitive advantage to the particular haven's banks in bidding for international flows of illegal money."[25] These might include "flee clauses," whereby trusts and International Business Companies automatically change jurisdictions once a request for information concerning that entity has been lodged by any law enforcement or tax authority, and bank secrecy so tight that it cannot be waived even with the account holder's permission.

As discussed in chapter 1, since 1989 money laundering has been the province of another collaborative project between the G7 and the OECD on financial sector regulation, the Financial Action Task Force (FATF), which has used the same "exclusionary" tactics against many of the same jurisdictions targeted regarding their tax regimes.[26] The future head of the ITIO claimed in December 2000 that there was a deliberate attempt to confuse the FATF campaign against money laundering and the OECD campaign relating to tax competition and that even some OECD officials failed to appreciate the differences between the various blacklists produced.[27] The FATF's habit of issuing its press releases on OECD stationery, using the OECD website and including the term "OECD" on its business cards, hardly helped clarify matters.[28]

Listed jurisdictions claimed that they were willing to cooperate with foreign criminal authorities and had a proven record of having done so in the past. They also argued that much more money is laundered within the G7 countries, particularly the United States, than in any tax haven.[29] The Black Congressional Caucus echoed this line in their March 2001 letter to Secretary O'Neill:

> What we have been facing is a successful international media campaign, developed by the OECD, aimed at painting a picture of money laundering and unsound regulatory practices. However, the anti-money laundering regulations of many of these countries have been successfully enhanced through the assistance of international funding agencies and the commitment of their own national resources.[30]

But as in the distinctions between tax avoidance and evasion, those making these ripostes have had only limited success. Writing for the Center for Freedom and Prosperity, one author conceded that "The OECD has been successful in demonizing the so-called tax havens by raising the false spectre of money laundering."[31]

The terrorist attacks of 9/11 saw this general association of secrecy with criminality extended to terrorism. The benefits attributed to a successful OECD campaign by its Deputy Secretary General expanded accordingly: "By promoting transparency and cooperative arrangements, our work will contribute to efforts to counter money laundering and the financing of terrorism, while strengthening the international financial system."[32] Gabriel Makhlouf, chair of the Committee on Fiscal Affairs, stated that the shock produced by the attacks resulted in a great deal more pressure on listed countries to sign up and compromise on banking secrecy (although some officials in targeted states dispute this claim).[33] A commentator from PricewaterhouseCoopers held that "Post-September 11, I don't think it's acceptable for any finance center to say that they value banking secrecy more than human life."[34] IMF interviewees referred to some officials in targeted states committed to financial secrecy as "living in a pre-9/11 world." The ITIO rushed out a statement pledging its support for efforts to combat terrorists' financial networks. Liechtenstein was forced to declare that "Tax harmonization is not an instrument in the fight against terrorism."[35] In fact al Qaeda cells in the United States seem to have run their activities on a very modest budget of less than a million dollars using unsophisticated but effective measures to raise and conceal funds inside the United States without resorting to international money laundering.[36] But the lack of evidence connecting tax havens with terrorists has done little to reduce its rhetorical effectiveness.

Despite the success in linking harmful tax practices with criminal activity of various kinds, the FATF and other anti–money laundering bodies were very keen to keep the issue of tax competition separate from money laundering. Significantly, the desire of those prosecuting the tax competition campaign to be associated with those responsible for countering financial crime has not been reciprocated. Indeed, the FATF and regional bodies like the Asia-Pacific Group on Money Laundering have gone out of their way to distance themselves from the OECD's initiative,[37] or, in the case of the Caribbean Financial Action Task Force, have been vocal critics.[38] The implication is that these bodies have observed the steadily declining fortunes of the OECD in this matter and have no desire to be tarred by association or have the clarity of their message muddled.[39] As the head of the Liechtenstein Bankers' Association has observed, many people argue in favor of tax competition, but no one argues in favor of money laundering.[40]

The OECD accused tax havens of inappropriate conduct by undermining the integrity of other countries' tax systems, by tempting away capital, and facilitating international criminal activity through financial secrecy and loose regulation. Tax havens fought hard to dissociate themselves from criminal activities, such as money laundering, and insisted that secrecy provisions were entirely reputable. The OECD had some success in linking tax competition with tax evasion, money laundering, and terrorist financing, and to this extent was able to exert considerable pressure on listed states (see chapter 4). Limiting this association, however, was the reluctance of anti–money laundering bodies to erase this distinction and associate themselves with tax and revenue issues. These bodies tended to damn the OECD campaign with faint praise.

Sovereignty and Nonintervention

Sovereignty and the concomitant principle of nonintervention is perhaps *the* foundational norm of the modern international system. The OECD introduced the issue of sovereignty in the 1998 report, but a concern with maintaining national sovereignty in the face of global capital flows is at the heart of broader concerns about globalization, as discussed in chapter 1. The problem faced by the OECD from the beginning of the campaign was that along with national defense, the power to tax and make fiscal policy is a quintessential prerogative of sovereign states. Anticipating these objections, the OECD took a two-pronged approach. The first was that the campaign against tax havens actually worked to bolster the de facto fiscal sovereignty of both member and nonmember states that would otherwise be ensnared in a race to the bottom. The second line of argument was that sovereignty not only involved a right to be free from outside interference, but also an accompanying duty to refrain from undermining the laws of other sovereign states. At its most basic, the need for action from the OECD, rather than individual states, was said to arise from the mismatch between interwoven global economic networks and fragmented national political and fiscal organizations. At times it seemed that officials in the OECD secretariat were dubious of the national control of tax:

> Tax reform must be examined from a global perspective because there is an incoherence in the relevance of national borders for trade purposes and, in turn, their relevance for tax systems. The same incoherence allows harmful tax practices to thrive. . . . All these principles—fairness, neutrality, efficiency, etc—must be interpreted on a global level if they are to achieved at all.[41]

The specter of the race to the bottom and the insufficiency of unilateral or bilateral responses to harmful tax competition augur for a world in which sovereignty is rather passé in the face of pressing political, economic, and environmental trends and challenges. Yet this strand of the contest did not see an opposition between an antisovereignty, pro-globalization OECD, on the one hand, and a reactionary group of targeted jurisdictions hanging on to the traditional prerogatives of the "Westphalian" state, on the other hand. Both sides acknowledged that growing cross-border economic flows were bringing about important, and largely beneficial changes in the international system, but also stood by the continuing value of state sovereignty, including fiscal sovereignty. Having committed to the same norm, each side portrayed itself as defending the concept and practice of sovereignty under threat from the machinations of the other. Each report, and most public statements from OECD officials, stressed that the initiative was in no way aimed at usurping state prerogatives over tax and that the structure of tax codes remained a political decision to be taken by national governments.[42] There were repeated statements by Jeffrey Owens and others in charge of the OECD's tax work that "this project is not about dictating to countries what their tax systems or tax rates should be."[43] The OECD argued that its actions shored up sovereignty under threat from what was termed "the dark side of globalization." The OECD's defense of sovereignty rested on a supposed "harmonization paradox": "The 'harmonization paradox' is that harmful tax competition actually reduces fiscal sovereignty. It could force a de facto harmonization of direct taxes at a zero/nominal rate, and a shift from direct taxes to consumption taxes."[44] By encouraging and pressuring other countries to abstain from harmful tax practices the OECD was protecting states' "true," "effective," or de facto fiscal sovereignty that would otherwise be undermined by the race to the bottom, leading to near-uniform taxes and the powerlessness of the voting public to influence economic policy making through nationally elected representatives.[45] Only by failing to sign on to the tax competition campaign would economic and specifically fiscal sovereignty be endangered.

Aside from the "harmonization paradox," the OECD and other commentators argued that because sovereignty is so important and valued, states should refrain from trying to undermine the sovereignty of others in the system. As the 1998 United Nations report on money laundering puts it:

> The concept of sovereignty as agreed to by the Member States of the United Nations, and as applied in international law, gives the sovereign State control over its territory, its citizens and its residents. A corollary of this concept is that no Member State should assist citizens or residents of another State in the violation of the laws of their home country.[46]

Specifically, tax havens should not pass laws and regulations designed to allow foreigners to beat the tax and legal codes of their home states by facilitating tax evasion and fraud.[47] More generally, sovereignty in tax matters does not obviate the requirement that states should abide by generally accepted rules. Or, in the OECD's ambiguous formulation contained in the 1998 report, "Countries should remain free to design their own tax systems, *as long as they abide by internationally accepted standards in doing so*" [emphasis added].[48] The questions of just what these standards are and who sets and interprets them comprised the crux of the struggle.

In response, those identified as tax havens argued that as sovereign states they had a clear right to set their own taxation laws, independent of the consequences for others, and that any interference with this right was plainly illegitimate and violated the principle of nonintervention. Targeted jurisdictions asserted that the OECD had no legal or moral right to legislate or enforce its chosen standards on nonmember states, or to claim a kind of supranational jurisdiction for itself. Of course, there is some irony in this position in that of the forty-one jurisdictions identified as tax havens in early 2000 (thirty-five listed in June plus the six others that made advance commitments), fifteen were not sovereign states in maintaining colonial ties or similar relations with the United Kingdom (Anguilla, Bermuda, the British Virgin Islands, the Cayman Islands, Gibraltar, Guernsey, Isle of Man, Jersey, Montserrat, Turks and Caicos); the Netherlands (Aruba and the Netherlands Antilles); New Zealand (Niue and the Cook Islands); and the United States (U.S. Virgin Islands). With the exception of the U.S. Virgin Islands and Gibraltar, however, each jurisdiction had full constitutional and practical autonomy in setting its own tax regimes, and the unilateral right to declare independence.

This sovereignty critique came from opponents across the globe. In their dissenting statements in the 1998 report, Luxembourg and Switzerland both cast doubt on how compatible the initiative was with the precepts of national sovereignty over tax matters.[49] The head of Caribbean Community stated that "the OECD members must understand that they do not have the right to legislate for countries other than themselves."[50] The Pacific Islands Forum annual summit reaffirmed "their sovereign right to operate offshore centers" as well as the "sovereign right of nations to establish domestic tax regimes of their own design and choosing" in 2000 and 2001.[51] The governor of the Samoan central bank pointed out to the OECD that "Samoa is an independent constitutional democracy which cherishes the common law rights of its citizens. It considers its Parliament to be supreme, its laws effective and the choices it makes for its citizens to be determinative."[52] Upon being listed as an "uncooperative tax haven" in April 2002, Liechtenstein declared that "Taxation is the responsibility of independent sovereign states."[53] Those jurisdictions that were British territories were quick to remind London about their traditional freedom to set their own taxes, a right that in some cases dated back for centuries. Meanwhile the Foreign Minister of Antigua and Barbuda asked,

> Should 41 jurisdictions around the world accept that the OECD has the right or authority to set itself up to make tax rulings which they expect nonmembers to follow? By doing this, would these 41 jurisdictions . . . not be opening the floodgates to a raft of other demands by an organization with no authority except the coercive power of its member states? [. . .][The OECD] has no legal authority to speak for the world or to establish norms or standards for any state except its members.[54]

Caribbean and Pacific states often recalled their long experience of colonial domination, rule by outsiders who had little knowledge of local conditions and even less interest in the local welfare. None too subtle parallels were drawn between the activities of previous imperial powers and the current OECD campaign. Thus the Prime Minister of Barbados was moved to remark at a conference on the OECD initiative,

> It is perhaps also timely to remind ourselves that the spark that ignited the war of independence and led ultimately to American nationhood was the refrain of "no taxation without representation," a rejection of the notion that an absentee colonizer across the ocean had the automatic right to impose a system of taxation on those who had no say in its construction and derived no significant benefit from the deployment of its proceeds.[55]

A report produced for the Commonwealth Finance Ministers' meeting in September 2000 echoed these concerns in a more circumspect fashion:

> Although the OECD has been at pains to explain that it does not intend to dictate to jurisdictions what their tax structures should be, the effect of failing to cooperate with the OECD's initiative will certainly compromise the sovereignty of jurisdictions to determine their tax policies. On this basis, it is possible to argue that the OECD initiative amounts to OECD member countries legislating on behalf of independent jurisdictions outside the organization, and therefore violates the sovereignty of these jurisdictions.[56]

To counter the OECD's tag of tax havens as unscrupulous free riders on global public goods, small island states painted a picture of an unimpressive spectacle in which the world's largest and most powerful states were ranged against tiny polities with fragile, dependent economies. They accentuated the grim economic circumstances they faced and the lack of alternatives for economic development, as well as the incongruousness of affluent great powers denying marginal developing states a chance for economic viability (the OECD had designed the initiative to exclude the important issue of capital flight from the developing world to its own members).[57] Given that industrialized nations provide development aid to all but eight of the thirty-five tax havens listed in the OECD 2000 report, how could these countries be both poor and vulnerable enough to attract aid flows, yet also vilified when they pursued one of their few options for economic advancement? Was it a case of "developed countries' gain, Caribbean pain"[58] driven by a "tax cartel" master-minded by a "rich countries' club"? The struggle was portrayed by the tax havens themselves, but also by many media observers, as the strong against the weak, the rich against the poor, the large against the small, in a David and Goliath struggle,[59] an unfair and dishonorable fight. While the inhabitants of Monaco, Bermuda, Liechtenstein, and Bahrain are hardly the wretched of the earth, and Iceland and Luxembourg are both OECD members, these exceptions did not alter the prevailing simplified image of the contenders.

In an article entitled "Tax Haven in Paris sets out to Bully Microdot in the South Seas" (alluding to OECD officials' tax free salaries) the author notes in tones of heavy sarcasm, "It is terrible to think that Britain, France and the United States are being roughed up by Vanuatu, but Larry Summers of the U.S. Treasury seems to think so."[60] The Cayman Islands representative at a UN forum spoke of the OECD "big bully syndrome," characterizing the initiative against harmful tax competition as "gunboat diplomacy at the dawn of the millennium," motivated by "pure, unadulterated self-interest" and a "might makes right" mentality with calls for transparency reminiscent of "1984 Big Brother is watching you." Bermuda and the British Virgin Islands made similar complaints at the same meeting.[61] At the UN Millennium Summit, the Prime Minister of Antigua and Barbuda accused the OECD in the General Assembly of "the most blatant disregard for the rules of international law." It was said further that "rules no longer apply" and that the OECD believed that "only might is right."[62] In early 2001 the Commonwealth secretariat called the OECD "dictatorial" and the campaign "coercive."[63]

Aside from the widely employed "bully" epithet, critics within the United States made much of the supposed world-spanning supranational ambitions of the "Parisian monstrosity."[64] Daniel Mitchell of the CFP and Heritage Foundation wrote: "The [OECD's] proposed recommendations would interfere with the right of sovereign nations to determine their own tax policies" and continued, "Such an effort contradicts international norms and threatens the ability of sovereign countries to determine their own fiscal affairs."[65] Despite the repeated denials by members of the OECD secretariat, the listed states' line on sovereignty found its way into Paul O'Neill's *Washington Times* statement of May 2001: "I am troubled . . . by the notion that any country, or group of countries, should interfere in any other country's decision about how to structure its own tax system. . . . The United States does not support efforts to dictate to any country what its own tax rates or tax system should be." Partially admitting the OECD's culpability, the head of the OECD Committee on Fiscal Affairs himself conceded that initially the campaign had a rather "Al Capone" flavor to it.[66]

Both sides thus sought to out-do each other in pledging their respect for the norms of sovereignty and nonintervention, the OECD arguing that far from infringing state prerogatives, it was in fact defending countries' practical fiscal independence. The vociferous response from the other side was that a cartel of rich and powerful states, motivated by the lowest kind of self-interest, was trying to bully small, developing countries into ceding control of their economic policies. Given the tiny size of the tax haven states, both relative to their opponents and absolutely, the OECD was forced to fight an uphill battle in winning observers' sympathies, as well as in countering the claim that it had arrogated to itself the right to legislate for others.

Consistency and Hypocrisy

Crucial to the credibility of any appeal to norms and the force of arguments is the issue of consistency. Actors that wish to achieve influence by their rhetoric and appeals to principle must maintain some consistency between their different statements, and between their statements and actions.[67] Listed jurisdictions repeatedly charged that rather than occupying the moral high ground, the OECD was in fact practicing a "do as I say, not as I do" selective morality, and that small nonmember states had been targeted precisely because they were small and vulnerable. In particular, critics contrasted the strongly positive value the OECD had given to competition overall with the implied negative value put on competition with respect to tax. A second major focus of attack was Luxembourg and Switzerland's refusal to be bound by the provisions of the 1998 report or any further work along these lines. The OECD was thus in the position of trying to impose standards on others which had been rejected by important sections of its own membership. The OECD was ultimately forced to concede in relation to both points.

Symbolizing the idea of "fair" and "unfair" competition was the idea of a level playing field, epitomizing not only efficiency-enhancing, but even more so morally virtuous competition. Indeed it is difficult to read even the shortest contribution to the debate from either side without running across some mention of the level playing field, as this has been a central metaphor. The ITIO titled its longest contribution to the debate *Towards a Level Playing Field.*[68] In October 2003, listed states and OECD representatives set up a subcommittee to define the concept; all parties agreed that "The level playing field is fundamentally about fairness."[69] The idea of the metaphor is that while winning is the aim for both sides, there are appropriate and inappropriate ways of doing so. Certain factors, such as skill, stamina, and leadership, should influence the outcome of the game, since this is considered a part of fair competition, while other considerations, such as the gradient of the playing field, should be neutral and constant for all players and not influence the game's outcome.

In the contest between the OECD and the targeted countries, both sides committed to the ideas expressed in the metaphor but differed as to which factors should be part of the competition and which should be held constant or neutral. The OECD argued that the status quo, in which tax havens competed on the inappropriate basis of tax and banking laws and regulations, tended to invalidate the result of the competition, and that the tax competition campaign only served to remedy the situation and create an environment where fair competition could flourish. Countries listed as tax havens inverted the problem, arguing for the legitimacy of tax regimes as part of their comparative advantage in the competition for mobile international investment and the accompanying government revenue. They presented the OECD campaign as an illegitimate attempt to tilt the field in favor of large developed countries. The governor of the East Caribbean Central Bank demonstrated this tendency to try to turn the tables: "We have to combine our resources to ensure we are not sunk by what is described as harmful taxation. We say it is harmful competition on their [the OECD's] part."[70]

The Prime Minister of Barbados asserted that the OECD was in favor of the market only when it worked to member states' advantage, and the campaign against tax competition was simply an attempt to reverse the verdict of free and fair competition: "Those who gain market share call it exploiting competitive advantage. Those who lose market share call it harmful."[71] Jurisdictions accused of being tax havens have often argued that the OECD was shifting the goal posts to the advantage of its own members, having found the competition too tough. "It is evident to most that the OECD intends to ensure that investment currently being channeled in countries such as ours is diverted back to their own economies."[72] The Democrat Black Congressional Caucus sent a letter to the Secretary of the Treasury holding that "Wealthy OECD nations should not have the right to rewrite the rules of international commerce on taxation simply because they are upset that investors and entrepreneurs are seeking higher after-tax returns."[73] The Pacific Islands Forum accused developed states of wanting to have it both ways with developing countries: to be able to cut development aid, but also prevent poor countries from exploiting their competitive advantage.[74] The head of the CARICOM secretariat claimed that the larger states saw "the level playing field as always where the OECD countries

are."[75] Putting this criticism in more structural terms the Cayman Islands Minister
for Finance observed:

> The perception of some on the outside of the current process is that the focus and scope
> of recent initiatives indicates that these initiatives are merely a means for large rich
> countries to preserve and project forward the existing global economic order at the ex-
> pense of smaller less developed countries . . . [and that] no economic diversification is
> to be tolerated if it potentially competes with the interests of large developed states.[76]

While stressing the revenue gains for developing countries which are not tax havens
and the overall global benefits of the initiative, which included more stable markets
and the combating of financial crime, Owens did admit part of this critique:

> Well let's be very pragmatic and look at the numbers. The conclusion of these agree-
> ments permits OECD member countries to enforce their tax laws more effectively. Re-
> member that the IRS estimates that the U.S. government alone loses U.S. $70 billion a
> year in taxes due to undeclared income held in tax havens. Let's also look at this project
> in context. This project means raising revenue without raising taxes.[77]

Relatedly, after the release of the 1998 report, the OECD ran into a flurry of accusations that it was hostile to tax competition as such, and was out to end this form
of competition by harmonizing taxes up toward the levels of the EU states, identified in some quarters as the driving force behind the whole project. The OECD has
had a long commitment to the virtues of competition, flexibility, deregulation, and
low taxes, and thus found itself in an awkward position in being seen to argue against
these very same principles when they were adopted by small countries. Thus the
Prime Minister of St. Vincent and the Grenadines's comment: "Tax competition is
really about whose treasury gets the money. The international financial community
urges competition and open markets but when we succeed they declare it unfair."[78]
Critics leaped to the defense of tax competition. The June 1999 BIAC response to
the 1998 report is a prominent example:

> The multinational business community speaks with a single voice when it puts forth the
> view that tax competition, generally, is a healthy phenomenon. . . . After all, countries
> do compete in other ways to attract business to their territories, so why single out tax-
> ation of one relatively limited form of activity as harmful?[79]

After discussing the tax cuts across the world in the 1980s, the statement continues
"The Report does convey an impression that the OECD is advocating a reversal of
this trend, thus encouraging higher taxes."[80] The response from the Australian
Chamber of Commerce and Industry was even more negative:

> The OECD's work on harmful tax competition is a barely-disguised effort to limit, if
> not eliminate, tax competition between countries, and to place a minimum platform un-

der the taxation systems of developed countries. . . . The underlying assumption of the OECD work is tax competition is a bad thing.[81]

Many other commentators in the specialist and general press, as well as officials in Switzerland and Luxembourg, also drew similar conclusions: that the OECD had come out against tax competition in general, and that the new project would create pressure to harmonize and/or increase taxes. Paul O'Neill included this point as another of his criticisms of the tax competition initiative up to 2001: "The United States simply has no interest in stifling the competition that forces governments—like businesses—to create efficiencies."[82]

OECD officials were quick to claim that these criticisms were a product of misreading its intentions and the 1998 report, innocently or intentionally, arguing that tax harmonization had never been on the agenda, that much, perhaps even most, tax competition was indeed beneficial, and finally that the organization was seeking to enhance rather than degrade the quality of competition between jurisdictions for international investment.[83] The number and diversity of those who had "misinterpreted" the 1998 report strongly suggests, however, that at least some of the authors did indeed believe that tax competition was most often harmful, that zero or low taxes in and of themselves were a problem, and that an upward convergence would be welcome in addressing these issues.[84] Indeed, several EU members had gone on record (and continue to do so) with these views in discussing tax competition in Europe. With the range of opinions on the matter even within the OECD, it is not surprising that the report contained ambiguities. But the similarity between some aspects of the 1998 report and antiglobalization critiques, most prominently the race to the bottom, and the emphasis placed on harmful tax competition and the lack of attention given to any other kind, means that it is not surprising observers drew these conclusions.

The OECD began to retreat from these aspects of the 1998 report. In 2000 the *Economist* reported: "Some officials at the OECD now regret ever using the phrase 'harmful tax competition.' As one of them puts it, 'As an economist, how can you ever say anything bad about competition?'"[85] Another OECD official noted that if an advertising firm like Saatchi and Saatchi had been commissioned to market the initiative, it never would have been called "harmful tax competition."[86] References to "unfair tax competition" and "harmful tax competition" gave way to "harmful tax practices," and by the November 2001 progress report, the OECD was criticizing harmful tax practices precisely because of their *anti*competitive effects, a line followed by some national tax authorities commenting on the issue as well.[87] The 2000 report and various public statements took pains to indicate that tax competition was a good thing that ought to be promoted.

The early defection of Luxembourg and Switzerland was all the more embarrassing in that these two members criticized the approach to "harmful tax competition" along the same lines as were subsequently taken up by the listed states. In its dissenting opinion, the Luxembourg government noted that:

> By voluntarily limiting itself to financial activities, excluding industrial and commercial activities, the Report . . . adopts a partial and unbalanced approach. . . . By taking an almost unilateral approach with respect to the prescribed measures, the Report gives the impression that its purpose is not so much to counter harmful tax competition where it exists as to abolish bank secrecy.[88]

Switzerland was even more critical, and almost vetoed the whole report, which it also described as "partial and unbalanced," before deciding to abstain:

> From our point of view, State intervention that distorts competition must be considered in all sectors and in the economy as a whole. . . . The Report recognizes that each State has sovereignty over its tax system and that levels of taxation can differ from one State to another. However, the same Report presents the fact that tax rates are lower in one country than in another as a criterion for identifying harmful preferential tax regimes. . . . Switzerland considers that it is legitimate and necessary to protect the confidentiality of personal data. . . . Finally, the selective and repressive approach that has been adopted does not give territories that make tax attraction a pillar of their economies an incentive to associate themselves with the regulation of the conditions of competition and will therefore fail to combat effectively the harmful excesses of tax competition that develops outside of all rules.[89]

Thus each element of the tax havens' critique of the campaign against "harmful tax competition" was foreshadowed: the rejection of any association between secrecy and criminal activity, skepticism toward the OECD's declared commitment to states' sovereign taxation rights, and selectivity and bias in framing the problem.

If guilt by association with transnational crime has been one of the most damning charges to be rebutted by listed countries, the charge of hypocrisy has dogged the OECD from the defection of Switzerland and Luxembourg at the beginning of the campaign, exacerbated when Belgium and Portugal also abstained from the November 2001 report (later joined by Austria). Targeted jurisdictions asked how the OECD could be acting to promote a level playing field when two of its members, some of the tax havens' main competitors, had from the beginning publicly and repeatedly stated that they would not be bound by the project. This concern was all the more prominent given the emphasis placed in the 1998 report on the mobility of capital and investors' tendency to seek out the most favorable regulatory environment. In rejecting the offer to make a commitment, the Marshall Islands statement reasoned that "If we commit to the OECD initiative, our foreign investors will head to the four OECD member countries that are not following OECD requirements. . . . The list has very little credibility because the OECD is not making the same demands of its own member nations as it is requiring of us."[90] A 2001 Pacific Islands Forum position paper stated:

> Listed Pacific nations ask that the OECD undertake the same level of constructive dialogue with non-OECD members as they undertook amongst themselves. We are not

asking for the OECD to set a lower standard for non-OECD jurisdictions. Indeed, an agreement that both OECD and non-OECD nations can commit to as equals is an equitable outcome and would remove any perception of disparate treatment of nations.[91]

In July 2001, the director of the ITIO requested "an assurance that the OECD is not asking them to do more than is being asked of OECD members."[92] Vanuatu employed a similar justification in explaining its noncompliance, given "that OECD member states have not committed to the standards that non-OECD states are being expected to implement, and given the economic distortions that the lack of a level playing field will create."[93] In the run-up to the 28 February 2002 deadline to avoid the "uncooperative tax havens" list, the ITIO put the issue starkly in a press statement entitled "Is the OECD Preparing Sanctions against Switzerland and Luxembourg or not?"[94] Even the World Bank called for measures to be "fully symmetric and apply equally to developed and developing countries."[95]

A *Financial Times* article is typical of similar sentiments carried in many other papers when it claimed:

> OECD members scarcely occupy the moral high ground. Although the tax havens plan is supposed to apply to them, two of their number—Switzerland and Luxembourg—have balked at it from the outset. It is also a bit rich of OECD members to complain about other countries' tax regimes distorting investment flows, while they compete fiercely with taxpayers' money to capture mobile investment projects. To set a credible example to the rest of the world, they need first to set their own houses in order.[96]

Concerns about hypocrisy and double standards between the OECD's treatment of nonmember havens as opposed to abstaining members also carried over to the specialist business press:

> Regrettably, the OECD's high-minded commitment to a level playing field (occasionally trumpeted to garner media support for the project) has not always translated into practical reality. In particular, the OECD has shown inappropriate reluctance to permit the implementation of commitments by OFCs [Offshore Financial Centers] in the context of the Harmful Tax Competition initiative to be conditioned on implementation of equivalent commitments by all OECD Member States, including Switzerland and Luxembourg.[97]

The OECD could not remain deaf to these complaints, especially when they were given credence by O'Neill in May 2001 and conceded even by those sympathetic to the overall thrust of regulating tax competition. In response, it attempted to defuse these charges of blatant hypocrisy. Senior OECD officials, including the Deputy Secretary General Seiicho Kondo and Gabriel Makhlouf, made nearly identical public statements in response to media questions on this issue:

> We know that the committed jurisdictions have concerns about establishing a level playing field in which no player gains an unfair advantage from practices that others have

shunned. We share these concerns. Financial services are extremely mobile, and it is not in our interest that harmful activities move from a committed jurisdiction to another which fails to meet our standards for transparency and the exchange of information. The OECD countries participating in this project have pledged to eliminate their own harmful tax practices by April 2003. By having a large number of onshore and offshore financial centers commit to the same principles, we have gone a long way toward achieving a level playing field.[98]

After side-stepping the Anglo–Spanish dispute over Gibraltar and accommodating U.S. reservations, the refocused initiative from mid-2001 granted the concession long demanded of the OECD: that members and nonmembers should be held to the same standards and the same timetable in terms of applying sanctions. Owens announced that "We have agreed that these defensive measures will not apply to uncooperative tax havens before they apply to the OECD countries that fail to remove the harmful features from their harmful tax practices."[99] When the ITIO's question about sanctions on Switzerland and Luxembourg (and potentially Portugal and Belgium as well, after their November 2001 abstentions) was later posed by journalists to Jeffrey Owens, he replied: "At the end of the day, there is only going to be one distinction: cooperative versus uncooperative."[100] OECD officials evinced great reluctance, however, in going into details, and studiously avoided mentioning Switzerland and Luxembourg by name in connection with failing to comply or the matter of sanctions: "A question about any member countries that may not commit is hypothetical at this stage. In any case, it would be a question for member governments to decide."

Targeted jurisdictions scored a notable success in ensuring they would not be committed to reforms unless these measures were also adopted by every OECD member state by way of the "Isle of Man clause." Originally the OECD had wanted each jurisdiction to commit by signing a common form letter drafted by the secretariat. The Isle of Man ignored this requirement, however, and in writing its own commitment letter in December 2000 it explicitly made any reforms conditional on every OECD member doing likewise. This innovation was copied by almost every other jurisdiction,[101] particularly those that signed up in 2002 to the much-reduced initiative, shorn of its most important provisions.[102] Thus the OECD became bound by a web of conditional commitments. But it remained unclear just how this conditionality, tacit or open, would work, as the head of the PIF pointed out:

> Those committing have all placed caveats requiring, at least, all OECD members to also commit and to fully implement the initiative. The OECD, in publicizing the commitment letters, has accepted these caveats. However, if the caveats are called into play, the method by which disputes regarding the OECD's assessment of its own members' implementation will be managed is unclear.[103]

Once again, the ITIO echoed these points.[104] After commenting that he was convinced that all the pledges were made in good faith (rather than on the assumption that Switzerland would torpedo the whole process and thus commitments would never have to be honored), Owens cautioned that "The OECD has negotiated all the commitments on the basis that there is no 'most favored nation treatment' concept. The OECD would not accept a commitment to progress by any one country that is conditioned on the actions of all other countries."[105]

Countries listed as tax havens also made more specific accusations of hypocrisy and double standards. They pointed out that in some cases the structure of their financial sectors had been designed by their former imperial rulers, the very same countries that were now most unyielding in their condemnation of these activities. Thus the New Hebrides (now Vanuatu) was jointly administered as a condominium by Britain and France until 1980, whose administrators saw little opportunity for economic viability beyond offshore banking.[106] Barbados developed its offshore financial center from 1977 on the advice of the IMF.[107] Even while France was urging tough action against tax havens, French authorities were suggesting that Corsica should become a tax haven to enhance its development prospects.[108] Banking secrecy and disclosure requirements, a priority for anti–money laundering as well as tax competition, also posed some uncomfortable parallels. Few countries get a clean bill of health on this score.[109]

For example, a 2005 U.S. Treasury Department report notes:

> A handful of U.S. states [Delaware, Nevada, and Wyoming are the three discussed] offer company registrations with cloaking features—such as minimal information requirements and limited oversight—that rival those offered by offshore financial centers. . . . The competition among [these] states to attract legal entities to their jurisdictions has created a "race to the bottom," and a real money laundering threat.

A subsequent Government Accounting Office report recommended that the United States learn from the Isle of Man and Jersey in tightening up its American regulations in this area.[110]

Given the patchy record of OECD member states themselves on the standards that supposedly comprised the internationally accepted minimum, not to mention the out-right rejection of the whole approach to tax competition and financial regulation by Switzerland and Luxembourg, the thirty-five countries listed as tax havens in 2000 were able to make considerable mileage out of the perception of hypocrisy and selective justice that clung to the campaign against harmful tax competition. After a great deal of adverse publicity, the OECD was forced into retreat in dropping the term "harmful tax competition," and agreeing that listed states were not obliged to make any reforms until all OECD members had done likewise.

Arguing about Arguing

While accusations of hypocrisy and double standards among the OECD countries were important in the debate about the potential results of the tax competition initiative, similar charges were central in the controversy about the conduct of the campaign itself. It was crucial for both sides to not only convince others that they were aiming for the right result, but also that they were going about advancing this result in the right (appropriate, legitimate) manner. Given that military force and economic sanctions had been ruled out, and in line with the OECD's technocratic identity and "expert" authority, this meant a combination of reasoned and moral suasion, or arguing. In turn, this imposed a set of rough standards of appropriate conduct that the OECD claimed it was upholding, whereas the accused jurisdictions claimed just the opposite, namely, that the OECD was in violation of its own standards. Thus both sides, and sometimes third parties as well, engaged in arguments about arguments. This is related to the way that results or decisions are said to be legitimate to the extent that a certain process was followed in reaching that end point. This process might be elections, judicial proceedings or a certain degree of consultation and participation by key actors.[111] Both sides sought to portray themselves as eminently reasonable, interested in genuine dialogue, punctilious in observing the norms of debate, and committed to achieving their ends by force of argument and rational persuasion. The OECD claimed that it was interested in widening participation on its tax competition initiative and keen to engage in dialogue with listed countries. In contrast, the latter charged that the OECD had violated the norms of debate by setting itself up as both equal participant and supreme arbiter of what was negotiable and what was nonnegotiable, of barring tax haven states from making their case in appropriate forums, and of failing to commit in advance to observing the result of the debate.

In deciding to allocate responsibility for curbing at least some kinds of tax competition to the OECD, the G7 countries made a bet on an organization with a particular identity that entailed particular strengths and weaknesses. The former included being an established institution with a membership broad enough to encompass the major rich countries but selective enough to exclude likely targets. Another strength was its long track record of fostering cooperation among members. The very strength of the OECD's reputation for impartial technocratic expertise, however, foreclosed options that would have been available to other institutions. Furthermore, having committed to the liabilities as well as the assets of the OECD, the OECD in turn had committed itself to follow the expectations involved in a rhetorical or argumentative approach. And if it was adjudged to have violated these expectations by third parties or some of its own members, the whole campaign would be endangered. It is useful to sketch out some of these norms concerning the appropriate conduct of arguments.

First of all, by embarking on a rhetorical path the OECD had to at least give a convincing impression that it was taking the process seriously and would abide by the result, that it was committed to the principle of "may the better argument win." Along these lines, Kratochwil holds that arguing involves a duty of abstaining from trying to break the other's will.[112] Similarly, Elster notes that "In rational discussion, the only thing supposed to count is the 'power of the better argument,' including arguments that are radically dissociated from the bargaining power of the parties."[113] The OECD had to grant its opponents a certain equality, to listen as well as talk, to refrain from claiming any special privileges or prerogatives, and to avoid the impression that the matter was already settled. This concession of equality dovetailed with the norm of sovereign equality and beliefs of appropriate conduct in the international arena. At a still higher level of abstraction, it relates to the way "The logic of appropriateness [requires] similar behavior from dissimilar actors because rules and norms may make similar behavioral claims on dissimilar actors."[114] It was incumbent on the OECD not only to convince others that it was genuinely aiming for a level playing field in tax competition, but also that there was an intellectual and rhetorical level playing field in place as well. Arguing also imposes a duty of consistency between statements made by the same speaker at different venues and at different times, and a further expectation of correspondence of words and actions.[115] In reading through the various press releases and public statements from participants in the controversy, it is striking how often the same few terms crop up with the same strong value loading, either positive or negative. Thus parties could do no better than to practice "dialogue" in a "multilateral," "inclusive" and "transparent" fashion with their "partners" whilst always avoiding "unilateral," "arbitrary," or "coercive" "dictates."

Perhaps the most explicit development of these shared norms made by any participant in the dispute was given by the Finance Minister of the Cayman Islands, though it could just as well have come from an OECD official:

> International relations have . . . evolved to the point where there is a legitimate expectation in the international arena that differences in perspective can be discussed and common ground found in order to resolve disputes and competing claims. . . . Engaging in meaningful dialogue is a vital element in this process, as is creating a nonconfrontational environment in which dialogue can occur. . . . [This] will refute any perception that "might makes right" and confirm the legitimacy of the process in which we are now engaged. It will also confirm to the international community that it is the rule of international law rather than "the rule of the big stick" that determines the outcome of the process.[116]

The corollary of the OECD's search for euphemisms for "sanctions" was its public commitment to dialogue. When asked how the OECD initiative would succeed, first on the list for Owens was "dialogue, more dialogue and yet more dialogue."[117] From the outset it was announced that, "International co-operation through a multilateral tax competition framework is the best way to ensure stability and the peaceful co-existence of different tax systems."[118] Owens later reiterated that, "We are in the business of looking at this in a constructive way, and the focus is very much on constructive dialogue."[119] The head of the Tax Competition Unit pronounced herself all in favor of "an extended dialogue with jurisdictions that are interested in a co-operative dialogue,"[120] based on the assumption that "Dialogue and broad cooperation will produce many positive results."[121] After the initial combination of indifference and hostility that greeted the release of the 1998 report, the G7 heads of state summit recommended an "intensification of dialogue." During the January 2001 meetings in Barbados, the World Bank called for more "discussion and dialogue" to bridge differences.[122] Finally, Jeffrey Owens made this commitment to inclusive dialogue even more explicit:

> The important thing is that as many people as possible have a seat at the table in setting what the rules would be. I see that as a general trend in a lot of our work. We must be opening up; we must become more inclusive; we must not just be inviting the countries to come and listen to what we have to say, but we've got to be inviting them and saying, "You are here as partners. We're interested in what your views are, and your views will shape things that come out of the OECD."[123]

In 2005 one participant joked that the password to enter an official OECD Global Tax Forum reception changed every hour: from "partnership" to "dialogue" to "peace, love and harmony."

Targeted countries were less impressed with the OECD's protestations of its sweet reasonableness. They were more likely to point out the huge asymmetries of power and wealth between the two sides and assert the intrinsically coercive nature of the exercise. Samoa claimed that "we are now faced with a threat to our international reputation and status in a process which appears to be a case of the strong dictating to the weak, the rich to the poor and the big to the small."[124] In criticizing the campaign, the ITIO stated that "It needs to be an inclusive process but at the moment the OECD is like a club of the rich telling the poor."[125] Speaking more broadly, the CARICOM secretariat said of its opponents that "The view seems to be that inherent in underdevelopment and small size is the inability and ineligibility to be on equal terms with the powerful OECD economies in international rule-making."[126]

Adverse publicity forced the OECD to modify its approach and make concessions, which it did until late 2001 without abandoning its core concerns. Makhlouf confirmed this change of tack:

> One of the most interesting things about the exercise has been that when it started it was pretty clear that member governments had decided that tax havens were a bad thing, therefore we would decide what was a tax haven and take counter measures against it. It seemed to suggest we would gear up to introduce some sanctions. The remarkable thing has been that the process has changed significantly since then. The idea of a "blacklist" has become a tool to promote change. We have found that many of the jurisdictions that have come under scrutiny are interested in changing.[127]

Outsiders were less circumspect. Guernsey officials recalled in July 2001 that "Without doubt, the approach was bullying, chaotic, badly thought out and badly organized when [the tax competition initiative] was launched two or three years ago. It started out with big countries telling small ones to do as they were told."[128] To remedy this exclusionary taint, a succession of OECD officials publicly declared that tax reform would be successful only if participation was broadened to include many more states beyond the thirty rich countries.

Yet this spirit of accommodation only went so far, and in the follow-up meetings of the Joint Working Group in early 2001 the OECD refused to give way on the basic elements of the 1998 report. The OECD worried that giving havens equal representation would lead to a "lowest common denominator" approach, stalling any momentum that had been acquired and wiping out the progress made so far.[129] It further opposed moving negotiations to the UN: "Multilateralism has, in this case, very clear limits since it would include in the negotiation countries that have nothing to do with the subject. Therefore we should not take the dialogue into a forum such as the United Nations."[130] Turning to the Commonwealth, a senior UK diplomat said that progress was being made "in spite of the Commonwealth" which "has been deplorable . . . hopelessly ineffective at dealing with the complex issues, and incapable of reconciling the divergent views of its members" (which, of course, included the UK itself).[131] A document leaked to the press, which the OECD later claimed had been faked by its opponents, included several passages that were very difficult to reconcile with the norms of argument listed above, saying in part:

> There must be acceptance of the OECD's interpretation [of how matters should proceed] . . . as a basis for agreeing to eliminate harmful tax practices. . . . Then both sides can discuss any remaining areas which are unclear. [We are] happy to continue the dialogue to avoid the impression that we are not prepared to discuss the initiative. [We are] happy to discuss the principles in a clarificatory manner only. But time is running out for the havens.

The document went on to say that some important Caribbean jurisdictions were "within spitting distance of committing" and that "This fact is an additional tight constraint on the OECD's room to manoeuver, even if [we] wanted to. Which [we] do not."[132]

The Commonwealth Secretary General Donald McKinnon was furious in his response:

> This minute clearly confirms the suspicions of many that the FAC [Committee on Fiscal Affairs] not only writes the rules, but wishes to be the prosecutor, judge, jury and jailor. . . . This memorandum suggests that the [Committee] is determined to obstruct genuine political dialogue. It has clearly the potential to derail the negotiations which lie ahead.[133]

In return, the Secretary General of the OECD replied to McKinnon: "To issue a public statement without having made any attempt to verify the accuracy of the source is most inappropriate. . . . [T]he issuance of your statement the day before the meeting has not increased the chances of a successful outcome."[134]

In the midst of this exchange, listed jurisdictions in the Joint Working Group, led by Barbados and assisted by the Commonwealth secretariat, put forth an alternative blueprint for improving international coordination on tax matters, which also served as a critique and a challenge. It urged the OECD to live up to the norms of argument it had put in play with the 1998 report and subsequent pronouncements. First of all, it was said that a genuine dialogue does not have a unilaterally imposed deadline, and thus the (then) July 2001 deadline had to be scrapped. Relatedly, since arguing involved staking the result on the power of the better argument and eschewing power-based strategies, the non-OECD half of the Working Group called for all references to sanctions to be dropped. A genuine dialogue, it was argued, could not take place in the shadow of coercion. Second, the OECD could not treat its partner in a truly equal fashion if it reserved itself the right of both participant and referee (prosecutor, judge, jury, and jailor). This claim to incompatible statuses was apparent in the OECD restrictions on the entry to the Forum on Harmful Tax Practices to jurisdictions that endorsed the principles of the 1998 report.

Instead the listed countries called for a new forum to be created which was open to all without preconditions, perhaps under the auspices of the United Nations. Finally, they also called for the 1998 report as the source of basic principles and definitions to be dropped and replaced by new mutually agreed principles of transparency, information exchange, and nondiscrimination. The benefits of such an inclusive process was said to be standards that would have more legitimacy than those just involving OECD members.

> The non-OECD members of the working group, established in Barbados after a high-level consultation on 8–9 January 2001 . . . remain committed to the creation of a consultative political process that includes the widest possible participation and to the creation of a truly global forum. The non-OECD members believe such a forum should consider the legitimate interests of all jurisdictions and establish standards that command the respect and support of the international community with respect to tax matters which have cross-border implications.[135]

The PIF echoed these sentiments: "Meetings in which all affected countries do not participate, although they may allow dialogue, do not fully achieve multilateralization and may act to divide the concerted efforts of affected nations to achieve a consistent dialogue with the OECD."[136] The newly created ITIO asserted that listed jurisdictions could bring considerable practical expertise to the table as well as normatively validating the exercise. "It is manifestly unfair to exclude the countries most affected by the OECD project. It is also thoroughly silly to exclude countries that have more hands-on experience of offshore issues than most OECD members." Earlier, in almost the only contribution by an NGO to the controversy, an Oxfam report that was critical of listed states nevertheless endorsed the need for a broader forum, calling for

> A genuinely inclusive approach fully involving developing countries in discussions; a multilateral approach to what are global problems; and strategies to help small, poor and vulnerable economies to diversify from a reliance on harmful tax practices and to comply with standards to prevent money laundering.[137]

Listed jurisdictions, individually, through their regional organizations and through the Commonwealth and the ITIO, continued to criticize the OECD's credentials as a partner in dialogue and the tax reform framework as a product of unilateral power rather than consensual give-and-take or bargaining as was appropriate for setting international standards. They characterized the OECD as going through the motions of argument, and only really wanting to discuss the details of how nonmembers should go about implementing the standards laid out in the 1998 report and developed subsequently by the secretariat. Lynette Eastmond, head of the ITIO, described the frustrations of the small states in dealing with the OECD, and once again portrayed it as violating norms of argument:

> Seminars and a meeting in Paris does not amount to dialogue in my opinion . . . participation is still a privilege. . . . Now compare this with how the European Union and the United States are engaging each other on the Foreign Sales Corporation issue which has to do with a tax incentive as well. They go to a legal framework, the WTO, they have arguments, they go before an independent tribunal, the U.S. puts something in place, the EU says they don't like it, they take it back to dispute settlement and then we will see what the outcome is. That is the way that countries should treat each other. . . . My view is that the trips to Paris the objective was to say, well, we spoke to them, but the response that most jurisdictions got was that OK, so when are you going to change your rules, there was no attempt to take on board what we had to say.[138]

Finally, this kind of accusation got support from an unlikely source when Frances Horner left the OECD initiative and contributed a paper for the United Nations' tax body. Commenting specifically on the initiative to regulate harmful tax competition, she wrote:

> The OECD making development issues a priority? The rich countries' club? Perhaps not. The OECD has evolved to become, principally, a policy forum to discuss, agree on, and promote the interests of the rich countries. . . . The OECD likes to claim that it develops the "rules of the game," but unfortunately not all the players are at the table. . . . If the OECD wants to be the facilitator of truly global rules of the game, it must find a way to put the developing world at the table with a real and meaningful voice.[139]

The procedural concessions described briefly above, and examined in more detail in the following chapter, saw the OECD concede to most of the demands made by listed states. Nothing better conveys the change of tack than the change in labeling states. Whereas some states in 2000 were called "tax havens," from 2003 onward they have been called "participating partners." These participating partners have identical rights with OECD members in the Global Forum, which in turn makes decisions by consensus. Furthermore, even those jurisdictions that refused to make even a minimal conditional commitment to the post-2002 initiative, or reneged on an earlier commitment, have still been eligible to participate. With sanctions off the agenda, all participants have only the "soft compliance" means that the OECD, and the vast majority of other international organizations, have traditionally relied on.

The OECD thus went to great lengths to portray itself as a reasonable partner for all those interested in dialogue and a cooperative approach to the issue. In response, tax havens and others drew attention to the degree to which the most critical issues had been declared nonnegotiable before the dialogue had begun, and pointed out the tension whereby the OECD claimed to be an equal participant in a debate while also jealously guarding its prerogative to judge the result. The OECD found it very difficult to maintain the campaign's focus and momentum while at the same time limiting itself to the role of an open-minded debater happy to rely on the force of argument alone.

The rhetorical contest in the period 1998–2002 tended to coalesce around recurring themes. Drawing on the public statements of participants and observers in the press and in reports, this chapter has traced the development of the main strands of the debate. Both sides sought to muster support from third parties by claiming their adherence to the same set of widely shared norms and principles, norms and principles purportedly violated by their opponents. Although the OECD managed to taint listed states by association with criminal activities, it was less successful in countering accusations that it was violating fundamental sovereign prerogatives of targeted states, applying double standards in the conduct of the campaign, and failing to adhere to the conventions of reasoned debate. In 2002, the OECD abandoned the main goals of the initiative, and the methods that marked the tax competition campaign out as a departure from traditional OECD practice. Chapters 4 and 5 analyze the outcome of the debate and theorize why the result of the rhetorical contest also determined the result of the overall political contest.

CHAPTER FOUR

Reputation, Blacklisting, and the Tax Havens

It has yet to be demonstrated why participants in the tax competition dispute, or in world politics generally, should care about what others think of them. In particular, why should participants be influenced by normative rules, given that these rules are not taken-for-granted axioms? This chapter and the next aim to elucidate the stakes of the struggle for the tax havens and for the OECD and to explain the different means employed by both parties. For the tax havens, the stakes were their reputations for stability and financial probity, vital for attracting investors. As discussed in chapter 5, for the OECD the stakes were its reputation for objectivity and scientific authority, vital for continued policy influence among governments and preeminence among economically oriented international organizations. Thus both sides had very important reasons to care about the result of the rhetorical struggle surveyed in the previous chapter. In terms of the means employed, the OECD relied on attacking the reputation of tax havens by making negative public judgments, or by blacklisting. The response from the other side, discussed in the following chapter, was to try for "rhetorical entrapment": targeted small states and their supporters seized on discrepancies between the OECD's professed values and conduct in the campaign against harmful tax competition.

The coverage devoted to surveying the rhetorical contest in the previous chapter is based on the claim that there are important negative consequences (internally or externally) that can arise as a result of these discursive interactions. Following from this, international actors will tend to adapt their actions to avoid these unfavorable consequences. But why should tax havens or international organizations care whether they have a good, bad, or indifferent reputation? Why should they care whether others see their conduct as legitimate or illegitimate? The pressures to avoid inappropriate behavior span a spectrum. At one end are internalized taken-for-granted norms. At the other is norm-compliant behavior almost entirely based on the disapproval of third parties and social sanctioning. Regarding the parties in relation to the tax competition controversy, it is argued while the internalization of norms and external social penalties both played a role, these pressures operated differently on each side. For the OECD internalized rules and socialization played an important part together with external pressures. For listed jurisdictions, however, external social sanctions were much more important than internal compliance pressures.

The Center for Freedom and Prosperity's (CFP) lobbying technique provides a good example of the difference between these internal and external mechanisms. The Director Andrew Quinlan speaks of an "inside-outside" strategy. Using the inside strategy, lobbyists first aim to convince legislators of the "compelling truth of our arguments," based on persuasion, or effecting an internal preference change. The outside part is the mobilizing of grass roots to generate electoral pressure (changing pay-offs by introducing external rewards and penalties).[1] Typically, Quinlan, Daniel Mitchell, Véronique de Rugy, and others tried to win over Congressmen and Treasury officials to the cause by presenting opposition to the OECD as both a principled *and* self-interested stance.[2] Speaking for the OECD, Jeffrey Owens has also argued that complying with the initiative is both "the right thing to do" and in the enlightened self-interest of tax havens.[3]

The first half of this chapter analyzes the stakes for tax havens, namely, keeping their reputations intact. Consideration is paid to how the lack of objective defining features of tax havens has meant that classification tends to be by "reputation test." I will argue that for targeted states a reputation as a safe and well-regulated destination for investors' funds is the single most important factor in attracting outside investment. My definition of reputation is broader than that current in the field. Unlike treatments derived from economics, I take reputation to be a relational concept rather than a property concept. It is emergent and intersubjective, rather than an aggregation of individual opinions. Finally, I argue that reputation is based on associations and feelings, rather than induction from an objective record of past behavior. In this way, reputation shares much with marketing and branding, as is briefly discussed with reference to the Cayman Islands and Liechtenstein.

The second half of the chapter is devoted to coverage of blacklisting, the main rhetorical means used by the OECD to try to elicit compliance from targeted states. A conceptual discussion of blacklisting is followed by evidence showing its effects on listed jurisdictions. I argue that blacklisting is a form of action, "doing in saying," in line with J. L. Austin and John Searle's ideas about speech acts. Such an action changes the world by changing (damaging) the reputations of tax havens. Rather than being cheap talk, inclusion on the OECD's lists of 2000 and 2002 imposed costs on small states. These lists have tended to reverberate and diffuse among states, financial intermediaries, and individual investors. Blacklisting damaged small states' reputations, which in turn tended to lead to capital flight or the fear thereof, and this created pressure to comply with the OECD's demands. Although this compliance pressure was generally not sufficient to win the day for the OECD, it did help avoid complete defeat by means of creating pressure for targeted states to agree to the much-reduced demands of the initiative from 2002. Evidence from this proposition is drawn primarily from interviews conducted by the author in fourteen affected jurisdictions in Europe, the Caribbean, the Pacific, and the Indian Ocean.

Though there were pressures on each side, blacklisting for the tax havens and rhetorical entrapment for the OECD, this did not mean the pressures were equal, as shown by the lop-sided result. In both substance and process, the tax havens generally won and the OECD generally lost. Although small states would have much preferred to stay off the June 2000 "tax havens" and the April 2002 "uncooperative tax havens" lists, blacklisting was generally not sufficient to induce targeted states to capitulate on the main issue: whether or not to abandon features of their tax codes that were designed to attract foreign investment from OECD countries. Conversely, the effects of the rhetorical contest surveyed in the previous chapter on the OECD, both directly and as mediated through third party opinion, did produce a comprehensive climb-down. In late 2001, the OECD renounced the central plank of the campaign to regulate international tax competition by dropping its objections to ring-fenced concessions for foreign investors who did not engage in substantive economic activity. In the language of the 1998 report, this gave tax havens a blank check to engage in continued "tax poaching" and fuel the fiscal "race to the bottom."[4]

Relating to process, from the initial position of exclusionary or top-down regulation the OECD conceded the principle of the level playing field through the "Isle of Man clause": no tax haven state was bound to make reforms until every OECD member state had committed to introduce identical measures on the same timetable. Because Switzerland and Luxembourg consistently refused to have any truck with the initiative, in effect tax havens were not committed to do anything at all. Furthermore, from October 2003 an additional condition was included, whereby the commitments of tax havens would become binding only if eight additional non-OECD countries made identical commitments. Thus by 2004, if any one of seventy-six jurisdictions refused to be bound by the new standards (the new nonmember eight plus thirty OECD members plus thirty-three "participating partners" plus five "uncooperative tax havens") the other seventy-five were off the hook. All this at a time when the OECD had renounced the threat of sanctions. Not surprisingly, in practice these stringent conditions and lack of enforcement powers have meant that the OECD has had to give up its plans for a "big bang" solution, whereby all jurisdictions go to the same tax information sharing standards on the same timetable.[5]

What's in a Name? International Organizations and Defining Tax Havens

International organizations gain a great deal of their power from the ability to label and categorize.[6] The OECD's efforts to regulate international tax competition since 1998 provide a classic instance of how international organizations can achieve influence by their authoritative command of language. OECD bodies like the Forum on Harmful Tax Practices and the Committee on Fiscal Affairs have molded the meanings and connotations attached to the term "tax haven," and have used this label to exert pressure on noncompliant jurisdictions by threatening their reputations. "Tax haven" is now regarded as a pejorative, an unfavorable judgment on a jurisdiction's stability, financial probity, and standing in the international community. The term "tax haven" is a persuasive exemplar of the power to label and name because there is so little agreement as to objective features that distinguish between tax haven and non–tax haven jurisdictions. Furthermore, the side of the distinction upon which states end up has important political and economic consequences. Reviewing the history of the concept, one scholar points out, "Almost every work dealing with tax havens begins with the author acknowledging the practical impossibility of clearly defining a tax haven."[7] The OECD has come close on several occasions to admitting that, rather than reflecting any particular cluster of banking, financial and fiscal laws or regulations, its judgments are a reflection of the identity projected by the particular state, or how that state is perceived in the eyes of third party investors and governments. The OECD has thus in a sense created tax havens by the particular way it has chosen to label.

A logical place to start in substantiating the claim that "tax haven" is a very malleable term is by reviewing the OECD's own attempts at definition.

> The concept of a "tax haven" is a relative one as any country can be a tax haven in relation to a particular operation or situation. . . . Attempts to provide a single definition of a "tax haven" are bound to be unsuccessful. . . . It can be argued that the "tax haven" concept is such a relative one that it would serve no useful purpose to make further attempts to define it.[8]

The same report did, however, go on to list features commonly associated with such jurisdictions: a low or zero rate of tax, strict bank secrecy, a large financial sector relative to the rest of the economy, modern communications, absence of currency controls and, significantly, being advertised as a tax haven.[9] As discussed earlier, the 1998 report admits (in a notable understatement) that the term "tax haven" "does not have a precise technical meaning,"[10] but it goes on to say:

> No or only nominal taxation combined with the fact that a country offers itself as a place, *or is perceived to be a place,* to be used by nonresidents to escape tax in their country of residence may be sufficient to classify that jurisdiction as a tax haven.[11] [Emphasis added.]

There is considerable circularity here, in that a major factor in leading third parties to perceive certain jurisdictions as tax havens is that the OECD has categorized them as such. The report then goes on to operationalize the term, looking at low or zero tax rates, lack of information exchange, lack of transparency, and investments that produce no substantial economic activity. The details were to be developed and applied by the Forum on Harmful Tax Practices set up in the wake of the report. It is thus significant that the OECD itself has admitted the relative and elastic nature of the term tax haven, candidly in a 1987 report, obliquely in 1998. It has previously stated that the term is applicable to many and perhaps all countries depending on the definition adopted. Finally, it has included a "reputation test," based on how third parties perceive a particular jurisdiction. A tax haven is a tax haven if enough of the right people think it is.

Similarly, national governments also have not had an easy time deciding what constitutes a tax haven. Tax specialists have expressed skepticism that such a classification could ever be made objectively rather than pressed into service in the pursuit of political goals.[12] Thus in the opinion of one member of the U.S. Senate Finance Committee in 2002: "It's kind of like defining pornography. As the Supreme Court said, you know it when you see it."[13] Two decades earlier, the IRS's Gordon Report was even more blunt in its reliance on reputation. The report also deliberately crafted its definition of the term to exclude large rich countries:

> The term "tax haven" has been loosely defined to include any country having a low or zero rate of tax on all or certain categories of income, and offering a certain level of banking or commercial secrecy. Applied literally, however, this definition would sweep in many industrialized countries not generally considered tax havens, including the United States. . . . The term "tax haven" may also be defined by a "smell" or reputation test: a country is a tax haven if it looks like one and if it is considered one by those who care.[14]

Other analysts concur with the OECD's 1987 judgment that the "complexity of modern national taxation systems, combined with greater capital mobility, has rendered practically every country in the world a potential tax haven from some type of taxation and regulation for residents of other countries."[15] Some have claimed that the United States and the United Kingdom are both tax havens. In the words of one of the most renowned commentators on international tax questions:

> It does not surprise anyone when I tell them that the most important tax haven in the world is an island. They are surprised, however, when I tell them that the name of this island is *Manhattan*. Moreover, the second most important tax haven in the world is located on an island. It is a city called *London* in the United Kingdom.[16]

The United States refuses to exchange information on interest earned by foreign depositors. In addition, certain states like Delaware, Montana, Colorado, and

Nevada offer easy incorporation with minimal reporting requirements, tax free treatment for nonresidents, and promote themselves on the strict limits they impose on information exchange with other jurisdictions.[17]

The City of London is one of the world's biggest offshore centers, which the British government has shown great determination to defend. In a quirk of the UK tax system, foreign domiciled individuals residing in Britain may avoid all tax on their foreign income.[18] Even Scandinavia, a bastion of social democracy and the welfare state, with some of the world's highest effective tax rates, provides similar examples. Danish holding companies can provide 100 percent exemption from tax on dividends and capital gains from selling shares for foreign investors, with no withholding tax and no stamp duty.[19] Sweden has recently begun offering similar tax concessions to compete for the same holding company market.[20] An important but seldom-mentioned feature of the OECD's initiative is that it does nothing to stop citizens and firms in developing countries from escaping their tax obligations at home by shifting assets to OECD countries, as opposed to non-OECD tax havens.[21] These examples have given rise to the charges of hypocrisy and double standards covered in the previous chapter.

Because of the extreme flexibility of the term, decisions on just which jurisdictions are tax havens involve a great deal of discretion, and thus leave much latitude for political factors to intrude on what is ostensibly a technical adjudication. Yet despite the difficulty of compiling an objective list of tax havens, being labeled as such has important effects. Thanks to the OECD's campaign, aided by the activities of the FSF, FATF, and other related initiatives, "tax haven" has become a pejorative term with which to threaten reputation and thus the viability of small states' financial sectors.

> The term "tax haven," recognized in the past as a neutral description for countries offering attractive low-tax regimes to attract financial services and other economic activities, has been reinterpreted by these two reports [OECD 1998 and 2000] to mean countries indulging in harmful tax practices.[22]

This reinterpretation has stuck. Tax specialists speak of the "international financial centers" that were "previously known under the now politically incorrect label of tax havens."[23] Another notes that "tax haven" and "financial center" are largely synonymous, but that the latter is "less pejorative and thus more politically correct."[24]

In this light, the 2002 edition of the Economist Intelligence Unit's authoritative survey of tax havens is an interesting example. The very first page begins:

> The term "tax haven" has become a controversial term. This report, like the previous nine editions, refers to fiscally attractive locations as "tax havens," for the sake of continuity and simplicity. This usage is entirely neutral and is not intended to imply any judgment whatsoever about the probity or otherwise of any particular tax regime.[25]

In stating, "To be, but not to be known as, a tax haven is the main challenge facing many small economies," the report belies its own claim that "the Anglo–Saxon tax haven, the French, Spanish and Portuguese fiscal paradise and the German tax oasis will smell as sweet by any other name." Another industry source reinforces the fact that tax havens may indeed smell sweeter by another name.

> The Central Banks and governments of the world's tax havens agree on one thing— they much prefer to be called *financial centers* than *tax havens*. The word *tax haven* conjures up the notion of tax evasion, money laundering and illegal drug profits, none of which a respectable tax haven wants to be associated with.[26]

More specifically, writing on the history of the Isle of Man's financial services in 1975, a senior governmental official entitled his book *Anatomy of a Tax Haven*.[27] Currently, however, the island's Insurance and Pensions Authority has a separate web page, "International Reputation," on which it notes its agreement with the OECD "to ensure that the Island is not regarded as a tax haven."[28]

Countries that came to feature on the June 2000 list (as well as Switzerland and Luxembourg) were quick to deny that they were tax havens. In a typical instance, the Bahamas told the OECD that it found the term "deeply offensive."[29] Accounting firm PricewaterhouseCoopers in Aruba explained a new package of laws operative from 2003 as necessary "to dispel the image of Aruba as a tax haven."[30] An interview with the head of the Malta Financial Services Authority noted "the island's progress from 'tax haven' to more European orientated regulatory environment."[31] The Chief Executive of the Guernsey Promotional Agency stated that "The biggest challenge is to remove the description of the island as an offshore tax haven and replace it with offshore financial center."[32] In sum, the lack of any definite match between the term tax haven and objective features had created the permissive environment for the OECD to reshape and employ the term in an attempt to enforce its solution to harmful tax competition. The OECD not only controlled the application of this label through its 2000 list, but was also able subtly to insinuate new and more negative connotations.

The Importance of Reputation

The success or failure of a tax haven is more dependent on its reputation than any other single factor. Tax havens are not undifferentiated units offering perfectly substitutable services, nor is price the most important point of competition between them. Some level of specialization occurs as jurisdictions seek to enter, or create, niche markets. Nevertheless, reputation is the main point of differentiation among a relatively large number of tax havens that are engaged in fierce competition with each other within and across regions.[33] Jurisdictions with more established financial centers assiduously cultivate their image as secure, stable, and well-run investment destinations. As a consequence, they are able to attract a greater volume of more lucrative business. Despite the prevalence of race-to-the-bottom thinking, in part promoted by the OECD, it is commonsensical that no amount of secrecy and protection from tax authorities will attract investors to jurisdictions in which deposits are thought to vanish into thin air. The 1998 UN report on money laundering and havens succinctly presents this balancing act:

> The more stringent and scrupulous one is about due diligence and vetting customers, the more likely it is that some customers will take their business to alternative venues that ask fewer questions and present fewer obstacles. On the other hand, if a haven develops too unsavory a reputation as a home for "dirty money" or a haunt of organized crime and drug traffickers, then not only will legitimate money go elsewhere as respectable companies move their businesses to avoid tarnishing their reputations but so too will more sophisticated criminals who want to avoid any taint by association.[34]

In a thorough and thoughtful piece on the multilateral initiatives, Gilligan comes to a similar conclusion: "Some investors may prefer more costly financial centers precisely because some may have a better reputation for stability, investor protection and transparent regulatory standards."[35] Interview material indicates that offshore regulators are well aware of this trade-off between under- and overregulation.[36]

Writing specifically on how the Bahamas and Cayman Islands have conscientiously sought to foster a positive image abroad, Alan Hudson notes that after the early 1980s "reputation and trust became all-important," easily dominating the tendency to engage in competitive deregulation to attract investment. The Caymans began marketing itself under the motto "Reputation is our most important asset."[37] This came after both locations became associated with drug trafficking in the 1970s and 1980s and lost business as a result.[38] After conducting dozens of interviews among regulators and investors in the region, Hudson reports that "reputation" was the most often used word by his informants in discussing selling points for a particular location. When questioned on what sort of qualities the country tries to project, a former Bahamian Attorney General replied: "Stability, stability, stability, stability, stability."[39] While successfully cultivating the notion that a favorable image pays dividends, it also leaves countries very vulnerable to scandals or adverse publicity. In particular, "The USA, through the statements of its politicians, news media and financial publications plays a central role in the production and distribution of representations of the Bahamas and Cayman OFCs, representations which contribute to making the places what they are."[40]

There is a wealth of other evidence to support this conclusion, with "reputation" featuring prominently and repeatedly in various offshore centers' general self-promotional material and in connection with blacklists. The home page of the British Virgin Islands International Financial Center states that "Reputation is our most important single asset. We are very proud and protective of it, and fully committed to maintaining and enhancing it."[41] Responding specifically to the Bahamas commitment to the OECD, which kept it off the 2002 blacklist, one official commented: "The Caribbean banking centers—and I certainly can speak for the Bahamas—have always been concerned about our reputation. Our institutions live by their reputations. We're pleased not to be on the list."[42] He later noted "Our reputation is crucial to our long-term development and we are determined to protect it."[43] An Antiguan regulator stated that reputation "is the most important thing" for the success of an offshore center.[44] A Mauritian private sector source explained that "your reputation is all you've got."[45] An IMF report on offshore activities in the Caribbean further supports this finding: "it is most likely that the major competitive factor in the current international environment is a country's established reputation."[46] FATF sources note the greater sensitivity of offshore centers to reputational damage compared with onshore countries.[47] These concerns extend well beyond the Caribbean, and again the emphasis is on how third parties view a particular jurisdiction: "the Isle of Man's position in the offshore financial center sector depends on being perceived as meeting the 'international norm.' If some practices are widely seen as unhealthy and harmful, then the island will have to fall into line." Products and pricing that might make sense on narrowly commercial grounds are rejected if they are felt to pose a reputational risk to the jurisdiction.[48] Even jurisdictions that would seem to have very little reputation to worry about still seem concerned. Thus the homepage of the Somali International Financial Center (not on the OECD's list), after noting the "liberal, proactive business environment" in the country, lists the five main advantages of Somalia, with the first bullet point being: "Reputable jurisdiction, not blacklisted, former British colony."[49]

The Concept of Reputation

"Reputation," according to the head of the Liechtenstein Bankers' Association, "is trust in advance."[50] As used by rationalist scholars, however, reputation is a record of an actor's past behavior, or more formally their past behavior in an iterated game. This rationalist understanding of the concept is so important that it "now stands as a linchpin of the dominant neoliberal institutionalist theory of decentralized cooperation."[51] Although settling on a working definition of "the degree to which a state reliably upholds its international commitments," after a far-reaching literature review Downs and Jones note that "no detailed justification of the traditional [rationalist] theory of reputation exists in the literature."[52] This traditional view holds that "Observers are like accountants who carefully tabulate the target's behavior and collectively give the target one reputation."[53] For this book, however, the concept of reputation is different on at least three important counts. First, reputation is used as a relational concept rather than a property concept. Second, reputation is intersubjective, a social fact, rather than just the sum of individual actors' beliefs. Third, reputation includes a range of feelings and associations, operating as much at the subconscious as conscious level and therefore not included in rationalist treatments.

Rather than trying to show that rationalist conceptions of reputation are wrong, the aim is to show that conventional views on the subject are excessively narrow and incomplete, something that some of the most thoughtful rational scholars working on the topic are happy to admit. Downs and Jones contrast a more social conception of reputation, "the extent to which a state is considered to be an honorable member of the international community," with the rationalist definition given earlier ("the degree to which a state reliably upholds its international commitments"). However, they note that "It is this rational dimension of reputation that is chiefly of interest to economists and most political scientists."[54]

The first point in arguing for this more expansive definition is to establish reputation as a "relational concept" (what others think of an actor) rather than a "property concept" (something that an actor can own).[55] Conceptually, very few would dispute this point, but in practice reputation is often written about like a good or commodity. An actor in Robert Axelrod's computer tournament, and in the legalization compliance models common in political science, economics, and law, is said to have a high degree of control over its reputation.[56] Actors have a choice: they can defect and therefore pay the cost to their reputations, or comply and build up social capital with respect to reputation in terms of cooperative behavior that accumulates over time, hence accumulating something that now belongs to and is controlled by them. Governments and central banks trade off the benefits of electorally popular macro-economic policies against the costs to reputation incurred among investors.[57] The danger of forfeiting reputation in terms of social capital or property is often the stake that makes actors' commitments credible.[58]

> According to the standard argument, a major—if not the major—reason why states keep commitments, even those that produce a lower level of returns than expected, is because they fear that any evidence of unreliability will damage their current cooperative relationships and lead other states to reduce their willingness to enter into future agreements.[59]

In his extensive discussion of the concept from an economist's point of view, highly reminiscent of conventional political science wisdom, Kreps notes:

> In transactions where one side must trust the other, the reputation of the trusted party can be a powerful tool for avoiding the transaction costs of specifying and enforcing the terms of the transaction. . . . Reputation works as follows: The trusted party will honor that trust because to abuse it would preclude or substantially limit opportunities to engage in future valuable transactions.[60]

Reputation is an "economic good" that can be invested in and sold.[61] It is a reflection of actors' choices, with the perceptions of third parties assumed to follow unproblematically and uniformly.[62]

This view, however, understates the autonomy of third party perceptions, and greatly overstates the control actors have over the way others see them. Compare the treatment of how Nevis would like to be seen by others compared with the way it is seen by (at least some) others:

> The Nevis Island Administration has maintained a conscientious and conservative approach to building a solid reputation and has developed recognized expertise in this area [of offshore financial services]. . . . Over the years, Nevis has jealously guarded its impeccable reputation and has continuously demonstrated its commitment to the development of a solid international financial services sector.[63]

> [Nevis] has a reputation as being a money-laundering haven for drug traffickers and other suspicious businesses (despite righteous denials by Nevis officials). The tiny island has some 9,000 offshore businesses—about one business per inhabitant—registered and operating under strict secrecy laws.[64]

This negative reputation is not a result of Nevis's defections in an iterated game. Furthermore, being an emergent and intersubjectively shared belief in the minds of third parties, it is something over which Nevis and other tax havens have only very limited influence.

A commitment to "social facts" as well as material reality has become a bedrock principle of constructivism.[65] In line with this concern, reputation is characterized by intersubjective features at least as much as subjective aspects. Reputations are clearly not brute material facts, so the question is whether they are solely the sum of individual beliefs, as rational choice theorists hold, or something more than this. Alexander Wendt's discussion of common knowledge is helpful in illuminating why reputations should be considered something more than just the sum of individuals' thoughts and beliefs.

> Common knowledge is subjective in the sense that the beliefs that make it up are in actors' heads, and figure in intentional explanations. Yet because those beliefs must be accurate beliefs about others' beliefs it is also an *inter*subjective phenomenon which confronts actors as an objective social fact that cannot be individually wished away.[66]

Wendt goes on to contrast the game theorist's notion of common knowledge, which is nothing more than the content of people's heads, to collective knowledge. The latter is based on but, having an emergent quality, also something fundamentally more than individual cognitions. As such, instances of collective knowledge are "knowledge structures held by groups which generate macro-level patterns in individual behavior over time."[67] This book argues that reputation is just such a collective knowledge structure.

The third point of difference with conventional conceptions of reputation is the inclusion of a much broader array of associations and information than "should" be relevant under rationalist concepts. In the conventional view, reputation is inductively derived from objective information (such as repeated moves in an iterated game). If actors' moves cannot be observed and remembered as information, then there is no reputation. As a result, the cooperation engendered by the "shadow of the future" breaks down. It is just this monitoring function that regimes are said to perform in fostering international cooperation.[68] Continuing in this vein, the more information that is available (the more iterations that have been played), the more important reputation becomes. For the actor making the commitment, as a reputation accumulates over iterations it becomes more and more valuable, and thus enables more and more credible signals to be sent. The credibility of this signal allays the fears that commitments will be dishonored and trust betrayed.

Compare this view with the comment of the Liechtenstein banker that reputation is trust in advance or instead of specific information. The word "Liechtenstein" should immediately be associated with ideas of security, reliability, confidentiality, and professionalism. Given that gathering information is costly, and that there are many alternative investment destinations, if instead "Liechtenstein" conjures up ideas of crime, money laundering, and suspicious practices it is unlikely that investors will look for more information to correct a bad first impression. These associations matter much less for people who have had dealings with the Principality for a long time, who know the banking and other financial legislation, who are familiar with relevant court decisions and economic trends, and so on. The relationship between information and reputation is reversed: from the rationalist point of view, the more information is available, the more important reputation becomes. From a more sociological perspective, exactly the opposite obtains: the less information available, the more actors are likely to be swayed by reputation. In line with this logic, tax havens, collectively a catalogue of the most obscure states and semi-states on earth, are thus particularly dependent on reputation. Even specialists can be stumped, as when a Belgian money laundering official asked at an international seminar whether there really was a country called Palau, only to be quickly assured by the Palauan representative that there was.[69]

Reputation as Branding

Rationalist explanations hold that people making investment decisions should be interested in some kinds of information but not others. Relevant information might include sovereign credit ratings, security of property rights, macro-economic indicators, auditing and record keeping requirements, trust and company formation fees, and so on. Relevant information would not include the color of the jurisdiction's logo, how the jurisdiction is portrayed in soap operas, films and popular novels, or the presence or absence of palm trees. Hence, to attract investment, tax havens should be very concerned about the first kind of information, useful for the rational investor, while they should be unconcerned about the second kind of information. The trouble is that tax havens spend more effort on the second kind of publicity and marketing than the first and are extremely concerned about negative publicity in areas that "should" be irrelevant to the rational investor. Some suggestive evidence to support this claim is presented below.

A more expansive notion of reputation, trust in advance of specific information rather than afterward, in some ways has more in common with marketing and "brand management" than game theorists' renderings.[70] Established jurisdictions in particular, such as the Caymans, Jersey, and Liechtenstein, obsess about reputation as "the totality of the thoughts, feelings, associations and expectations that come to mind when a prospect or consumer is exposed to an entity's name, logo, products, services, events, or any design or symbol representing them."[71] Asked to explain why the British Virgin Islands has registered almost as many International Business Companies as the rest of the world combined (over 700,000 in 2005), one member of the Caribbean financial services industry noted: "It's a brand, like Coke. There are plenty of other colas around but people prefer Coke." In words that closely echo the opinions of officials in tax havens channeling huge flows of intangible wealth between one onshore country and another, van Ham observes: "In the end, location brands may consider their image more important than their 'assets.' In fact, a successful location brand may do without any territory whatsoever."[72]

Liechtenstein is a prime example of reputation as branding. The Principality was linked with several scandals in the 1980s and 1990s and also appeared on the OECD's June 2000 list of tax havens, the April 2002 "uncooperative tax havens" list, and the Financial Action Task Force Non-Cooperative Countries and Territories list in June 2000. An article in the *Guardian* reports, "Officials wearily conceded that most people have either never heard of Liechtenstein, or know about it for the wrong reasons."[73] In response, as well as carrying out far-reaching and expensive regulatory reforms, the Principality has deliberately tried to re-brand itself, the campaign centering on a new aubergine logo. As one government official explained: "aubergine is a serious color." The head of the Liechtenstein Bankers' Association has bemoaned the problem created by German soap operas that routinely portray evil characters stashing their money in the Principality.[74]

Continuing this theme of concern, or obsession, with reputation as affected by popular culture is the "Grisham Effect" on the Cayman Islands. The government felt moved to issue a point-by-point refutation of John Grisham's popular novel *The Firm*, dealing with a nefarious law practice based in the Caymans.[75] This episode has gone down in local lore as a salutary lesson concerning the dangers posed to the islands' reputation by unflattering popular cultural references.[76] An article entitled

"Perception versus Perception" in the *Cayman Financial Review* is centered on the impact of "blockbuster movies, books, and other media that include the obligatory negative mention of such [offshore financial] centers."[77] The article continues:

> Traditionally, offshore centers have seemed to let the poor perceptions persist, with some hope that at worse [*sic*], they do not have a significant negative impact on business. More recently, we have seen a major change across jurisdictions with the use of marketing and public relations bodies and an increase in public-sector funding of such initiatives. There is a clear recognition that maintaining a financial center that is commercially successful means maintaining one that has integrity, enshrined not only in its laws, but also in how it is perceived internationally.

After discounting the role of regulatory improvements in solving this perception problem, the author goes on to note that "Crucially, these [marketing] efforts provide an alternative perspective to individuals that do have an influence on the policy environment onshore, such as politicians and technocrats within OECD-based think tanks that are affected by the media just like everyone else." Some evidence to this effect is provided by an IMF official commenting on the reputation problems of tax havens like the Caymans; after all, he said, "just think of the movies."[78]

These same marketing priorities are also reflected in less established jurisdictions as well. The comment that "perception is more important than reality" is a constant refrain in interviewing those from the public and private sector involved in offshore finance. The Antigua and Barbuda financial services regulators for a long time placed much greater emphasis on their marketing function than their regulatory duties.[79] Both private sector and government officials in Vanuatu attribute the relatively poor performance of the offshore sector to lackluster marketing,[80] a judgment also common to other Pacific jurisdictions and beyond.[81] Finally, a survey of jurisdictions' main financial services home pages reveals a profusion of palm trees and an equally conspicuous lack of hard economic and financial data.[82]

Reputation is the main asset of a tax haven but also its main vulnerability. Small states cared about the result of the rhetorical struggle with the OECD first and foremost because, to the extent they lost, their reputations suffered, and thus their ability to attract foreign investment declined. Having completed the first main task of this chapter, examining the stakes for small states, the remainder covers the means used by the OECD to threaten this precious commodity in creating compliance pressure. By far the most important of these was blacklisting, an example of a speech act. The three sections below explain the concept of speech acts, demonstrate the mechanisms by which blacklists were diffused, and, finally, present evidence that blacklists as speech acts created material economic damage in targeted states.

Words as Actions

With direct reference to the campaign against tax havens, the *Economist* noted that "Few countries wish to end up on the OECD blacklist, but the group's bark may well be much worse than its bite. It has no legal authority, and can only issue recommendations." A counter to this view of a strict separation between words and actions is the work of J. L. Austin, particularly as contained in his aptly titled book *How to Do Things with Words*.[83] Austin begins by outlining the shortcomings of the view that language is just there to report facts and describe, and thus can always be judged in terms of true or false. In addition to these descriptive roles, Austin looks at a class of utterances he terms "speech acts." The notion of speech acts is not entirely foreign to International Relations; pioneer constructivists like Kratochwil and Onuf discuss it at some length,[84] but it has generally been associated with broader notions of communicative action.

For Austin, examples of speech acts include promising, warning and apologizing. So, for instance, "When I say, before the registrar or altar, etc., 'I do,' I am not reporting on a marriage: I am indulging in it."[85] Saying "I name this ship the Queen Elizabeth" while smashing a bottle of champagne against the prow is not to describe naming the ship but rather it is to actually do it. These are instances of "performative utterances" in that by saying something speakers are actually doing something, they are performing an action.[86] Austin maintains that performatives like "I do" are restricted in that they must be said in the right way (audibly, not as a joke), in the right circumstances (in a church, at the altar), by the right person (the groom or bride, not the priest or a passer-by). Most relevant for the issue at hand is the class of "verdictives" or judgments. These may occur when for example a referee pronounces a player offside or a jury foreman declares a defendant guilty.[87] These utterances do not report on or describe whether a person is offside or guilty but instead they are acts of passing judgments or verdictives. The force of the judgment depends on the right sort of person performing this action, saying the words in the appropriate context, and performing the right rituals in order for the verdictive to be recognized as legitimate. Thus the orientation of third parties begins to intrude, as do conceptions of appropriate roles or identity, a vitally important point that is taken up in the discussion of the link between the OECD's identity and its effectiveness in chapter 5.

John Searle also creates a typology of speech acts, of which the class of "assertive declarations" is particularly relevant to the practice of blacklisting; it is similar to Austin's verdictives. Assertions are statements about the world that may be judged true or false according to evidence, like "North Korea has nuclear weapons." Declarations, in contrast, "bring about some alteration in the status or condition of the referred to object or objects solely in virtue of the fact that the declaration has been successfully performed."[88] Assertive declarations are a combination, and again the examples of a judge or umpire are relevant:

The judge and the umpire make factual claims: "you are out," "you are guilty." . . . But, at the same time, both have the force of declarations. If the umpire calls you out (and is upheld on appeal), then for baseball purposes you are out regardless of the facts of the case, and if the judge declares you guilty (and is upheld on appeal), then for legal purposes you are guilty.[89]

In the same way, blacklisting a person or country brings about a change in the condition of that person or country solely by virtue of the blacklist having been published. A jurisdiction becomes blacklisted (whether fairly or unfairly, accurately or not) and by that action alone its reputation is changed. Thus rather than the verdictive being a description of, or signal for, an action that has changed, or will change some part of the world, it *is* an action that changes some part of the world.

As detailed in the section on defining tax havens above, the lack of any agreed definition means that official judgments by the Forum on Harmful Tax Practices and Committee on Fiscal Affairs, later endorsed by the OECD Council of Ministers, were making facts rather than just reporting on them, and were performing actions, not just describing objective phenomena. Through labeling and relabeling the world, the OECD has remade it. This was recognized both by those jurisdictions adjudged to be tax havens as well as media observers. It undermined any distinction between "mere words" (blacklisting) and "real action" (sanctions). Speaking of the combination of OECD, FATF and Financial Stability Forum blacklists in mid-2000 one observer held that:

> The combination of the three blacklists . . . has restrained capital movement and has resulted in concrete steps by banks and financial institutions to close accounts or require depositors to visit in person to provide additional identification if they wanted to maintain their accounts. . . . Clearly, in a practical and legal sense, the issuance of blacklists are not merely "naming and shaming," but the imposition of economic sanctions.[90]

Tax havens themselves were even more forthright about the damage caused by blacklisting, and saw the resulting economic damage as part of a premeditated OECD strategy of applying pressure against noncompliant jurisdictions. The Commonwealth has echoed these concerns in identifying "the potential for systemic impact and damage to their reputation suffered from the linkage [by the OECD] with the listings by the UN and FATF."[91] More wide-ranging comments by George McCarthy, Finance Minister of the Cayman Islands, illustrate how the participants in the controversy have been well aware of the impact of language and rhetoric, independent of strictly material inducements or threats. "Language is very powerful. The Book of Proverbs (Chapters 12 & 18) teaches that words can play a decisive role, whether for good or evil. They can be as destructive as sword thrusts or the means of healing."[92]

The Mechanics of Blacklisting

Blacklisting by the OECD was a speech act that served to exert pressure on re-calcitrant small states via threatening their reputation in the eyes of international in-vestors. This section explains how blacklists reverberated down through three levels: states, financial intermediaries, and individual investors, with the last-mentioned partially covered in the discussion of reputation as branding above. At each level the blacklists tended to be reproduced and rebroadcast both laterally (from one state to another, one financial intermediary to another) and vertically (down from states to financial intermediaries, and from states and these intermediaries to individual in-vestors). Following this discussion, the next task is to demonstrate the effects of OECD blacklisting on targeted states. It is both easier and more useful to look at how those in targeted states perceived the effects of blacklisting, both anticipated and actual, than to try to measure the objective effects of blacklisting. Evidence of these perceptions is drawn from interview material from twelve affected jurisdic-tions. The differing sensitivity of targeted states is examined by dividing them into three groups. The first group comprises those that made commitments to the max-imalist OECD program before the concessions of late 2001. The second, larger group consists of those that rushed to make a commitment to the reduced initia-tive before the deadline for the April 2002 "uncooperative tax havens" list. The last groups are the holdouts that defied the deadline and thus appeared on the 2002 list. Although different jurisdictions were affected in different ways, nowhere was black-listing a matter of indifference.

Being named as a "tax haven" in June 2000 or "uncooperative tax haven" in April 2002 by the OECD did not create any obligations under international law, nor un-der the domestic laws of member states. Yet in practice these blacklists were rapidly adopted and reproduced among member and nonmember states. Many countries have long taken action against tax havens on a unilateral basis by compiling national blacklists.[93] These countries have faced the same problems identified above in de-ciding just which jurisdictions qualify as tax havens. Forming a definition is very dif-ficult because it can require studying dozens of foreign tax codes. As a result, there is a tendency for national tax authorities to rely on preexisting lists, and increasingly those produced by international organizations like the OECD. A Pacific Islands Fo-rum report claims that the OECD 2000 list of tax havens was incorporated in na-tional blacklists in countries including Argentina, Brazil, France, Italy, Peru, Mexico, Spain, and Venezuela, which have often neglected or refused to remove ju-risdictions even after they had made commitments to the OECD in 2002.[94] Officials in the Caymans, Isle of Man, and St. Kitts and Nevis share this complaint.[95] The Australian Tax Office states openly: "The Tax Office definition of a tax haven is based on the criteria used by the Organisation for Economic Co-operation and De-velopment."[96] Most of the jurisdictions targeted by the OECD put a high priority on securing their removal from such national blacklists, and thus have been concerned and angered about what they have characterized as the unhelpful influence the OECD has had on this process of de-listing.[97] Indeed, this issue attracted more attention than any other at the November 2005 Global Tax Forum meeting.[98]

National blacklists of tax havens may specify a range of countermeasures. There may be a duty to report all transactions with listed jurisdictions, or punitive withholding taxes may be applied to such transactions. Deductions that would otherwise be possible may be disallowed when transactions involve listed jurisdictions. Citizens residing in tax havens may be liable for personal income tax even after they have cut all other ties with their home country. Aside from general blacklists of tax havens, other countries maintain more focused blacklists, often as part of their Controlled Foreign Corporation or transfer pricing regulations.[99] There is a general suspicion in listed jurisdictions that officials compiling these national blacklists often do so without a great deal of care and attention, and are susceptible to incorporate whatever lists are available. Perhaps the best example is when Venezuela copied the Mexican blacklist, only to discover, after the fact, that the Mexicans' list included Venezuela, and thus the latter blacklisted itself.[100]

Blacklists of tax havens have proliferated in the United States in response to the controversy over U.S. businesses reincorporating in Caribbean tax havens to reduce corporate income tax (so-called corporate inversion) and because of concerns about the financing of terrorists. These blacklists prescribe unfavorable treatment for jurisdictions identified as tax havens, but they generally do not include a procedure for determining which jurisdictions qualify. As a result, once more there is a tendency to defer to existing lists, and again particularly those compiled by international organizations. For example, even the USA Patriot Act, in many ways the epitome of unilateralism, identifies jurisdictions "of primary money laundering concern" based on "the extent to which that jurisdiction is characterized as an offshore banking or secrecy haven by credible international organizations or multilateral expert groups," most prominently the OECD. Officials in tax haven states have expressed concern about the tendency for language taken directly from OECD reports to appear in U.S. legislation and regulations.[101] Other countries, including some tax havens, have, in turn, often tended to take their cue from the United States and other leading OECD members.

Aside from the state-to-state level, the effects of blacklisting on reputations have reverberated through accountancy, insurance, banking, and legal firms as well as other corporate service providers. These private actors may have been taking their cue directly from international organizations, or indirectly from national governments rebroadcasting these listings. Large multinational financial services firms maintain their own informal blacklists and methodologies for practicing due diligence, keen to preserve corporate reputations. Reflecting this apprehension, some foreign financial service firms have withdrawn from particular blacklisted jurisdictions rather than be tainted by association (see the section on Vanuatu below).[102] Others have applied special restrictions to transactions from blacklisted jurisdictions, or imposed extra fees to cover the cost of increased scrutiny, even when these measures are not required or recommended by their respective national governments. Firms may simply refuse to process transactions from listed jurisdictions as these dealings become more trouble than they are worth. The Prime Minister of Liechtenstein spoke of the effects of international organization blacklists reverberating in the private sector as follows:

> If an American bank, for example, would not do transactions with Liechtenstein any more, this would be a problem. And even if these states say "OK, you are on the right track," you still have to fear that some overeager bank says "we had better break off relations." The damage is done in either case.[103]

Once particular jurisdictions are listed, they may be placed as key terms on privately produced anti–money laundering software designed to raise "red flags" and enhance scrutiny. And like many national lists, jurisdictions may not be removed from private lists even after being given a clean bill of health by the relevant international organization.

This sensitivity to reputational damage by association with a listed jurisdiction is particularly evident among publicly listed companies, which provide most of the high margin business and the much sought after substantive activity that creates spin-off benefits for the local economy. High margin business might include off balance sheet vehicles, hedge funds, mutual funds, and other collective investment schemes that often involve the physical presence of a reasonably large number of lawyers and accountants. This physical presence is in contrast to low-margin pure "booking center" activity whereby tax havens are providing a legal fiction for transactions and assets that are practically located onshore (through International Business Companies and offshore banks). Nauru's four hundred banks, whose only material incarnation was a plastic name tag on a wall in a small shed on the island, are a prime example.[104] Also, private client banking relying on secrecy to facilitate tax evasion is also seen as a low-margin, static, and scandal-prone market.[105] The same is true of selling International Business Companies for a few hundred dollars in annual fees per company.[106] But as well as being the most highly sought after business, institutional clients are also the most sensitive to reputational tainting by association with blacklisted jurisdictions, as such connections may pose a threat to their share price.[107] Unlike private clients, the presence of listed companies in tax havens is usually much more public, known to both regulators and shareholders. Banks are especially cautious on this score, given the vital role of confidence for their functioning.[108]

The effects of differing levels of sensitivity between institutional and individual investors can be seen in the varying reactions of listed jurisdictions. Those with the most institutional presence have often been the least willing to resist the OECD (Bermuda, the Caymans, the Isle of Man).[109] In contrast, the Pacific jurisdictions have been among the most recalcitrant, given that they have very little institutional business and are supported by local providers. Samoa, Niue, and the Cook Islands forced the extension of the 28 February 2002 deadline for the "uncooperative tax havens" list, while Vanuatu, Nauru, and the Marshall Islands refused to agree to even the much reduced demands for information exchange.[110] In the Cook Islands, the differing priorities between public and private companies can be seen at a more micro level. Subsidiaries of foreign owned and publicly listed trust formation companies have been in favor of granting the OECD and FATF's demands, whereas locally owned private companies have been unwilling to bear the higher regulatory costs of compliance.[111] Civil law jurisdictions like Andorra, Monaco, and (to a lesser extent) Liechtenstein, tend to rely on banking secrecy, rather than more complex financial products generating a visible corporate presence, and have also proved more resistant (which is not to say invulnerable, see Liechtenstein below) to the reputational effects of blacklisting.

Also, individual investors may also steer clear of, or withdraw from, listed jurisdictions after hearing directly or indirectly of international organization blacklists. Regulators and private sector sources in targeted states often portray offshore investors as nervous and risk-averse people, easily spooked by bad publicity. The new more confrontational strategy on the part of the OECD from 1998 was very much designed to generate publicity and media attention,[112] and indeed the lists achieved just this, not only in the specialist financial journals but also the general press. Alternatively, investors may have caught wind of these initiatives through the resulting advisories and press releases from their national governments and tax administrations. Financial advisers may have a duty to advise clients about blacklists that include specific jurisdictions. The increase in fees and processing time for transactions with blacklisted states sometimes imposed by banks elsewhere created further disincentives for individuals looking to conduct business. Individuals that remain can drive a harder bargain with local regulators and corporate service providers, as in the case of Antigua and Barbuda (see below). And, remembering the "Grisham effect," blacklists may exert their influence via unlikely media, from travel guides to Hollywood thrillers.

The Effects of OECD Blacklisting

The OECD failed to achieve its original aims in prosecuting the campaign against harmful tax competition. It failed to prevent tax havens using special tax and regulatory concessions to lure in nonresident investors not engaged in any substantial economic activity offshore, identified as the main threat to OECD states' revenue base in the 1998 report. Furthermore, the OECD was forced to abandon its exclusionary strategy and revert to its conventional methods of consensual negotiation and inclusiveness. However, this defeat does not mean that inclusion on the original

2000 list or the "even blacker"[113] 2002 "uncooperative tax havens" list was a matter of indifference for those jurisdictions targeted. It was a matter of serious concern and in many cases was believed to have caused economic damage. But until the crucial concessions of 2001, targeted jurisdictions generally saw the damage of the OECD's blacklisting as outweighed by the cost of the new regulations demanded. Originally, many established and newer jurisdictions in the Caribbean, the Pacific, and Europe perceived the OECD's demands as an invitation to commit financial suicide,[114] a point the OECD later obliquely conceded.[115] As one Caribbean official put it to the author: "It's hard to believe that a report that calls for your extermination is a reasonable proposition." But the equation changed once the OECD's most important demands were dropped, and the costs of blacklisting allowed the OECD to save face by securing the commitment of the majority of jurisdictions to the truncated initiative in early 2002. Both the Commonwealth and the Pacific Islands Forum encouraged members to make a conditional commitment to the OECD (i.e., conditional upon Switzerland and Luxembourg making the same concessions), specifically to avoid reputation damage flowing from appearing on the 2002 "uncooperative tax havens" list.[116]

An early instance of coordinated blacklisting against Antigua and Barbuda in December 1999 demonstrates the damaging consequences that can result from such an attack on reputation, and the process of reverberation down to and among financial intermediaries and individual investors. The United States and Britain decided to issue advisories against the country after a high-profile scandal in Antigua and Barbuda involving the Russian-administered "European Union Bank."[117] Making matters worse, an offshore bank owner was appointed to head the local banking regulatory body.[118] Speaking at a conference in Trinidad and Tobago in December 2000, a spokesman for Antigua and Barbuda outlined the impact of these advisories, warning his colleagues "God forbid that you share this experience." The Anglo-American advisories acted as a trigger for other countries to issue similar cautions (including other havens like Jersey). Shortly after they were issued, the Bank of New York, Bank of America, Chase Manhattan, and HSBC Banks all terminated their correspondent banking relations with Antiguan institutions. Those banks that continued to provide correspondent banking services raised their fees by 25 percent, on the grounds that they had to take extra precautions against illegal money. Thanks to a sudden drop-off in interest in the country by foreign investors, the number of offshore banks declined from seventy-two at the end of 1998 to eighteen in December 2000, causing revenue and job losses.[119] Investment professionals and bankers in the United States and Britain were obliged to warn clients about the advisories, many of whom instead chose other Caribbean jurisdictions, while those investors that persevered tended to drive a harder bargain with Antiguan authorities.[120]

Further evidence for the effectiveness of blacklisting is drawn primarily from interviews conducted in twelve targeted jurisdictions in Europe, the Pacific, and the Caribbean (Antigua and Barbuda, Aruba, Barbados, the British Virgin Islands, the

Cayman Islands, the Cook Islands, the Isle of Man, Jersey, Liechtenstein, Montserrat, St. Kitts and Nevis, and Vanuatu), supplemented by interviews with the OECD, and observers in other international organizations (FATF, IMF, World Bank, Pacific Islands Forum, ITIO, the Commonwealth, UN Ad Hoc Committee of Tax Experts, and UN Office on Drugs and Crime).

The discussion of the blacklists' impact is organized by dividing jurisdictions into three groups, depending on the timing of their commitments. Most of the evidence presented is from interview material from the twelve jurisdictions, but this is supplemented by supporting evidence from other listed countries. Of this sample of twelve, the first group is comprised of the "early committers," the Cayman Islands, the Isle of Man, and Aruba, who signed up to the original conditions of the initiative, i.e., before the OECD had made the important concessions in 2001. The second group is comprised of those jurisdictions that rushed to sign up in the weeks and days before the deadline for the "uncooperative tax havens" list, but also after the OECD had made fundamental substantive and procedural concessions (Antigua and Barbuda, the British Virgin Islands, the Cook Islands, Jersey, Montserrat, and St. Kitts and Nevis). The third group, the holdouts, refused to concede and thus appeared on the "uncooperative tax havens" list (Liechtenstein and Vanuatu). In terms of the distribution of commitments by timing for all forty-one affected jurisdictions, six jurisdictions made an advance commitment before the June 2000 list plus five others before the November 2001 OECD report formalizing the concessions (the eleven early committers). A further twenty jurisdictions pledged their cooperation February–April 2002. Seven states appeared on the "uncooperative tax havens" list in April 2002, of which two subsequently reversed this stance before 2006. Within groups there are important variations in the impact of the lists and the reasoning behind decisions on whether or not to defy the OECD. Nevertheless, these breakpoints in the campaign shed light on how blacklists affected different jurisdictions.

Of the twelve case studies, the Cayman Islands was the only jurisdiction to make an advance commitment before the original June 2000 tax haven list was released. Sources in both the public and private sectors confirm that fear of the effects of blacklisting was crucial in motivating this decision.[121] Having been classified in the lowest tier of the Financial Stability Forum's study of the perceived quality of regulation in May 2000, and then included on the FATF's money laundering blacklist, officials worried that a third listing could cause major damage to the financial sector. In particular, there were concerns that New York banks might cut correspondent banking relations. There was also a fear that being on the wrong side of so many international organizations could arouse the ire of the United States government. In general, the Caymans was keenly aware of the potential reputational damage resulting from its inclusion on blacklists. Because the Caymans was so heavily involved in international banking, and because banks are most concerned with issues of confidence and reputational risk, it was felt that the jurisdiction was particularly vulnerable to this kind of adverse publicity. More optimistically, although the 1998 report was regarded as inaccurate, ill-thought out, and unreasonable, it was also vague, and the feeling was that there was room for the Caymans to maneuver with regards to specific concessions. Bermuda also made an advance commitment to avert appearing on the 2000 list. This move reflected the urging of its business community, which feared damage to its reputation by being classified as a tax haven. Bermuda then used its absence from the list as a selling point in its promotional material.[122]

European Union dynamics predominated for Aruba and the Netherlands Antilles (which committed to the OECD after the June 2000 list but before the concessions of 2001), specifically the EU prohibition on ring-fenced special tax concessions for foreign investors as part of the Code of Conduct exercise. Holland (along with the UK) was the worst offender on harmful tax practices, and was very keen for the Dutch Caribbean islands to fall into line with the EU measures to spare it further embarrassment. Constitutionally, each part of the Kingdom of the Netherlands enjoys equal status, but financially the Caribbean segments are dependent on Holland, which made clear its preference for Aruba and the Antilles to comply and abolish ring-fencing. Because pressure from Holland made the reforms inevitable, it was felt that there was little point in continuing to pay the price of being blacklisted by the OECD as well. Both jurisdictions had set out to negotiate removal from Latin American blacklists as a priority, and, as discussed above, appearing on the OECD list tended to make this goal more difficult.[123]

The Isle of Man released a statement in December 2000 noting its agreement to be bound by the terms of the OECD initiative (subject to the clause about Switzerland and Luxembourg's agreement to do the same). Manx officials had been considering the move since before June 2000. In the context of the parallel initiatives on money laundering (FATF) and prudential regulation (FSF), the government came to the conclusion that such multilateral regulatory initiatives were destined to remain a permanent feature. The conclusion was that internationally accepted norms and standards regarding offshore centers were changing, and that the island should put itself on the right side of these trends. Direct confrontation was regarded as a bad strategy compared with conditional cooperation.[124] The latter approach aided the Isle of Man's removal from national blacklists, again a priority, and also was seen as more likely to allow for input into the process of international standard setting.

As discussed earlier, the OECD initiative was transformed by the concessions it made from the second half of 2001. These concessions were the most important factor in motivating the twenty jurisdictions that made commitments to the OECD in the first four months of 2002. However, the prospect of remaining on the 2000 list of tax havens, and even more so of being included on the new "uncooperative tax havens" list, promised for the end of February but only released 18 April 2002, was also significant. The 2002 list was seen as more threatening than the 2000 list. A common sentiment was that "everyone was on the 2000 list," and thus it was less damaging. But as more and more jurisdictions committed themselves ahead of the 2002 deadline, those that did not do so risked inclusion in an increasingly small, deviant, and stigmatized group. Given the high degree of competition for a limited pool of investment, there were fears that investors would be more likely to avoid or withdraw from a blacklisted jurisdiction if the next island along was free from such a taint. Less tangibly, the moral support that came from a common front and strength in numbers also provided individuals with reassurance that they were in the right in resisting the OECD. For each jurisdiction that signed up this reassurance incrementally drained away.

Centers like Antigua and Barbuda, Barbados, the Bahamas, Grenada, Dominica, Mauritius, Montserrat, St. Kitts and Nevis, and the Cook Islands had experienced a decline in business in 2000–2001, and although some of this decline was attributed to other factors, there was also a belief that uncertainties connected with the OECD initiative had been important.[125] Observing these trends, in early 2002 the Cook Islands, Samoa and Niue decided that there was little point continuing to hold out without the support of the Caribbean.[126]

Seven countries refused to make even a conditional commitment to information exchange in 2002 and thus appeared on the "uncooperative tax havens" list. Nauru and Vanuatu reversed this decision and made commitments in 2003, while as of 2006 Andorra, Liechtenstein, Monaco, the Marshall Islands, and Liberia were still holding out. Vanuatu is a particularly significant case in that it avoided the FATF blacklist but was included by the OECD in both the 2000 and 2002 lists. The government and accounting industry in Port Vila were particularly vocal critics of the OECD initiative along themes laid out in chapter 3. More than this, however, they initially saw blacklisting as a positive advantage in commercial terms, providing free advertising for Vanuatu as a tax haven and putting it on the map.[127] Contrary to these early expectations, the offshore industry suffered increasing damage that locals, in hindsight, attribute to the listing, and these losses in turn explain the volte-face in signing up to the OECD initiative in 2003.

From around the time of the second listing in 2002, HSBC, Barclays, and several New York banks refused to process transactions from Vanuatu. KMPG also distanced itself, despite having previously had an office in Port Vila. The National Bank of Vanuatu began to have great difficulties transacting business in U.S. dollars, and had to buy currency from local branches of Australian banks, creating delays and extra fees. Clients of local accounting firms also started to ask for their correspondence and transactions to be rerouted via other jurisdictions to obscure any connection with Vanuatu. Responding to these new negative associations, the leading local trust provider company dropped "Vanuatu" from its name, and those in the industry began to suspect that the term "Vanuatu" had been included as a "red flag" in suspicious transaction reporting software.[128] Thus rather than attracting extra business from its defiance of the OECD, the country saw a substantial decline after 2000. While in 2000 some 1,226 new International Business Companies were formed, in 2001 the total was 557 and in 2003 only 447. In 2000 only 167 companies were struck off (almost always because of nonpayment of fees), but by 2003 this had increased to 847.[129] The number of offshore banks, which had peaked at 150, was of 2005 down to 7.[130] Fourth quarter revenues to the government from the offshore sector were down by 26 percent in 2003 on their 1999 level.[131]

The other holdouts in the region, Nauru and the Republic of the Marshall Islands, provide some similarities. Nauru also had planned to resist the OECD before capitulating in December 2003. In this case, however, in the absence of interview data, it is impossible to even approximately assess the impact of the OECD listing separately from the torrent of bad publicity following Nauru's involvement in a Russian money laundering scandal, the FATF listing, and strong bilateral pressure from the United States from 2002. Nauru currently has no solvent banks at all and has experienced complete economic collapse. The Marshall Islands, depending more heavily on its flag of convenience industry, rather than the offshore sector as such, calculated that it could beat the OECD initiative by relying on its Compact of Free Association with the United States and compensation payments for atomic testing.[132] Again reliant on its flag of convenience registry rather than offshore financial services, Liberia has generally lacked a sufficiently functional government to make any response to the OECD at all, and has infinitely greater problems in any case.

Liechtenstein stands out as an exception in that it has steadfastly refused to make even a highly qualified commitment to the OECD, and thus has been listed as an uncooperative tax haven since 2002. Even after the FATF de-listing in 2001, as of 2004 *Anstalt* (a trust-like entity) formation in Liechtenstein was still below its 2000 level, while from 2000 to 2002 the net income of Liechtenstein banks fell from 549 million Swiss Francs to 251 million, taxes paid from 64 million to 27 million, and assets managed from 112 billion to 96 billion.[133] Service providers in Switzerland were less willing to advise clients to invest in Liechtenstein, and Singapore forbade some banks from the Principality from opening branches because the country was still blacklisted by the OECD.[134] The head of the Liechtenstein Bankers' Association has referred to the continued OECD listing as "destabilizing,"[135] a damning indictment remembering the Bahamanian official's emphasis on the importance of stability.

Both this chapter and the next answer two questions for the OECD and the tax havens: What were the stakes of the struggle? What were the means by which the struggle was waged? This chapter has examined the stakes for the jurisdictions labeled as tax havens, particularly their reputations in the eyes of potential foreign investors. It has also analyzed the OECD's practice of blacklisting as a form of speech act that constitutes action in and of itself. Blacklisting has had impact through damaging jurisdictions' reputations and attractiveness as investment destinations. Reputation as a concept is argued to be the totality of thoughts, feelings, and associations held by third parties in connection with a referent actor or place.

The section on the definition of tax haven demonstrated that there are great difficulties with settling on a generally accepted procedure for distinguishing tax havens from "normal" states. Instead there is often an explicit or implicit reliance on a reputation or smell test, how third parties perceive a jurisdiction. This plasticity has given the OECD latitude to exert an authoritative claim in classifying jurisdictions as tax havens and has helped to enhance the negative connotations of this term. Negative labeling is so important for tax havens because their reputation is their single greatest competitive asset. Despite the failure of the OECD to achieve its main substantive and procedural aims as laid out in 1998, blacklisting was sufficient to induce a majority of listed states to sign up to a very much more modest set of regulatory reforms, and thus helped the OECD avoid complete failure. Blacklisting has an impact as it diffuses and reverberates down and across three levels: states, financial intermediaries, and individual investors. It produced pressure to comply as tax havens either anticipated future economic damage if they did not make a commitment, or interpreted a decline in business as a result of blacklisting. Evidence for this claim has been predominantly taken from interview material. Judging from this material, there has been significant variation between those jurisdictions making early commitments, those in the rush before the 2002 blacklist, and the seven holdouts.

This chapter asked what were the stakes of the struggle for tax havens, and what were the means employed by the OECD? The next reverses these same concerns: what were the stakes for the OECD, and what were the means employed by its opponents? In place of reputation for financial probity and soundness, the OECD had to preserve its reputation for impartial expertise, crucial for its influence over the policy process. Listed states and others sought to gain leverage from this point by a strategy of rhetorical entrapment, seeking to convince third parties that the OECD was being untrue to its own professed values. Unlike the campaign of blacklisting, this campaign of hoisting the OECD on its own petard was decisive in resolving the struggle for global tax standards.

CHAPTER FIVE

The OECD Rhetorically Entrapped

In international politics, as in everyday life, the reception of a statement depends as much on who is making it as on what is said. "Who says?" is a common question for people assessing the credibility of a claim, piece of information, or argument. This question of the identity of the speaker in evaluating the impact of a speech act has been raised in connection with norms. Risse holds that "It makes a difference in the UN Security Council whether the United States or Cameroon pushes a certain argument,"[1] but provides little explanation as to why. Critics of the constructivist program have faulted its practitioners for failing to address the issue whereby "Norms backed by the United States are likely to become more widespread and effectual than otherwise similar norms originating in Luxembourg."[2] This chapter assesses how the outputs of the OECD, including the 2000 and 2002 blacklists, are invested and infused with its reputation as an institution. The OECD's ability to influence politicians, transnational policy communities, corporations, journalists in the specialist and general press, and ultimately investors has been closely linked to its standing as an impartial, "apolitical" and technocratic institution. In this way, Austin's analogy of marriage vows discussed earlier is again relevant: the effectiveness of speech acts depends on them being said by the appropriate person (bride and groom, not the priest or a passerby) in the appropriate circumstances. Blacklisting of tax havens by the author, the French government, Oxfam, or the UN Ad Hoc Committee of Tax Experts would not have had the same effect as blacklisting by the OECD, even if it were based on exactly the same analysis and written in exactly the same words.

But this strength is also a weakness. The converse of these benefits conferred, the

127

extra credibility engendered by the authority of the speaker, is that the OECD is also constrained to act in a manner appropriate for such an institution and in line with the expectations it has built up in the forty years of its existence. The OECD's status has thus proven to be a double-edged sword. On the one hand, this status adds particular weight and effectiveness to the OECD's endorsements and criticisms of the whole array of economic policies, including how jurisdictions regulate their financial sectors. But on the other, it ties the OECD's hands and has provided a point of entry for critics to attempt rhetorical entrapment. This reputation, a strength that is also a vulnerability, constitutes the stakes for the OECD in the rhetorical contest surveyed in chapter 3. To the extent that third parties were persuaded by targeted states and other critics that the OECD was being untrue to its own values and was acting inappropriately in the tax competition campaign, the OECD suffered a loss of institutional standing that would directly feed through to a lack of institutional effectiveness. Rhetorical entrapment was binding because to ignore the verdict of the rhetorical contest, to be seen to defy the underlying norms, would for the OECD damage its reputation, diminish its authority, and devalue the currency of its influence.

The first half of this chapter concerns the stakes for the OECD in terms of its reputation, and the second half looks at the means employed by its opponents in terms of rhetorical action. I begin with a brief sketch of how international organizations in general, and the OECD in particular, embody and epitomize notions fundamental to the modern era such as rationality, bureaucracy, and science. The tenets of their identity and their reputation as impartial, expert, rational-legal bureaucracies infuse and valorize the products of international organizations like the OECD (models, country reviews, statistics, etc.), and thereby tend to make these outputs authoritative in the eyes of observers and policy makers. Institutional effectiveness—in this case, the OECD's influence on national economic policy making—is thus crucially dependent on this reputation being preserved intact. If the organization were to damage this reputation, being perceived to behave in a manner incompatible with the expectations that accrue to such a role, it would have few if any other means available to achieve its goals. Additionally, it would be vulnerable to institutional rivals and competitors, a fate that has befallen the OECD in the area of tax regulation.

The chapter then focuses on Schimmelfennig's concept of rhetorical action, the strategic use of norm-based arguments. Returning to the public contest surveyed in chapter 3, the OECD was rhetorically entrapped by its own norms; its opponents were able to convince a transnational audience that the tax competition campaign ran contrary to the OECD's proper role. Unless the OECD changed course, it was faced with increasing damage to its reputation and thus its institutional effectiveness. The most visible evidence of the damage to the OECD's institutional standing has been the entry of other institutions with the aim of regulating tax at an international level. These new entries have been explicitly or implicitly premised on dissatisfaction with the OECD tax competition campaign and have served to erode the OECD's dominance in this area. I argue that the potential for the weak to use the principles of the strong stems from the irreducible ambiguity of language. Dominant actors can set prevailing norms and principles, but they cannot prevent the advancement of contrasting interpretations by subordinates for subversive ends. Thus the agent-centered notion of rhetorical action is tempered by the fact that effective dissent can only take place within the broad terms that entrench existing inequalities. I conclude with an investigation of why, given its particular vulnerabilities, the OECD was chosen as an institutional home.

International Organizations as Rational-Legal Bureaucracies and OECD Identity

In general, constructivist scholars have relied on the idea, implicitly or explicitly, that the norms that shape actors' decisions and behavior are ultimately bound to their identities, and vice versa.[3] Certainly with respect to the OECD, it is apparent that expectations of appropriate conduct held by those inside and outside the secretariat reflected and reproduced its institutional identity. Similarly, how the OECD achieves political influence over member and nonmember governments by means of persuasion, socialization, and model building extends directly from and redounds back on this same identity. Above all, the OECD epitomizes the impartial, technocratic international organization devoted to the production and dissemination of scientific knowledge. As such, the OECD has a much more narrowly functional identity than states, even the tiny states it has clashed with over tax competition. In turn this image is closely linked with the knowledge-based authority or "epistemic authority"[4] that it wields. Finally, this image also represents the stakes for the OECD and the point of leverage for its opponents. To the extent that the OECD is seen to violate expectations of appropriate behavior or deviate from its role, it risks damaging its standing and authority, in turn reducing its influence over policy, imperiling its budget, and continued institutional survival.

Before expanding on these points, a definition is required. Political science often suffers from a multiplication of overlapping and underdefined terms. In relation to constructivism, Finnemore has noted that "Conceptually, the relationships among principles, norms, institutions, identities, roles, and rules are not well defined so that one analyst's norm might be another's institution and a third scholar's identity."[5] In this chapter "identity," "reputation" and "authority" all feature. But what are the conceptual relationships between them? The concept of reputation, or what others think of an actor, has been amply discussed in the previous chapter. To have an identity is "to have certain ideas about who one is in a given situation."[6] Hopf writes of the connection between the two, holding that, "identities are congealed reputation."[7] For our purposes, reputation is largely external to an actor, whereas identity is more internalized. To be sure, identity formation is premised on interactions with others (socialization). To this extent, identity is relational. But identity is first and foremost an actor's self-perception, rather than how an actor is perceived by others. In turn, authority, like the other two concepts, is a social construct, whereby actor A receives deference and/or obedience from actor B and both parties believe that the form of this relationship is right and proper. This contrasts with unwilling subordination to brute force.[8] In describing this particular type of relationship, authority is a more specific concept than either identity or reputation. Thus to say "applying sanctions against tax havens was incompatible with the OECD's identity" means that this course of action was incompatible with the way the OECD had come to see itself, in part as a product of its interactions with others. To say that "applying sanctions against tax havens has damaged the OECD's reputation" means this has resulted in the negative perception of the OECD by other actors. This may or may not have made them less deferential toward the organization. To say that "applying sanctions against tax havens has damaged the OECD's authority" means that as a result of this action other actors felt less of an obligation to defer to or comply with the OECD's judgments and expressed preferences.

Those writing in a sociological vein, particularly Barnett and Finnemore, have emphasized the degree to which international organizations epitomize the trends and values that define modernity.[9] Prominent among these are ideas of rationality, bureaucracy, and science. Rationality is generally meant in the Weberian sense of rational-legal authority—rational as it is based on reason and rationally debatable.[10] According to Weber, "bureaucracy could be seen as the most thoroughly rationalized institution of the contemporary world."[11] Rule according to rational-legal bureaucracies is said to be based on hierarchy in that there is (1) a division of labor according to superiors and subordinates; (2) continuity whereby career officials are employed on a long-term basis with potential for regular advancement; (3) impersonal prescribed rules that are free from arbitrary personal or political factors; and (4) merit or expertise: staff are hired and promoted according to achievement and control knowledge in archives.[12] Rule according to such ostensibly de-politicized, technocratic principles has become a defining characteristic of politics in the modern era and the central points of what sociological institutionalists refer to as "world culture."[13] Coupled with the rise of such rational bureaucracies has been the influence of science and scientific expertise in policy making.

How do these very abstract notions of rationality, bureaucracy, and science relate to international organizations in general and the OECD in particular? Although these notions have had crucial importance in the formation of the modern state, they have been instantiated to an even greater degree in international organizations. States may rely on foundational myths, nationalism, or charismatic leaders to command allegiance and establish their authority, as well as rational-legal bases. Because international organizations have no such myths to fall back on, "international bureaucracy fulfils the criteria of legal-rational legitimation more than any other; not in terms of efficiency, to be sure, but with regard to personal detachment and neutrality."[14] More directly, international organizations often explicitly or implicitly contrast their rational-legal credentials relative to their state members and creators. International organizations portray themselves and are generally seen by others as being less prone to arbitrary, subjective, self-seeking behavior.[15] Lacking the myths and coercive resources of states, intergovernmental organizations are commonly communities of experts sworn to advance the common good against narrow personal or national benefit. This tight association between international organizations and notions of rationality, bureaucracy, and science is long standing.

> Historians of intergovernmental organization and international integration note that for the last two centuries at least, the ideology most often used to justify new, powerful, and autonomous international institutions has been a kind of "scientism," the argument that there are socially beneficial, technical tasks that should be handed over to "experts" to be done for us.[16]

Just as the typical international organization can be seen as the embodiment of techniques of modern rule, so too the OECD can be seen as an exemplar of the type. Founded in December 1960 the OECD came into being in September 1961 with three main goals: to foster economic growth, employment, and rising living standards in member states; to promote "sound economic expansion" of both member and nonmember states; and to assist in expanding world trade "on a multilateral, nondiscriminatory basis in accordance with international obligation" (article 1). Its membership roll is a conventional measure of which countries have "arrived" in terms joining the club of the most advanced and prosperous states. As a community of professional economists, the organization issues a steady stream of statistics and studies of particular policy areas or countries which generally constitute the internationally accepted standard. It does not issue loans like the IMF or World Bank, nor act as a venue for tough economic bargaining like the World Trade Organization. Relying on its reputation for impartial expertise, the OECD instead achieves its goal of promoting economic development by persuading policy-makers in member and nonmember states with arguments based on economic theory. Because decisions within the OECD can only be passed unanimously, and the OECD has traditionally not had any enforcement powers (which makes the campaign against tax havens such a departure from past practice), the OECD can only influence policy change through consensual deliberation and the force of ideas. Thus, harking back to the discussion of the idealized international organization, Salskov-Iverson holds that "[The OECD's] power rests on the acceptance of its discourse; its research-based opinions provide it with expert status and enable it to canvass support for its 'objective,' universally applicable knowledge, which transcends time and space."[17]

Writing on the founding principles of the OECD, Martin Marcussen relates that the institution was designed to act as an epistemic community, with the objective to "develop a common value system at the level of civil servants in the OECD countries that should form the basis for consensually shared definitions of problems and solutions in economic policy-making."[18] Thus relating to its typical internal conduct, the OECD corresponds closely with various works on transnational epistemic communities.[19] Braithwaite and Drahos judge that "The OECD is the single most important builder of business regulatory epistemic communities,"[20] while the Committee on Fiscal Affairs has the same degree of preeminence in international tax regulation.[21] To this extent the OECD has stayed true to the intentions of its founders in the early 1960s:

> As a financially and politically independent body, the OECD would be able to distance itself from national controversies and dedicate itself completely to science. According to this point of view, the OECD exists in a vacuum which allows it to formulate, refine, and diffuse new policy ideas. *This it can do most effectively if it possesses a high degree of scientific authority and a reputation of political neutrality.*[22] [Emphasis added.]

Despite the emphasis placed on the way others perceive the OECD, the OECD's self-image and identity have also been vital in constraining its conduct in the contest with tax havens. The organization is pressed toward appropriate behavior by internal mechanisms as well as the force of external opinion. For example, when the OECD has tried to take on the role of bargaining or brokering international agreements, it has sometimes done poorly because of a lack of aptitude. Aside from trying to regulate tax competition, the other prominent example has been the effort to produce a Multilateral Agreement on Investment (MAI), ensuring the principle of nondiscrimination for foreign investors, aborted in late 1998. The reasons for the failure of this project go far beyond the scope of this book, but it is worth noting some parallels.

In both instances the same features that seemed to make the OECD a good institutional home for the project ultimately contributed to its undoing. The OECD committees involved had a long history of problem-solving dialogue free from political fall-out; they had a formidable level of expertise; and the participants were used to working together closely and shared similar views on a wide range of issues.[23] In a judgment also relevant to the tax competition project, Tieleman notes that "Most of the MAI-negotiators are investment specialists not used to viewing from a political perspective the concepts that they consider logical and essential parts of an investment discipline."[24] When public opposition was aroused and politicians began paying attention to safeguard the national interest, those in the secretariat did not know how to respond to external NGO pressure. The trade editor of the *Financial Times* ascribed the collapse of the MAI to the failure to "gain wider popular legitimacy for [the OECD's] actions by explaining and defending them in public."[25] Nor did it know how to deal with the shift from a problem-solving discussion to self-interested bargaining by member states; "the OECD has not had much success in using the same regulatory, negotiating types of diplomatic techniques that other organizations apply."[26] To this extent, institutional identity and socialization have meant that OECD staff are both disinclined to deviate from their usual scientific style of reasoned persuasion, but also unsuited to bargaining behavior common in other organizations. Despite important differences between the initiatives on investment and tax competition, in each the apolitical, technocratic nature of the OECD was seen as an asset, but this identity turned into a serious liability that hampered the response to unanticipated opposition.

A lack of aptitude for diplomacy and crafting compromises between winners and losers was also apparent in the first couple of years of the tax competition project. Those officials in Caribbean and Pacific targeted states, as well as the Commonwealth secretariat, were offended by what they saw as the overbearing and gauche manner of those from the OECD.[27] The former group often regarded these failings as a result of technocrats' unfamiliarity with proper diplomatic etiquette. Small state officials accused OECD officials of not knowing the proper protocol for visits by heads of state and government, of walking in on meetings to which they had not been invited, and provoking needless opposition by their high-handed manner. Caribbean officials favorably contrasted the negotiating style adopted by the United States government (no stranger to high-handed action in the region) with that of the OECD. Those from small states, very sensitive to slights, repeatedly complained that they were being snubbed as their Prime Ministers and Ministers were never met by counterparts from OECD countries, only by staff from the secretariat. Even worse, politicians from targeted states were sometimes left cooling their heels in the OECD headquarters, waiting for an audience. Officials from the secretariat have obliquely acknowledged these complaints. They have emphasized the degree to which they have learned from their initial approaches when they had been "set to broadcast but not to receive" and adopted an "Al Capone" style of negotiation. Once again, professional role expectations shaped behavior not just by a fastidious distaste for certain methods or an ineluctable group-think but also as a matter of aptitude. Experts research and politicians log-roll as a matter of inclination and ability.[28]

Compared with the powers of international organizations that can log-roll, broker deals and disburse and withhold credit, not to mention those of sovereign states, this reliance on consensus and a Fabian faith in reasoned argument to change people's minds may seem a ticket to irrelevance. But the OECD has in fact had great success shaping economic policy,[29] especially in the area of tax. Its model double tax treaty, transfer pricing and information exchange guidelines have become the global standards.[30] Given that the OECD has this particular identity (a paragon of scientific virtue and impartiality, a body of technocrats producing and disseminating economic knowledge), how does this translate into achieving institutional goals? How is this identity relevant as a point of vulnerability to be exploited by opponents of

tax havens? The following section explains how the reputation and scientific authority of the OECD are inseparably linked to the means by which it achieves institutional goals. Once again the OECD exemplifies the link between reputation and
effectiveness more generally for other international organizations. In a social world,
how much you can get done depends very much on how others perceive you.

OECD Tools of Influence

The tools by which the OECD achieves its aims are listed in the statement of purpose contained in its home page. "Dialogue, consensus, peer review and pressure"
are all said to be "at the very heart of the OECD." Its output consists of dozens of
models, manuals, reviews, guides to best practice, surveys, forecasts, and statistics.
Each of these relies for its impact not just on the factual content, but also on the reputation of its institutional progenitor, perceived as (in a revealing phrase) "the authority" among international organizations devoted to the study and measurement
of economic policy. Positive verdicts or high rankings on the various international
"league tables" are loudly trumpeted by governments, while more critical attention
is often seized on and amplified by opposition parties and pressure groups. The
OECD's Program for International Student Assessment (PISA), a survey of educational achievement in member states' schools, serves as a good example. A ranking
near the bottom of the OECD members in the 2000 PISA precipitated a national
crisis of confidence about the German educational system, leading to far-reaching
changes in schools and universities, and even spawning an eponymous television series.[31] The British government made much of its eighth-placed ranking in mathe-
matics in PISA 2000, but went out of its way to suppress its twentieth-placed
ranking in 2004.[32]

In acting as a forum where informal interaction in the corridors and elsewhere
complements more formal meetings and discussions, the OECD is among the most
active international organizations practicing what Adler has described as "seminar
diplomacy."[33] When policy makers have yet to form a clear idea of their own interests, or are clear about their interests but uncertain about how to promote them, the
OECD has often been able to provide the necessary direction in its conferences and
meetings, involving approximately forty thousand senior national policy makers
each year.[34] Apart from acting as a venue for national-level officials to meet and share
ideas, the OECD is explicitly devoted to spreading a liberal ideology, including beliefs about the limited role of government, the value of open markets, the benefits of
competition, and the need for deregulation across a variety of sectors.[35]

It is instructive to look at the OECD's own analysis of its techniques for spreading its values, particularly peer review and peer pressure. This analysis provides insight into standard operating procedures, but also highlights how poorly the strategy

to push tax havens into compliance fits with these procedures. In contrast to just providing a venue for national policy makers to meet and talk, peer review and peer pressure involve regular institutionalized interaction, a great deal of support work by the secretariat, and a level of shared values. Peer review is the bread and butter of the OECD's institutional life: "There has been no other international organization in which the practice of peer review has been so extensively developed as the OECD."[36] So closely is the OECD associated with this practice that it has been dubbed "the OECD technique."[37] The mechanisms are described as follows:

> Peer review relies on the influence and persuasion exercised by the peers during the process. This effect is sometimes know as "peer pressure." The peer review process can give rise to peer pressure through, for example: (i) a mix of formal recommendations and informal dialogue by the peer countries, (ii) public scrutiny, comparisons, and in some cases, even ranking among countries; and (iii) the impact of all the above on domestic public opinion, national administration and policy makers. The impact will be greatest when the outcome of the peer review is made available to the public, as is usually the case at the OECD. When the press is actively engaged with the story, peer pressure is most effective.[38]

This internal OECD paper observes that peer review is not necessarily limited to member states, and has been regularly used in promoting policy change in nonmembers. The report also emphasizes, however, several important preconditions. It stresses that peer pressure is not designed as a conflict resolution mechanism, and can never be coercive or adversarial. "Naming and shaming" risks "shifting the exercise from an open debate to a diplomatic quarrel."[39] Pagani continues, "Examiners have the duty to be objective and fair, and free from any influence of national interest that would undermine the credibility of the peer review mechanism."[40] The process and standards must be "credible" (legitimate) in that they are endorsed by all parties before the particular studies get under way. Lastly, the parties being reviewed must trust the reviewer and the process and regard them both as impartial. Needless to say, each of these prerequisites has been missing in the tax haven campaign and much of the tax haven case has been built on the discrepancies. In turn, these discrepancies have been crucial in the result of the struggle, as is examined in the last section of this chapter.

Institutional Reputation as Institutional Effectiveness

In common with most other international organizations, the OECD's institutional effectiveness is inseparably bound up with its institutional reputation. "Public and elite opinion pays attention to the OECD because it is viewed as an authoritative source of expert policy advice."[41] It is the very apolitical presentation of international organizations' initiatives that often gives them their political impact.[42] Similarly, the cultivation and maintenance of such a reputation is a crucial source of leverage for many other international organizations as well:

> IO officials are able to couple their expertise to claims of "neutrality" and an "apolitical" technocratic decision-making style that denies them the possession of power or a political motive. In short, IOs have authority in global politics and the ability to shape international public policy because of their "expertise," and our acceptance of their presentation of "self" as apolitical and technocratic.[43]

The link between institutional reputation and institutional effectiveness is nothing new for governmental and nongovernmental organizations. Writing in the 1860s, the founders of the Red Cross were emphatic in stressing that, to be effective in fulfilling its mission, the organization had to be perceived by warring parties as strictly impartial and exclusively humanitarian. To the extent that this reputation was compromised, the Red Cross would be unable to achieve its goal of tending to the wounded.[44] Because the International Committee of the Red Cross lost this reputation of neutrality and was seen as favoring U.S. ends in the eyes of some insurgent groups in Iraq, it was attacked and had to withdraw from the country in 2004. Similarly dependent on a reputation for neutrality for operational success are UN peacekeeping missions; a "pathological" fixation with maintaining this reputation played an important part in contributing to UN inaction in response to the Bosnian and Rwandan genocides.[45] Moving closer to the OECD, Price notes of NGOs: "The source of influence relies upon the status of experts as providers of objective knowledge; where such objectivity is compromised, often so is their influence."[46]

Staying within role expectations is essential for the OECD's ability to propagate its values and policy solutions among national governments. The scientific or epistemic authority[47] of the OECD infuses and valorizes its outputs. In this manner, the institution's reputation among its audience is inseparable from its continued effectiveness. The closeness of the link between the reputation of the institution and the influence it is able to wield is insightfully brought out by Porter and Webb:

> The reputation of OECD statistics among scholars is so good that typically the statistics are used without the author feeling any need to justify them as valid measures of the indicator in question. Similarly, OECD reports are widely used as authoritative statements of knowledge in many policy areas, again often without the author seeing any need beyond the label "OECD" to justify the authoritative character of the knowledge contained therein.[48]

The authors go on to talk about the OECD's concept of Producer Support Estimates (PSEs), a measure of the total "monetary value of gross transfers from consumers and taxpayers to producers arising from agricultural policies."[49] PSEs and PSE percentages, the proportion of total agricultural income derived from these gross transfers, are now the standard measures of agricultural support.[50] This measure enjoys widespread acceptance and is authoritative even among those (a majority) that have not gone back and checked the derivation of this concept or the particular calculations, because it is generated by the OECD.[51] Analogously, the IMF's figure that money laundering flows represent 2–5 percent the value of world GDP has gained acceptance in the media and among policy-makers alike, despite the fact that this figure was worked out almost literally on the back of an envelope, and that the few experts in the area agree that this is pure speculation.[52]

In both cases, these outputs are accepted among observers and have influenced the policy process because they are backed by the institutional reputation of their authors. People do not need to see the support (nonexistent in any case for the money laundering figure) because of the reputation link. With reference to the OECD and the IMF among many others, observers judge the speech by the reputation of the speaker and only secondarily by the content of what is said. Conversely, if policy makers or other commentators do go back and independently collect the necessary information to reconstruct these findings in order to assess them on their inherent merits, the reputation of the speaker becomes irrelevant. Thus parallel to the finding of the previous chapter, and opposed to the conventional view, reputation can be important in inverse (not direct) proportion to the amount of information available.

For the OECD, just as its reputation underlies and validates its practices and conduct, its practices and conduct reproduce its reputation. This reciprocal constitution has meant that expectations about appropriate behavior for the OECD have generated strong pressures to stay "in character," and these pressures have been exploited by tax havens trying to bolster their own case. The penalty for straying too far beyond these expectations is damaging institutional standing, which also entails a decline in institutional effectiveness. OECD models are followed because of what the OECD is seen to be; if the organization is seen to deviate from these ideals much of the reason to follow its recommendations is diminished. To the extent that the OECD compromises its expertise, impartiality, inclusiveness and/or pro-market credentials, it discredits and devalues the pedigree of its outputs.[53] It has little else to fall back on. Scholars and scientists succeed by the force of their ideas and exposition: "Science as authority is much more influential than scientists as a pressure group."[54]

These findings illustrate the link between the effectiveness of particular pronouncements in bringing about policy change, and the reputation of the process and the institution that produced them. Furthermore, they lend weight to more general findings about international organizations' reliance on legitimacy and meeting expectations of even-handedness and inclusiveness[55] and are congruent with more general work on legitimacy.[56] As then Canadian Finance Minister Paul Martin said of new international financial standards: "They will work only if the developing countries and emerging markets help to shape them, because inclusiveness lies at the heart of legitimacy and effectiveness."[57] Sounding like a rather platitudinous hope, the experience of the OECD tax competition campaign tends to bear this verdict out.

Reputational Damage and Institutional Competitors

Chapter 3 surveyed the main themes of the rhetorical contest wherein tax havens were able to appropriate and subvert principles the OECD put into play. This contest ended in defeat for the OECD, as it dropped the main plank of its campaign and admitted targeted states to the decision-making process on equal basis with OECD members. The previous discussion explained why the OECD's reputation is essential to its policy influence and achievement of institutional goals. But as in the case of assessing the impact of reputational damage to tax havens stemming from blacklisting, there are difficulties linking the prospect or actuality of reputational damage with the OECD's defeat.

The evidence presented in chapter 4 connecting blacklisting with reputation damage and compliance pressure, was a mix of interview material relating to key participants' interpretations and observations, matched with observable data such as the diffusion of the OECD blacklist and bank and company statistics. Interview sources inside and outside the organization are unanimous in judging that the OECD got much more than it bargained for in terms of the degree of opposition aroused by the tax competition campaign. There was a further consensus that this opposition forced the policy and procedural concessions made from 2001. But there are also material indicators of the reputational damage sustained by the OECD. Since 2001 the OECD's dominance of international tax regulation has been challenged by new rivals. Just as in the case of blacklisted states, the interpretation put on capital flight is more important than measuring the disinvestment in isolation; similarly, it is important to probe the reasons behind the increased institutional competition for the OECD in the tax field.

The primary motivation for new entrants into the international tax policy area was the perceived shortcomings of the OECD in the tax competition campaign. For one set of actors, the campaign changed their perceptions of the OECD from positive (or at worst indifferent) to hostile. Not surprisingly this negative shift included the forty-one jurisdictions that had either made an advance commitment or were listed in June 2000. But a similar shift in perception occurred for a large number of U.S. think tanks and legislators mobilized by the Center for Freedom and Prosperity. More subtly, however, the OECD's reputation was affected in the eyes of other international organizations involved in financial regulation, such as the IMF, World Bank, United Nations, FATF, and the like. These bodies were broadly sympathetic to the OECD's aims in the tax competition initiative.[58] But from 2000–2001 there was a feeling that the OECD could no longer play an "honest-broker" role in international tax regulation, nor would its policy advice in this area be accepted as disinterested or impartial (and thus authoritative), given the ill-feeling that the campaign had engendered.[59] This damage to the OECD's reputation, the resulting short-comings in its institutional capabilities, and the continuing pressure from the G7 and others for tightened financial regulations, meant not only was there policy space for other international organizations to move into, but also pressure for them to do so.[60]

After the "attack of the alphabet" in 2000 (the OECD, FATF and FSF lists), tax haven states, particularly the more established centers in the Caribbean and Europe, pondered how to best look after their long-term interests in the new environment of international regulatory activism.[61] There was a realization that even if the OECD initiative collapsed completely, tax havens could not return to the status quo ante, and that regulatory pressure was likely to be applied from other international organizations. The first preference of tax havens was the unavailable status quo, in which they were able to set their own laws and standards in tax, finance, and anti–money laundering matters without outside interference. The least attractive situation was a repetition of the top-down exclusionary approach, whereby small states were pressed to comply with standards designed without their participation. Given that many tax havens felt that it was inevitable that tax and financial regulations would be set by international organizations, they resolved that the best available option was for these negotiations to be set in open-membership institutions in which they had a voice.[62]

The most logical, if not practicable, route for forum shifting was the creation of a World Tax Organization, along the lines of the World Trade Organization, that had universal membership and made decisions by consensus. Such an institution would overshadow the OECD and let at least those tax havens that are fully sovereign states set standards with OECD and G7 members on a more equal basis. Barbados called for such a body at the UN Monterrey summit on financing development in late 2002 (as did the earlier UN Zedillo Report in 2001), but this was regarded as a nonstarter given the sensitive nature of fiscal sovereignty. For those jurisdictions that had membership, the United Nations provided a possible substitute venue. The League of Nations had a leading role in international tax matters, especially laying the ground work for the first double taxation treaties. The UN inherited some of this work, though as with so many of the UN's activities the Fiscal Committee fell victim to Cold War rivalries, and was down-graded to an ad hoc committee (the UN Ad Hoc Committee of Experts on International Co-operation in Tax Matters). The ad hoc committee held meetings and published a model tax convention for double tax treaties, but those involved admit that this convention has been less influential than the OECD's.[63] After the OECD initiative, however, Caribbean countries worked to have the ad hoc committee reinstated as a full committee. In practical terms, an ad hoc committee had only a few members from each region on a rotating basis (at one stage Jamaica for the Caribbean, not a tax haven and not interested in the OECD initiative), rather than universal membership. Furthermore, representatives had to pay their own way to attend meetings. Thanks to agitation from the Caribbean, this reinstatement took place 11 November 2004, and a new venue for international tax regulation, and competitor for the OECD, was the result.[64]

Another new institution set up in late 2001 was the International Taxation Dialogue, an international organization of international organizations comprised of the OECD, World Bank and International Monetary Fund, with the UN as an observer. It was designed "to encourage and facilitate discussion of tax matters among national tax officials and international organizations." This new body was not the result of pressure by states targeted by the OECD. However, in being advertised as a "more inclusive" forum for sharing views and experience on tax questions (open to 184 countries) there was a deliberate contrast to the closed "rich countries' club" of the OECD. Although getting off to a slow start, the International Taxation Dialogue has begun sponsoring global conferences for tax administrators and engaging in the same sort of "seminar diplomacy" as practiced by the OECD.

Aside from its participation in this club of international organizations, the International Monetary Fund has also assumed the leading role in auditing, regulating, and extending technical assistance to offshore centers, effectively supplanting the OECD in this area.[65] The IMF first entered the field on the recommendation of the FSF in 2000. The IMF explicitly distanced itself from the substantive goal of the OECD initiative, namely, regulating tax competition fostered by ring-fenced concessions to foreign investment not engaged in substantive activity. The initial IMF report also recognized a "deep concern" with regards to the FSF's three-tiered classification of offshore financial centers[66] and has since been critical of blacklisting in public and in private.[67] Once again in deliberate contrast to the OECD's coercive strategy, the IMF emphasized that its assessments of offshore centers were voluntary, with no threats of sanctions or blacklisting. Findings remained the property of the jurisdictions assessed: "The coverage of OFCs depends on the number of volunteers; and on experience as the program gets under way. The aim is to convince as many OFCs as possible that it is in their interest to be volunteers."[68] Although the IMF does not provide equal representation to large and small states, it does at least provide a much broader membership and a greater opportunity for voice than the OECD, as reflected in its consensual approach. Like the International Taxation Dialogue, the IMF involvement in regulating tax havens did not come about at the behest of the tax havens themselves, but it was strongly influenced by their opposition to the OECD. The IMF represents an authoritative, richer competitor for the OECD in this policy area.

Reputational damage to the OECD as a result of the conduct of its campaign against tax havens thus led to the creation of an open membership body with equal voting rights on tax standard setting (the UN Committee of Tax Experts), and the rise of institutions that deliberately repudiated the OECD's confrontational approach (the International Taxation Dialogue and IMF offshore audit program). But perhaps the most threatening unintended consequence of the OECD's high-profile strategy of tackling tax havens is from the groups created to oppose the initiative. The International Tax and Investment Organisation (ITIO, later renamed the International *Trade* and Investment Organisation), created to coordinate tax havens' opposition to the tax competition campaign in early 2001, has already been discussed in chapter 3. The ITIO was founded to share information among targeted jurisdictions, coordinate responses to the OECD among targeted states, and conduct research on issues of general interest.[69] In 2005 it established a permanent secretariat in Barbados. Although short of funds and active only sporadically, the ITIO has sought to remove the aura of impartiality and disinterested expertise that is so important for the policy impact of the OECD's pronouncements on tax and financial policy making.

More important, in the United States a coalition of right-wing American lobbyists, assembled to fight the tax competition initiative, and enjoying strong congressional support, has turned its efforts to blocking all U.S. government funding to the OECD ($60 million, or 25 percent of its budget). If successful, this move would endanger the survival of the OECD as a whole. As well as the Center for Freedom and Prosperity, the Cato Institute, the American Enterprise Institute, and the Heritage Foundation, a coterie of other similarly minded lobbyists now no longer perceive the OECD as an impartial technocratic institution advancing science and economic development. Instead, they regard the OECD as a highly ideological body bent on imposing its anticompetitive and wealth-destroying policies as far as its power will reach. The CFP's Director, Andrew Quinlan, had earlier claimed that ten days of lobbying would be sufficient to have the OECD's funding from the United States cut and redirected toward a more electorally high-profile issue like the Head Start program for school children.[70] In fact, cutting off "the organization [that] attempts to choke the economy that feeds us all"[71] has proven more difficult than this, though language condemning the OECD's "anticompetitive" tendencies was inserted into the Senate Appropriations Bill in late 2004. The clear defeat of the Congressional efforts to cut off OECD funding in 2004 is only a limited consolation to the OECD. Thanks to the efforts of the CFP, many members of Congress know of the OECD only because of its tax competition initiative and perceive it in a thoroughly negative light. The campaign to cut off funding forced the Secretary General of the OECD to drop his other duties and travel to Washington, D.C., specifically to lobby against this proposal. Among opponents, the hope is that the OECD will eventually decide that having to return to Washington each year to defend its funding is more effort than the initiative against harmful tax competition is worth. Thus although the OECD's funding looks safe for now, it would be overly sanguine to dismiss the enemies it has created since 2000 as being powerless cranks.

Finally, there is the question of to what extent the Global Forum on Taxation remains an OECD body. First, the non-OECD "participating partners" (i.e., tax havens that have made a conditional commitment to information sharing) now outnumber OECD members. Second, this imbalance is set to increase only as other third party jurisdictions are invited to join. Since October 2003 the Global Forum (along with its subcommittees), rather than any purely OECD body, has been the most important body in steering what remains of the tax competition initiative.[72]

In crudest terms, the OECD's blacklisting of tax havens damaged their reputations and often led to a decline in new investment and the flight of existing capital from blacklisted jurisdictions. Equally, however, the tax havens' rhetorical campaign against the OECD damaged its reputation, leading to the entry of new competitors and opponents into the area of international tax and financial standard setting. In some cases this happened indirectly, as in the case of the International Taxation Dialogue and IMF, when the OECD came to be seen as too compromised by its confrontational tactics to reach out and be trusted by nonmember jurisdictions. Elsewhere, the reaction was more direct as targeted states and their allies deliberately sought to forum shift (to the UN) or formed new links to attack the OECD's credibility at the international or domestic level (ITIO and CFP, respectively).

Rhetorical Action and Weapons of the Weak

In the sections that follow, I substantiate the conceptual links between the public contest, the OECD's dependence on its reputation, and its policy defeat. I will do this with reference to the concept of rhetorical action, showing how the strategic use of norm-based arguments can enable the weak to capitalize on the principles of the strong. So far this chapter has examined the stakes for the OECD, why the result of the rhetorical contest surveyed in chapter 3 mattered to the organization.

The result of the public contest was important for the OECD's reputation, and this reputation was in turn important for the OECD's ability to achieve its institutional objectives, primarily its influence on policy making. In part the backdown from 2001 onward reflected the anticipation of reputational damage, analogous to the case of the Cayman's advance commitment to avoid being blacklisted. But also in part this retreat was a response to reputational damage. Although inherently difficult to measure, the entry of several other international organizations into the policy area of multilateral tax and financial regulation is suggestive of this damage, particularly as interview evidence tends to support the view that these new entrants were responding to the perceived failings of the OECD campaign. I will show in conceptual terms how weaker actors can defend their interests against the strong through the use of rhetoric. The aim is to explain why the kind of arguments summarized in chapter 3 can be consequential.

Both sides deliberately used language in such as way as to advance their contrasting political ends. For the tax havens, these ends were ultimately economic, safeguarding their offshore sectors against what they felt to be impossibly heavy-handed and unfair regulations. For the OECD, entrusted with the responsibility for prosecuting the campaign, these ends included defending the tax revenues of its members in line with the overarching goal of the initiative, but also advanced the standing of the organization itself. This standing or status was thus both a means to an end, and an end in itself. However, neither side had a free hand in designing their rhetorical strategies. Both were restricted by the presence of dominant principles or generally accepted beliefs. The tax havens were especially constrained, as these dominant principles more often than not had the effect of advancing the interests of the powerful; tax havens were largely forced to fight on terms set down by their opponents.

Frank Schimmelfennig's idea of "rhetorical action" is particularly helpful in explaining the themes and significance of the debate covered in chapter 3. A central claim is that the inherent ambiguity of language means that the strong can be tripped up by their own principles. Subordinates can effectively critique their superiors on the grounds that the latter are failing to live up to their own standards. Notions of "critique within hegemony" and "rhetorical self-entrapment" are particularly important in developing this idea of the subversive potential of dominant principles.

Thomas Risse writes that arguing is a separate domain of political action, distinct from the logic of appropriateness (doing the right thing) and the logic of consequences (calculated action to achieve particular interests).[73] More relevant than the logic of arguing as such, however, Risse also speaks of actors using rhetoric, a hybrid form of action:

> The logic of consequentialism is present to the extent that actors use rhetoric to convince others to change their interests, identities, or views of the world. The logic of appropriateness prescribes what is considered a legitimate truth claim in a given public discourse and, thus, circumscribes the boundaries of this discourse.[74]

Importantly for the case at hand, Risse also raises the possibility of "rhetorical self-entrapment." This occurs when actors' arguments are made in public and are subject to challenge. Actors that are self-entrapped in this way may be bound to adhere to their public position even when it runs counter to their preferences. Schimmelfennig takes this line of reasoning further,[75] dealing with "rhetorical action" that once again combines elements of consequentialism together with appropriateness in "the strategic use of a norm-based argument."[76] According to Schimmelfennig:

> Political actors are concerned about their reputation . . . and about the legitimacy of their preferences and behavior. Actors who can justify their interests on the grounds of the community's standard of legitimacy are therefore able to shame their opponents into norm-conforming behavior and to modify the collective outcome that would have resulted from constellations of interests and power alone.[77]

Schimmelfennig illustrates this idea by using the example of the eastward expansion of the European Union to include poor post-Communist states. Here the preferences of existing EU member states have been determined by material self-interest, but the decision to admit new members is in line with prevailing community norms. Despite existing member states' reluctance to admit a large number of poor entrants and the lack of material bargaining power possessed by states wishing to accede to the Union, the latter were able to shame the former by employing basic community values. In this case the values were the EU's professed desire to encompass all European market democracies. Braithwaite and Drahos characterize this sort of entrapment as providing an opportunity for others to employ "political ju-jitsu"; weak actors can use the power of the strong against those same powerful states.[78]

The correspondence with the case of regulating international tax competition is close: material self-interest explains the conflicting preferences held by each side, but norms seem to explain the result. Rhetorical action enables the circle to be squared.

> Rhetorical action presupposes weakly socialized actors: On the one hand, the actors are assumed to belong to a community whose constitutive values and norms they share. This collective identity generates a general commitment to the community and a general interest in upholding and disseminating its values and norms. On the other hand, it is not expected that collective identity shapes concrete preferences. . . . The causal mechanism of rhetorical action then describes how the actors are brought to focus on their collective interests and honor their obligations as community members. The medium of this influence is legitimacy. . . . The weakly socialized actors assumed here, however, do not take the standard of legitimacy either for granted or as a moral imperative that directly motivates their goals and behaviors. They confront the standard of legitimacy as an external institutional resource and constraint. As such, it affects both the mode of interaction between political actors and their relative power over outcomes. As for the mode of interaction, the legitimacy requirement allows and forces the actors to argue. They are obliged to justify their political goals on the grounds of institutionalized identity, values and norms. In other words, the standard of legitimacy serves as a "warrant" or "backing" for the validity of arguments in political discourse. Actors whose self-interested preferences are in line with community norms have the opportunity to add cheap legitimacy to their position. They will argumentatively back up their selfish goals and delegitimize the position of their opponents.[79]

Marc Steinberg sees more powerful actors as setting the dominant cultural and discursive features of the landscape; however, the ambiguity and nonexclusive nature of rhetoric and culture means that weaker actors have the opportunity to appropriate and subvert the language and values of the strong to even up the balance between them. Although elites may dominate the economy and maintain their monopoly of the means of violence, their control of linguistically mediated culture, ideas, and norms is always contested and uncertain. The practical upshot of this is that those challenging the dominant elite generally do so using a vocabulary and values developed by the elite themselves.[80] The very principles put into play by the strong can be used to trip them up. James Scott has written along very similar lines.[81] Again, he argues that the gaps and potential for multiple interpretations of principles laid down by the dominant leave room for a great deal of discord and conflict between rulers and ruled, even to the point of revolution.[82] Weaker players, motivated by conviction or self-interest, can further their own ends by seeking to hold the strong to earlier rhetorical commitments made by the latter. Reminiscent of Braithwaite and Drahos's idea of "political ju-jitsu," using the principles of dominant actors to defeat those same actors, Scott speaks of "symbolic ju-jitsu" along the same lines.[83]

A particularly relevant concept for the struggle by tax havens to resist being regulated by the OECD is that of "critiques within hegemony":

> One reason [these critiques] are particularly hard to deflect is simply because they begin by adopting the ideological terms of reference of the elite. . . . They clothe themselves in the public professions of the elite, which now stands accused of hypocrisy, if not the violation of a sacred trust. *Having formulated the very terms of the argument and propagated them, the ruling stratum can hardly decline to defend itself on this terrain of its choosing. . . . Any dominant group is, in this respect, least able to take liberties with those symbols in which they are most heavily invested. . . .* Many radical attacks originate in critiques within hegemony—in taking the values of ruling elites seriously, while claiming that they (the elites) do not. To launch an attack in these terms is to, in effect, call upon the elite to take its own rhetoric seriously. Not only is such an attack a legitimate critique by definition, but it always threatens to appeal to sincere members of the elite in a way that an attack from outside their values could not.[84] [Emphasis added.]

For Scott, the most effective opposition from weak actors comes not from an attempt to supplant or replace the hegemonic ideology, but to work within it; for elites this is "the ideological equivalent of being hoisted on one's own petard."[85] Thus the subversive comment from the Pacific: "*Harmful* tax competition? You're the OECD, you love competition,"[86] and the resigned response from the secretariat: "As an economist, how can you say anything bad about competition?"[87]

There are definite connections with the emphasis on consistency dealt with in the section of the previous chapter examining norms of argument.[88] By this measure, the "Washington consensus," that stresses robust competition, financial deregulation, the liberalization of capital flows, and the legitimacy of market outcomes occurring in the context of a level playing field, definitely constitutes a dominant discourse among economic policy makers. Accentuating this identification is the way these values are emphasized in the OECD's Convention and practices. The specific principles put into play by the 1998 report, and subsequent statements by officials relating to the tax competition initiative further cemented the links between these general principles and the OECD. Tax havens and their supporters took these themes and used them to undermine the OECD campaign.

Why Delegate to the OECD?

The effectiveness of rhetorical entrapment and "critiques within hegemony" in the tax competition case does not mean that the weak can routinely overpower the strong in international relations or politics generally. Dominant principles do usually favor rulers' interests, and although these principles are elastic and ambiguous, they are not infinitely malleable. As damaging as it may be to obtain a reputation for hypocrisy, this is often a price that states and others are willing to pay in the pursuit of other advantages.[89] Western Europe may have been bound by their earlier pronouncements to support (or at least not oppose) the accession of East European countries to the EU. But the rich countries are seemingly happy to preach free trade and practise agricultural protection. Furthermore, a large number of governments trumpet human rights principles they have never had any intention of observing. The success enjoyed by states labeled as tax havens can be seen across a wide range of circumstances, as Scott's work illustrates. But this success is also a product of especially favorable circumstances, of which none was more important than the features of the OECD discussed in the first half of this chapter. With these vulnerabilities in mind, however, the question is why the OECD was chosen as the institutional home of the initiative? Why didn't core states anticipate the problems that subsequently arose and take steps to prevent them?

In 1996 the G7 opted to entrust the investigation of "harmful tax competition" to the OECD, and subsequently the Committee on Fiscal Affairs was also responsible for designing and implementing the strategy to resolve the problem. In turn, the Committee opted for a rhetorical approach to gaining the adherence of nonmember jurisdictions. The OECD seemed like the logical institutional home for such an issue. It had a long standing interest and formidable technical expertise in issues relating to taxation as well as financial and banking regulation. Its deliberative and consensual style, and apolitical technocratic identity, were also well suited for such a potentially controversial topic, namely, dealing with one of the fundamental prerogatives of the sovereign state in an area of sharply differing policies. The OECD also had the right degree of inclusiveness. Its membership was wider than the G7 and able to incorporate and co-opt a reasonably large number of countries, but yet, unlike the UN, IMF, or World Bank, not so broad as to include developing states that would render the already difficult task of building compromises on such a delicate issue almost impossible. In short, under highly uncertain conditions, the United States, the EU and Japan took their best guess concerning the optimal institutional location for the tax competition initiative. This decision subsequently pushed them into endorsing a particular strategy to address the problem.

Ironically, the tenets of OECD identity that subsequently offered critics so much latitude for entrapment also constituted the reasons why the OECD seemed like such a logical institutional home for the initiative in the first place. By associating efforts to regulate harmful tax competition so closely with the OECD, decisions taken early on foreclosed other alternatives further down the track, as major changes to the structure and conduct of the campaign entailed progressively higher costs. In some sense, the choice was also a default. Since there was no World Tax Organization, the OECD and the Committee on Fiscal Affairs, in particular, were the best substitute available at that time. The primary positive factor recommending the

OECD to take charge of the campaign to regulate international tax competition, however, was that it seemed well suited to helping core state members achieve a working consensus on a politically delicate topic. In the early days, the priority of reaching a generally agreed position among member states on just what harmful tax competition was and what should be done about it looked much more daunting than inducing tiny nonmember tax havens to cooperate.

The vexed history of cooperation on tax matters inside the European Union provides a cautionary tale concerning the difficulties of coordinating tax policies, even in the context of a long history of joint policy making, pooled sovereignty and powerful supranational institutions. As discussed in chapter 1, the European Commission had been routinely rebuffed in its attempts to secure a role in tax policy. Britain and Ireland particularly have been adamantly opposed to tax harmonization (i.e., "leveling up") as promoted by Germany and France, who have looked askance at lower-taxing EU members efforts to "poach" tax revenue from them. In contrast, the OECD had a long history of promoting policy convergence in such areas as double taxation agreements and transfer pricing guidelines with none of this controversy or adverse publicity (or indeed much publicity of any kind). The quiet deliberation of like-minded experts behind closed doors, and the voting rules that gave every member a veto, meant that governments had little to fear either in terms of adverse press reaction and electoral consequences, or from being strong-armed into policy initiatives they felt to be inimical to their interests. The Committee on Fiscal Affairs in particular had a long track record of just this kind of incremental policy work.

It was not impossible, however, for the member states to escape the institutional and associated normative confines of the OECD. Why was the initiative not simply relocated and relaunched after it ran into difficulties? First of all, the OECD itself was very reluctant to admit failure, putting the best possible gloss on the various reverses and maintaining its ability to see the campaign through to the end. Criticisms by targeted states and others were described as "misunderstandings" by the OECD secretariat, and the backdown in 2001 as merely a "refocusing" or "evolution" of the campaign. Second, a great deal of political capital had been invested in the campaign; to change institutional venues would be an undeniable admission of failure that would leave the effort in an even worse position than if it had been started from scratch. At the stage when the OECD judged that it was losing the rhetorical contest and the sympathy of third parties, and some of its own member states, a key reason driving the secretariat on was the damage that a complete collapse of the initiative would cause the organization.[90] The main justification for excluding tax havens (not wanting to lose the work invested in the period 1996–2000) would have also been lost. Third, if the campaign had been relaunched any time after the departure of the Clinton administration and Lawrence Summers, it is unlikely that the United States and EU would have been able to reach any sort of workable agreement. With the spate of trans-Atlantic quarrels during the first term of the Bush administration, the Republicans' control of Congress, and the influence of the Center

for Freedom and Prosperity and its allies, a less propitious environment for negotiating international tax cooperation can hardly be imagined. The hostility of the
executive and legislature to exchanging information on interest payments to nonresident account holders is indicative, as is the rancor over the U.S. Foreign Sales
Corporations tax case in the WTO. Last and most importantly, asking why OECD
member states did not foresee in 1996–98 what happened in 2000–2001 understates
the degree of uncertainty faced by political decision makers. These individuals face
highly volatile negotiating environments, involving many different actors, underspecified preferences, and a chronic lack of information on the likely effects of various regulatory packages. The distorted picture of international negotiations given
by ignoring these kinds of limitations is indeed one of the main lessons to be taken
from this study.

The last two chapters have covered the four-fold task of detailing the stakes of the
contest and the means employed by the OECD and tax havens during the course of
the struggle for global tax standards. For listed jurisdictions, the stakes have been to
defend their reputations as stable and well-regulated destinations for foreign investment from the deprecation of the OECD. Even in the absence of credible threats
of economic sanctions, tax havens could not be indifferent to the way they were portrayed by the OECD for fear of losing valuable business. By blacklisting and attacking the reputations of tax havens, the OECD exploited this vulnerability. Rather
than these public negative judgments being "mere words," they comprised acts
equivalent to sanctions in damaging financial sectors and contributing to capital
flight; the OECD's bark *is* its bite.

The stakes for the OECD were its reputation as an impartial technocratic institution. As an international organization premised on an expert, apolitical character,
the OECD could not let claims that it was deviating from its role and *raison d'être*
go unanswered without undermining its own effectiveness and perhaps even its survival. The OECD's identity and mode of operation were central also to the means
by which listed jurisdictions sought to counter the campaign against them. By taking the OECD at its word, both in terms of its founding principles and in its more
specific procedural commitments in the tax competition dispute, tax havens were
able to bolster their position by convincing third parties and member state representatives that the organization was not being true to its own ideals. A combination
of internal role conflict and external social sanctioning was sufficient to split the
OECD and decisively defeat the key components of the initiative. Cameroon and
Luxembourg, as well as the Cayman Islands and Vanuatu, are at a disadvantage to
the United States in advancing norms, and thus they must instead try to appropriate U.S. norms in pursuit of their own ends. Working from this perspective helps to
resolve the problem of how norms are conceptually independent of material power
considerations, yet also practically related.

CHAPTER SIX

Implications for Policy and Theory

T he November 2005 meeting of the Global Forum on Taxation was notable for its politeness and amity. There was so little controversy that the two day meeting finished half a day early. Journalists expecting a repeat of the insults, tears, and high drama that had characterized previous meetings between the OECD and tax havens left disappointed. At the concluding press conference, the chair of the Committee on Fiscal Affairs and the Samoan Central Bank Governor (formerly a strident critic of the OECD) were relentlessly upbeat about the feats of dialogue and partnership that had been achieved. Andrew Quinlan even bought Jeffrey Owens a drink as the two discussed the areas of agreement between the Center for Freedom and Prosperity and the OECD. What had happened to the hostility and rancor, why the outbreak of peace and harmony?

To go back to the beginning, in 1998 the OECD had come up with a daring, innovative and ambitious strategy for regulating an important new issue, harmful tax competition, which centered on a confrontation with tax havens. But by 2005 the OECD had been forced back on a strategy that was eminently conventional, relying on inclusion and consensus to achieve incremental progress on tax information exchange. Within this period, the organization prosecuted a rhetorical campaign against targeted tax havens after key decision makers had been persuaded that the economic coercion, that had been threatened earlier, was not an appropriate response. Both sides in the contest sought to legitimate themselves and mobilize public disapproval against their opponents. In different ways, tax havens and the OECD were both crucially reliant on the way they were perceived by third parties, the former in terms of their reputation for financial probity, the latter in terms of its reputation for impartial expertise. The OECD struggled to reconcile the tax competition initiative with its status as a community of apolitical, pro-market experts. Opponents appropriated the very principles from which the OECD drew its authority to erode support for the campaign. The organization saw splits among its members, suffered role conflict within the secretariat, and lost standing in the eyes of third parties. Rhetorical entrapment, a form of "political ju-jitsu," saw the principles of the strong used for the purposes of the weak. The use of rhetoric by targeted states was strategic but not cynical. Small states were genuinely convinced that they were being treated unfairly and in a manner fundamentally at odds with just standards of international behavior.

This concluding chapter is evaluative. First, I assess the impact of the campaign to regulate harmful tax competition. A decade after the G7 had first raised the issue, what impact has the initiative had? There are three possible yardsticks of success: the original aims of the 1998 report; those of the scaled-down initiative after November 2001 focusing on information exchange; and the counterfactual "What if there had been no initiative at all?" Second, and more broadly, I assess the future of tax havens and general prospects for international regulation in the areas of tax and financial services. International regulation of tax and financial services will continue to increase, but such processes are unlikely to rely primarily on the top-down confrontational means used by the OECD and the FATF. Despite increasing challenges, most of the world's tax havens will survive, if only for a lack of other economic options. Third, this chapter summarizes and evaluates the theoretical and conceptual implications of the study. The globalization thesis of a fiscal "race to the bottom," premised on increased capital mobility and international collective action problems, has little explanatory power. Finally, I argue that an approach centered on language and social facts is in no way incompatible with the conclusion that conflict and power are central features of the international arena.

Assessing the Results, 1996–2006

The OECD initiative was novel and important in terms of its ends and means. In its first incarnation, the central goal of the project was to stop harmful tax competition that was said to threaten OECD member states' tax systems. Primarily, this involved dissuading tax havens from using their tax and financial codes to attract foreign investment that was not devoted to substantial economic activity. Supplementing this aim, member states were enjoined to review and abolish any harmful preferential tax regimes they might have. These were defined as special nontransparent tax breaks, available to foreign investors but isolated from the domestic tax system (ring-fenced). Unlike its treatment of nonmembers, the OECD's approach to addressing the supplementary goal of member state harmful preferential regimes was very much in line with standard practice. The nature of the general problem, particular instances of such, and the remedies were all defined by self- and peer-assessment. Decisions were made by consensus, and countries could opt out of the project (as did Switzerland and Luxembourg, joined later by Austria and Belgium), or even veto it in its entirety, without any penalty or sanction being threatened.

In contrast, the procedure for dealing with tax havens was very unconventional and broke new ground for the OECD. Nonmembers were excluded from defining the general problem and the particular instances. The standards drawn up in response were developed without any input from those affected by them, and non-compliance was to be met with threats of blacklisting and economic coercion. From late 2000 onward, however, the unconventional features of the OECD's approach to tax havens began to be stripped away, until the procedure for dealing with non-member states was almost exactly the same as that for dealing with member states. From December 2000, the OECD conceded that havens could make their commitments to reform conditional on member states introducing identical measures. From mid-2001, sanctions were only to be applied to nonmember tax havens if they were also applied to uncooperative OECD member states. Given the political impossibility of the OECD imposing sanctions on its own members, this meant that "defensive measures" would never be applied, even to those jurisdictions that failed to meet the 2002 commitment deadline or subsequently reneged on their commitment. Thus the various "final" deadlines came and went without sanctions being applied. From 2002, the committees designing the model information exchange agreement and defining the level playing field were comprised of equal members of OECD and non-OECD jurisdictions and these bodies operated by consensus. From 2003, the OECD formally conceded that "participating partners" could not only make reform conditional on member states doing the same, but also on the cooperation of third parties like Singapore, Hong Kong, and Dubai. In terms of process, the "participating partners" had got everything they wanted. Thus by late 2005, it was no surprise that the meeting in Melbourne looked as staid and uneventful as any other OECD meeting.

Aside from the shift from an exclusionary to an inclusive process, what has the initiative actually achieved? As noted, there are three possible benchmarks against which to judge results. The first is against the aims laid out in the 1998 report in which case the initiative clearly failed. The second is to look at the initiative in its post-2001 guise, and particularly the commitments the OECD obtained from the majority of targeted states in 2002 concerning the exchange of tax information. At first blush a major advance, these commitments have subsequently turned out to be less than meets the eye. The final standard—and the OECD's preferred benchmark—is a comparison with the counterfactual, imagining that the initiative had never been launched. Before looking at the results in relation to nonmember tax havens, it is worth briefly looking at the results the OECD achieved internally.

By 2004, the forty-seven "potentially harmful preferential tax regimes" identified in member states had either been given a clean bill of health (thirteen), or had been modified to remove their harmful features (fifteen), or had a date set for their abolition (eighteen). These tax regimes included arrangements for leasing, financing, insurance, fund management, corporate headquartering, distribution and service centers, and shipping. The remaining issue is Luxembourg's 1929 holding companies, to be the subject of further discussion.[1] Many of the most important and contentious examples of harmful regimes identified by the OECD were, however, modified or abolished due to extraneous factors. Prominent among these was the European Union's own internal efforts to eliminate special tax breaks, or, in the case of U.S. Foreign Sales Corporations, a World Trade Organization ruling. There are also suspicions that the forty-six out of forty-seven result flatters the OECD. Some member state practices which are clearly ring-fenced tax concessions have nevertheless been allowed, such as Australian Offshore Banking Units and Canadian International Banking Centers. It was determined that "these potentially harmful regimes were nevertheless not actually harmful on the basis that they do not appear to have created actual harmful effects."[2] New Zealand offshore trusts, a classic tax haven product, received no attention.[3] Similarly, Limited Liability Companies offered by Delaware and several other U.S. states, one of the most effective vehicles through which to evade tax for non-U.S. citizens, were never mentioned.[4] In sum, the OECD achieved progress on this front, but less than first appearances might suggest.

As I have demonstrated, the maximalist goals of stopping haven-driven tax competition, as laid out in the 1998 report, were clearly not achieved. The lynchpin of this effort was the clause aiming to prevent jurisdictions using tax concessions to attract investment not devoted to substantial economic activity. Tax havens regarded this "no substantial activity" clause as a clear threat to their survival and the most dangerous and objectionable feature of the whole initiative. Subsequently, the OECD conflated the "no substantial activity" clause with the prohibition on ring-fencing, though there is no necessary reason why ring-fenced concessions cannot involve substantial activity or why insubstantial activity has to be off-limits to domestic investors.[5] By the time of the November 2001 report, the OECD had abandoned the efforts to prevent insubstantial "booking center" or "brass plate" activity and ring-fencing among tax havens (though not among its own members).

This book has concentrated on the fate of the initiative in its original form 1998–2002, but it is also important to assess the success of the relaunched, scaled back project. This was exclusively focused on information exchange. Although modest, relative to the very ambitious aims outlined in 1998, securing commitments from thirty-three historically secretive tax havens to collect and exchange information, according to uniform standards and a uniform timetable, would still mark a very significant achievement for the OECD. These commitments are all the more notable because in their original form they amounted to small states agreeing to bear the expense of collecting information to help OECD member states increase their tax revenue. With very few exceptions, tax havens do not need tax information from large states, so in practice the exchange would be one way. Small states were to receive nothing in return, except avoiding further blacklisting. One particularly informed observer (not especially sympathetic to the OECD) writing in 2002 saw this result as a crushing defeat for tax havens:

> It looks as if, in the end, the OECD got what they wanted, and more, despite having been brought to a near stand-still by mid-summer 2001. . . . The offshore havens have now entered a brave new world of financial transparency with a whimper. Most are doing so in an orderly way, akin to queuing for lifeboats. The cries are muted. . . . It is likely that many of today's tax havens will not be fit enough to survive.[6]

The author goes on to suggest that the deadlines for exchanging criminal and civil tax information (the end of 2003 and the end of 2005 respectively) constitute "bright line tests for future survival."[7]

With the wisdom of hindsight, it is possible to see that the consequences of agreeing to exchange tax information have been far less earth-shattering than first thought. It is worth remembering that all such commitments were made conditional (either at the time or retroactively) on Switzerland and Luxembourg agreeing to exchange information also. Additionally, most of these pledges were also made conditional on "uncooperative tax havens" being subject to "defensive measures" (to counteract the tendency of capital to move from compliant to noncompliant jurisdictions where secrecy was still intact). Neither of these conditions has ever been met. Thus just counting the number of commitments without taking into account their conditional nature is a very misleading measure of success, particularly when it is unlikely that the relevant conditions will be fulfilled. Indeed, there are strong suspicions that some tax havens only made their conditional commitments because they believed they would never actually have to live up to concessions promised, thanks to Swiss intransigence.

Progress on tax information exchange has largely occurred on a bilateral basis, between individual OECD member states and individual tax havens. Such agreements are now negotiated on the expectation of mutual benefit. With the important exception of the United States, countries interested in gaining information from tax havens have had to compensate these small states for the costs involved in order to clinch an agreement. Many committed jurisdictions have stalled or, like the Bahamas, simply refused to sign any such agreements with OECD members (the United States again excepted), on the grounds that there is still no level playing field in place.[8] Rather than working to a uniform timetable, since 2004 all states were merely "encouraged" to meet the 2005 target date for exchanging civil information with all OECD members. Not one has. Thanks to its assertive, unilateral economic diplomacy, the United States has signed a slew of Tax Information Exchange Agreements with such jurisdictions as the Cayman Islands, the Bahamas, Aruba, the Isle of Man, Panama, the Netherlands Antilles, the British Virgin Islands, and Antigua and Barbuda, among others. But no other OECD member has had anything like the same degree of success.

This situation marks a big change from the scenario imagined in 2002. Given that information exchange is now decided bilaterally on the basis of mutual advantage and in the absence of coordinated pressure, the OECD as such has a much reduced role. The multilateral core that justified the OECD's involvement in the first place has been radically diminished, despite the 2004 report once again asserting the "inherently global" nature of the problem.[9] After 2002, the "brave new world of financial transparency" has receded far into the future. A final caveat is to note that even in a world of perfect transparency, it is uncertain how many tax havens would be put out of commission, or how much extra revenue would be gained onshore. Fewer and fewer havens depend on secrecy, and it is likely that the revenue losses from corporate tax planning within the law are much greater than those resulting from simple tax evasion premised on nondisclosure.[10]

According to the OECD itself, the initiative to regulate harmful tax competition can be judged a success, predominantly because it has created momentum for future incremental progress that would not have existed had the initiative never been launched.[11] In particular, the organization points to the likelihood that further information exchange agreements will be concluded with small states. It is of course difficult to access this counterfactual claim, especially remembering the concurrent anti–money laundering and EU tax campaigns that had partially overlapping objectives with the OECD project. This line also suits the interests of the OECD, which would be loath to admit that it had wasted ten years of work. But it does seem that the OECD initiative has been consequential.[12] Although the achievements in the field of global tax regulation are so far modest, this issue now features much more prominently on the international agenda than it did in the early 1990s or at any time previously. Reflecting a fundamental change, a large majority of tax havens have realized that now and in the future it is not a matter of whether their activities must meet international standards, but how these standards are decided and who gets a seat at the table in making them.

Policy Implications for Global Regulation

This section makes some observations and cautious predictions on both the prospects for global regulation in tax and financial services and the future of tax havens. There will be more and more global regulation of taxation and financial services. The other international organizations that have recently entered this policy field have embarked on a long series of studies, audits, assessments, classifications, guidance notes, and technical assistance programs. This work is supported by national governments, motivated by lingering fears about globalization-induced erosion of the tax base, and continuing onshore suspicions about offshore complicity in financial crises and crime. These concerns are now kept in the public eye by anti–tax haven NGOs, especially the Tax Justice Network, an increasingly important media presence and source of policy expertise.[13] Although the International Organization of Securities Commissions (IOSCO) has dropped hints of a future blacklist,[14] the coercive approach to regulating offshore centers pioneered by the OECD is unlikely to feature as prominently in the future as it did 1998–2002. This trend is briefly discussed with reference to anti–money laundering programs.

As the most direct attack on tax havens ever made, the exclusionary approach employed by the OECD marked a considerable departure from the standard practices of intergovernmental organizations. For large states and their clubs, the attractions of such a top-down or exclusionary multilateral strategy for standard setting are clear. Unilateral measures are inadequate because with global issues, such as international tax competition, problems are displaced rather than solved. But traditional multilateral approaches tend to involve high transaction costs and lowest common denominator solutions. Exclusionary standard setting offers the prospect of squaring the circle: global coverage, low transaction costs, and rigorous and effective standards. It also gives the favored few the opportunity to write global rules to reflect their national interests.

For all the novelty of the OECD's tactics, however, the initiative against harmful tax competition was not entirely unique. It shared crucial common features (inspired by the U.S. Treasury Department) with the FATF's similarly exclusionary effort to improve anti–money laundering regulations in nonmember states. In assessing such an approach, the FATF offers a second case, independent of the particular details of the OECD's experience. On one hand, interview sources are unanimous in agreeing that the FATF's Non-Co-operative Countries and Territories list exerted pressure on targeted jurisdictions in the same way as the OECD's blacklists, but to an ever greater extent.[15] As discussed in chapter 3, being associated with money laundering was a much greater source of stigma than being associated with low taxes, and thus there was little room for rhetorical entrapment by listed states. Yet in November 2002 the FATF decided to suspend its blacklist. Several reasons were given for this decision.

Most favorably, it has been said that the FATF had knocked the worst troublemakers into line by blacklisting, and thus, mission accomplished, it could return to the conventional means of persuasion, peer assessment and so on.[16] A different view is that administering the list was considerable work and put great strain on the secretariat's eight- to ten-person staff, only two of whom directly managed the list. Another variation was that although blacklisting was certainly effective in hurting noncompliant states, it did nothing to help those targeted set up an effective anti–money laundering regime. The most common view, however, which is not necessarily incompatible with the reasons above, is that the same sorts of norms relating to consistency and equality in argument that were important in the OECD case also applied to the FATF. A frequent objection, if only expressed *sotto voce*, was that the process of blacklisting states who were not members of the FATF was biased, especially as members have had very uneven records of compliance with their own recommendations in this area. Additionally, those in other international organizations regarded blacklisting as inconsistent with prevailing norms of international behavior. The Asia-Pacific Group on Money Laundering has expressed "philosophical difficulties" with blacklisting.[17] According to the UN Office on Drugs and Crime, "Culturally, it's not what we do."[18] IMF officials have referred to this practice as "against the nature of the Fund."[19] World Bank anti–money laundering officials are categorical that they would never blacklist.[20] The boards of the latter two organizations made their disapproval of the Non–Co-operative Countries and Territories list clear, and made their cooperation with the FATF in this area conditional upon the suspension of the listing process. Given the vastly greater staff and budget of the Bretton Woods institutions, and the greatly expanded complexity of both the new anti–money laundering standards, and the methodology for assessing them from 2004, the FATF had little choice but to accede to a more inclusive approach.

The regional anti–money laundering bodies, UNODC, World Bank, and IMF all go out of their way to emphasize the voluntary, nondiscriminatory, and cooperative nature of their programs. IMF assessments of offshore centers are only undertaken following an invitation from the jurisdictions concerned. The wording of reports, and particular conclusions as to whether certain standards have been met, must be agreed by assessors and assessed. The reports may not be published without the consent of the government concerned. When problems are identified, encouragement and technical assistance are the order of the day. In other words, these techniques are very similar to the processes of peer review carried out within the OECD as described in chapter 5. As long as there is a strong and broadly accepted normative consensus concerning the desirability of global regulation, such as suppressing money laundering and terrorist financing, such a nonconfrontational approach looks well-suited and likely to succeed. Where such a consensus is lacking, for instance, with regard to regulating tax competition, the prospects for inclusive strategies are much less favorable.[21] Yet, as the OECD initiative indicates, direct confrontational strategies that create absolute winners and losers who know the stakes may do no better. This means that those who hope to achieve major advances in international tax coordination are still stuck with the problem outlined at the very beginning of this book, namely, that economic changes have created a greater demand for global tax regulation but that traditional sovereign prerogatives continue to make such coordination very difficult.

Despite their success in resisting the OECD, in small states hoping to achieve economic viability and development through international financial services, the outlook for the future is surprisingly pessimistic.[22] It is quite common to hear the opinion that within the next decade the number of tax havens will have been cut from between thirty and forty to a dozen or fewer. There is a recognition that the anxieties that motivated large developed states to embark on the initiative against harmful tax competition have not gone away. The cross-border trade in financial services is growing strongly. The public profile of tax havens as a policy issue is enhanced by the eye-catching figures associated with them. For example, the total wealth in such jurisdictions in 2005 was claimed to be as high as $11,500,000,000,000.[23] The comparative moderation of new initiatives for regulating tax haven activity does not mean that small states interested in using their tax and regulatory advantages to attract investment can rest easy. Three challenges stand out for small states looking to defend their economic interests with respect to the global regulation of tax and financial services.

First, small states may have rhetorically entrapped themselves by depending so heavily on the notion of the level playing field, ever the centerpiece of their case. Uniform regulations may have highly disproportionate effects. Large companies can employ dozens of lawyers and other specialists to comply with complicated and burdensome regulations in a way that is impossible for smaller enterprises. Analogously, if the international standard mandates very large and expensive offshore banking supervision agencies, for example, this would pose far more of a problem for small countries than for OECD members. Such regulations would thus tend to drive all but the most mature havens out of the market, while also presenting substantial barriers to entry for any potential newcomers to the field. The Basel 2 accords on international banking supervision rules and intellectual property rights regime may be examples of uniform standards that nevertheless create a much bigger problem for small states than for large.[24]

Second, in looking to shift global standard-setting from closed membership clubs (the OECD, FATF and FSF) to more open bodies (WTO, World Bank, IMF, United Nations), small states have given up their original ambition to set their own tax and financial laws in line with national priorities and in isolation from the rest of the world. This development bears a close resemblance to the notion that states reluctantly give up powers to international organizations only when the status quo option of splendid isolation is removed.[25] Taking account of informal power hierarchies or "invisible weightings" based on economic size, inclusiveness, and a seat at the table for small states rarely means a truly equal voice.[26] The unequal allocation of expertise is probably still more important than the uneven distribution of these informal weightings in explaining how inclusive rule-setting can entrench the dominance of the few core countries at the expense of the large majority on the periphery. Many if not most of the small poor countries dragged into the OECD campaign do not have enough qualified officials to participate actively in the steadily proliferating number of standard-setting bodies on anything like equal terms. In this sense, small states are handicapped by their lack of knowledge more than their lack of military power or market size.[27]

Finally, despite their successes from 2001, tax havens have generally been reluctant to make common cause with each other and have been consistently bad at mobilizing the support of the private actors who depend on the facilities they offer. Many within small states admit that perhaps it was only the extreme threat that the OECD initiative was seen to represent which was sufficient to create some solidarity within and between regions. A more subtle strategy of divide and rule could well have succeeded where the OECD was denied. In failing to consolidate their success in terms of institutional gains, small states leave themselves vulnerable to future multilateral regulatory initiatives.

These future challenges are real and pose significant threats to the viability of many tax havens. Some, like Tonga, Niue, and Nauru have withdrawn from the market for international financial services.[28] Others, like Dominica, Grenada, Montserrat and others in the East Caribbean have experienced substantial declines.[29] Yet at the same time, much of the pessimism regarding "the death of tax havens" looks overblown.[30] Established centers like the Channel Islands, the Isle of Man, the Cayman Islands, Bermuda, and others continue to experience steady and sometimes spectacular growth in complex financial products. Even some centers relying on the bulk sale of relatively simple International Business Companies, like the British Virgin Islands, Samoa, and the Seychelles have seen an uninterrupted rise in the number of company formations and the associated fee revenue.[31] These successes are likely to continue to inspire imitators, like recent entrants Anjouan, Brunei, and Botswana.[32] While the United States and the European Union may have made it harder for their citizens to use tax haven products, new markets for the services of havens have arisen in post-Communist Europe and China; the fact that the British Virgin Islands is the second biggest source of Chinese foreign direct investment indicates the huge sums of money that are "round tripped" to and from China via the Caribbean.[33] Probably the biggest factor keeping tax havens in business, however, is the lack of alternatives for many small island states, particularly in light of rich country agricultural protectionism and declining aid flows. Even when the dominant industry is doing very well (for example tourism in Aruba, oil in Brunei) there is a need to diversify. "What else would you have us do?" is a common response from island states to complaints from onshore about their offshore financial industries. For as long as the answer is only "go back to growing bananas"[34] (or the equivalent), offshore finance will remain a popular option among small states. Tax havens look to be around for a long time to come, and thus so does the underlying potential for conflict between large and small states that sparked the OECD harmful tax competition initiative.

Theoretical and Conceptual Implications

Of the lessons to be drawn for International Relations scholarship, the first relates to globalization broadly defined, and particularly the importance of interstate collective action problems. The second concerns implications of the study for realism, power political economy, and redistributive regulation. The final part of this section returns to some of the criticisms of constructivism referred to in the introduction.

International tax competition for financial services has particular importance for work on globalization. The structure of the issue closely mirrors that of general globalization stories, as intangible assets and financial services are especially mobile, and the fierce competition among dozens of jurisdictions for this business implies an especially severe international collective action problem. If the ability of states to tax was actually threatened by tax haven–driven tax competition, this would be an epochal development justifying many of the sweeping claims made by commentators about globalization. But the moral of this book with regards to globalization is that the sky is not falling and does not look likely to. Even if tax havens and harmful tax practices had remained unchallenged, the steady long-term rise in the share of government revenue and spending belies the notion of a "fiscal crisis of the welfare state."[35] To the extent that such a fiscal crisis does look likely, relatively prosaic factors like aging populations and domestic resistance to pension reforms would seem to be the culprits, not exotic islands in the sun or alpine financial havens. Conversely, the idea that a more vigorous campaign against tax havens will yield major new government revenue is equally a mirage. In this way the book tends to support other studies that find the most remarkable thing about globalization stories is the way they have caught popular and elite imagination despite uncertain empirical support.[36] Having reviewed international cooperation (and conflict) relating to tax matters since the mid-1990s, it would seem that the importance of collective action problems has been overdone in International Relations.[37] Despite the prisoner's dilemma analogy in the OECD's initial report, and the chilling effect of anxiety about disinvestment from high-regulation to low-regulation countries, conflicting preferences have been much more significant in retarding cooperation than fears of being cheated.[38]

Realism and constructivism are generally presented as being incompatible rivals, with little conversation between them. But to agree with realists about the prominence and prevalence of interstate struggles in the political and economic realm should not have to entail downplaying the importance of norms, culture and identity. Emphasizing the importance of language does not amount to a claim that the international arena is some kind of ideal communication situation characterized by states earnestly working toward reasoned consensual understandings. The conflict over regulating tax competition was not to establish a self-enforcing contract or to determine who could get a bigger share of the winnings. The global tax standards at stake created winners and losers in absolute terms.

An anomaly for realists, however, was the active and autonomous role played by the OECD secretariat. The degree of resistance from small states also shows that the idea of power must be expanded beyond material resources.

More generally, the development of the struggle over global tax standards casts doubt on conventional assumptions in the field about actors' ability to correctly anticipate future events. Approaches emphasizing strategic decisions by utility maximizing actors generally underestimate the effects of "bounded rationality." Although, according to Stephen Krasner, "stupidity is not a very interesting analytic category,"[39] it may well be a very prevalent empirical one. As long as "stupidity" includes getting it wrong on highly complex issues in an environment of information overload, misjudging the interactive effects of policy decisions, and being prone to creating unintended consequences, behavior and decisions that fall into this category may be very common. Too often scholars start with the presumption that, "on average, voters vote intelligently with respect to their interests; legislators organize sensible coalitions, given their interests; and nation-states voluntarily enter alliances that, on average, improve their positions."[40] Tax policy making has been replete with serendipitous successes and unforeseen failures. Examples range from the early tax havens, the eurodollar and eurobond markets, to U.S. 401k pensions and the EU Growth and Stability Pact. In retrospect it is all too easy to see that delegating the conduct of a coercive campaign to the OECD was not a good idea, that small states' "ignore it and it will go away" attitude to the initiative from 1998–99 was unwise, and that the label "harmful tax competition" was impolitic. Even in hindsight, those on both sides freely admit that they were feeling their way in the struggle over tax standards and that if they had their time again, things would be very different.

This book has also responded to several important criticisms of the constructivist research program. The first issue is why actors modify their actions in line with shared conceptions of appropriate behavior for a given actor in a given context. From the late 1980s, scholars have argued that compliance pressures span a spectrum, from fully internalized, taken-for-granted rules that are followed as a matter of habit, to those resting on external social sanctioning, including a wide variety of intermediate points involving greater or lesser combinations of each.[41] Because compliance pressures may be produced by a combination of internal and external mechanisms, and because norms themselves may be underspecified, ambiguous or in conflict, there is room for choice and contingency. Norms may be "up for grabs" and contested. Individuals reason and argue with others about the appropriate course of action and may mobilize social sanctions to shore up various proscriptions and prescriptions. Those involved must reconcile their conduct with prevailing standards not only to the satisfaction of their peers but also to maintain their own self-image.

The main conceptual innovations presented concern rhetoric and reputation. The concept of rhetoric, the use of language for political ends, has featured throughout the book in several ways. When actors are unsure as to the appropriate course of action, they may be persuaded by a process of moral reasoning, as in the case of economic coercion in chapter 2. As a speech act, blacklisting is an action that changes the world by changing the status of the referent, as discussed in chapter 4 with reference to the attractiveness of tax havens to foreign investors. Chapter 5 considered rhetorical entrapment, how tax havens were able to convince third parties that the OECD was not living up to its own declared principles. Language has an irreducible ambiguity, and principles enunciated by dominant actors may subsequently be employed at their expense.[42] Views which hold that dominant principles inculcate a false consciousness among subordinates neglect the extent of the fragmented, internally inconsistent, and contested nature of these values and beliefs.

Although the concept of reputation already enjoys a prominent place in the field, I have argued that the definition must be broader. Rather than an inductively derived record of past behavior akin to a commodity, reputation is relational, intersubjective, and based on a wide range of connotations and associations. In broadening the definition along these lines, this notion of reputation allows for a more social view of international politics and political economy. It also brings the understanding of this term closer to everyday usage.[43] Rhetoric and reputation usually work together. The OECD's blacklists threatened the reputations of tax havens. The cost for the OECD of the tax havens' "critique within hegemony" was its reputation for impartial expertise. The impact of speech often depends primarily on the reputation of the speaker. In turn, the reputation of the speaker may be affected by its own or others' rhetoric.

Both critics and practitioners have urged that constructivist work become more attentive to the micro aspects of their explanations and the use of evidence. In line with these calls, most of the major claims made in chapters 2, 4, and 5 have been supported with evidence gained through much international fieldwork. The debate covered in chapter 3 is based on an extensive survey of public material. More generally, the book has been styled as a piece of problem-driven and policy-relevant research, rather than a clash of irreconcilable ontologies or epistemologies.

The potential for the powerful to be entrapped by the stratagems of the weak, the slipperiness of meaning and language, and the unpredictability of policy effects mean that the control of dominant actors is never unchallengeable and their projects rarely go exactly according to plan. But international political economy is still most commonly a matter of the strong regulating as they will and the weak suffering as they must. The interplay of rhetoric and reputation may just as readily entrench inequalities as undermine them. In 2005, authorities in the Indian city of Rajahmundry struck upon the idea of collecting back taxes by hiring troupes of drummers to play outside debtors' homes to publicize their debt until they paid up. As tax takings hit an all-time high, one official enthused, "I am very happy with this result and from now on we will take up this drum beating drive twice a year. . . . In September we will send the drum beaters to recover the half-yearly taxes and again in March for the remainder." The view from someone on the receiving end was predictably very different: "It is humiliating for poor people like me who are not in a position to pay the dues for financial reasons. . . . It is such an insulting situation to have drum beaters doing this that it might force us to commit suicide."[44] Even absent armed force and disparities of material wealth, there is no reason to think that a more social view of politics and economics entails a world of greater harmony or justice.

NOTES

Introduction

1. Lloyd Gruber, *Ruling the World: Power Politics and the Rise of Supranational Institutions* (Princeton: Princeton University Press, 2000); Daniel W. Drezner, "Who Rules? The Regulation of Globalization," paper presented at the American Political Science Association Conference, Boston, September 2002; Daniel Drezner, "The Hidden Hand of Economic Coercion," *International Organization* 57 (2003): 643–59.

2. Michael N. Barnett, "Historical Sociology and Constructivism: An Estranged Past, A Federated Future?" in *Historical Sociology of International Relations,* ed. Stephen Hobden and John M. Hobson (Cambridge: Cambridge University Press, 2002), 99–119. For some of the outstanding recent exceptions, see Jacqueline Best, *The Limits of Transparency* (Ithaca: Cornell University Press, 2005); Mark Blyth, *Great Transformations* (Cambridge: Cambridge University Press, 2002); Leonard Seabrooke, *The Social Sources of Financial Power* (Ithaca: Cornell University Press, 2006); and Craig Parsons, *A Certain Idea of Europe* (Ithaca: Cornell University Press, 2003).

3. Benjamin J. Cohen, "International Finance," in *Handbook of International Relations,* ed. Walter Carlsnaes, Thomas Risse, and Beth A. Simmons (Thousand Oaks, CA: Sage, 2002), 443.

4. Martha Finnemore and Kathryn Sikkink, "Taking Stock: The Constructivist Research Program in International Relations and Comparative Politics," *Annual Review of Political Science* 4 (2001): 391–416; James Fearon and Alexander Wendt, "Rationalism vs. Constructivism: A Skeptical View," in *Handbook of International Relations,* ed. Walter Carlsnaes, Thomas Risse, and Beth A. Simmons (London: Sage, 2002); Michael Tierney and Catherine Weaver, "Principals and Principles? The Possibilities for Theoretical Synthesis and Scientific Progress in the Study of International Organizations," paper presented at the conference titled Theoretical Synthesis in the Study of International Organizations, Washington, D.C., February 2004.

5. Gary King, Robert O. Keohane, and Sidney Verba, *Designing Social Inquiry: Scientific Inference in Qualitative Research* (Princeton: Princeton University Press, 1994); Henry E. Brady and David Collier, eds., *Rethinking Social Inquiry: Diverse Tools, Shared Standards* (New York: Rowman and Littlefield, 2004).

6. Jennifer Milliken, "The Study of Discourse in International Relations: A Critique of Research Methods," *European Journal of International Relations* 5 (1999): 225–54; Jutta Joachim and Bertjan Verbeek, "International Organisations and Policy Implementation: Pieces of the Puzzle," paper presented at the ECPR Joint Sessions Workshop, Uppsala, Sweden, 2004.

7. Charles C. Ragin and Howard S. Becker, eds., *What Is a Case? Exploring the Foundations of Social Inquiry* (Cambridge: Cambridge University Press, 1992).

8. David Kreps, "Corporate Culture and Economy Theory," in *Perspectives on Positive Political Economy*, ed. James E. Alt and Kenneth A. Shepsle (Cambridge: Cambridge University Press, 1990), 90–143; George Downs and M. Jones, "Reputation, Compliance, and International Law," *Journal of Legal Studies* 31 (2002): 95–114.

9. Leslie B. Samuels and Daniel C. Kolb, "The OECD Initiative: Harmful Tax Practices and Tax Havens," *Taxes* 79 (2001): 241–42.

1. Death, Taxes, and Tax Havens

1. Charles Tilly, *Coercion, Capital, and European States, A.D. 990–1992* (Oxford: Clarendon, 1992).

2. Charles Adams, *For Good or Evil: The Impact of Taxes on the Course of Civilization* (Lanham, Md.: Madison, 1993).

3. Susan M. Roberts, "Small Place, Big Money: The Cayman Islands and the International Financial System," *Economic Geography* 71 (1995): 237–56; Ronen Palan and Jason Abbott, *State Strategies in the Global Political Economy* (Pinter: London, 1996); Mark P. Hampton, *The Offshore Interface: Tax Havens in the Global Economy* (Basingstoke: Macmillan, 1996); Mark P. Hampton and Jason P. Abbott, eds., *Offshore Finance Centers and Tax Havens: The Rise of Global Capital* (West Lafayette, Ind.: Ichor, 1999); Mark P. Hampton and John Christensen, "Offshore Pariahs? Small Island Economies, Tax Havens, and the Re-configuration of Global Finance," *World Development* 30 (2002): 1657–73; International Monetary Fund, *Offshore Financial Centres*, IMF Background Paper (Washington, D.C., 2000); International Monetary Fund, *Financial Sector Regulation: The Case of Small Pacific Island Countries*, IMF Policy Discussion Paper, Asia Pacific Department (Washington, D.C., 2001); International Monetary Fund, *Caribbean Offshore Financial Centers: Past, Present and Possibilities for the Future*, Working Paper, Western Hemisphere Department (Washington, D.C., 2002); Bill Maurer, "Complex Subjects: Offshore Finance, Complexity Theory and the Dispersal of the Modern," *Socialist Theory* 25 (1995): 113–45; Bill Maurer, "Cyberspacial Sovereignties: Offshore Finance, Digital Cash, and the Limits of Liberalism," *Indiana Journal of Global Legal Studies* 5 (1998): 493–519; Ronen Palan, "Trying to Have Your Cake and Eating It: How and Why the State System Has Created Offshore," *International Studies Quarterly* 42 (1998): 635–44; Ronen Palan, "Tax Havens and the Commercialization of State Sovereignty," *International Organization* 56 (2002): 151–76; Ronen Palan, *The Offshore World: Sovereign Markets, Virtual Places, and Nomad Millionaires* (Ithaca: Cornell University Press, 2003); Caroline Doggart, *Tax Havens and Their Uses*, 9th ed. (London: Economist Intelligence Unit, 1997); Caroline Doggart, *A Study for the Implications of the HTI, FATF, and FSF for the Independent Caribbean*, UK Department for International Development (Caribbean) (London, 2001); Caroline Doggart, *Tax Havens and Their Uses*, 10th ed. (London: Economist Intelligence Unit, 2002); Gregory Rawlings, "Mobile People, Mobile Capital, and Tax Neutrality: Sustaining a Market for Offshore Financial Centers," *Accounting Forum* 29 (2005): 289–310; J. C. Sharman, "South Pacific Tax Havens: Leaders in the Race to the Bottom or Laggards in the Race to the Top?" *Accounting Forum* 29 (2005): 311–23.

4. Thomas P. Azzara, *Tax Havens of the World* (Nassau: New Providence, 2003); Walter Diamond and Dorothy Diamond, *Tax Havens of the World* (New York: Matthew Bender, 1998); Hampton and Abbott, *Offshore Financial Centers*, 1; Palan, *Offshore World*, 37; *Tolleys Tax Havens*, 2nd ed. (London: Butterworth, 1990); *Tolleys Tax Havens*, 3rd ed. (London: Butterworth, 2000); J. C.

Sharman and Gregory Rawlings, *Deconstructing National Tax Blacklists,* Society of Trust and Estate Practitioners (London, 2005).

5. Jorri Duusma, *Fragmentation and the International Relations of Micro-States* (Cambridge: Cambridge University Press, 1996).

6. Palan, "Trying to Have your Cake and Eating It," 638; see also Sol Picciotto, "Offshore: The State as Legal Fiction," in *Offshore Finance Centers and Tax Havens,* ed. Mark Hampton and Jason Abbott (West Lafayette, Ind.: Ichor, 1999).

7. Philippe Braillard, Oleg Guy Betcher, and Graziano Lusenti, *Switzerland as a Financial Center: Structures and Policies: A Comparison at the International level* (Dordrecht: Kluwer, 1988).

8. R. T. Naylor, *Hot Money and the Politics of Debt* (New York: Simon and Schuster, 1987).

9. Alan C. Hudson, "Placing Trust, Trusting Place: On the Social Construction of Offshore Financial Centres," *Political Geography* 17 (1998): 915–37; Alan Hudson, "Offshoreness, Globalization and Sovereignty: A Postmodern Geo-Political Sovereignty?" *Transactions of the Institute of British Geographers* 15 (2000): 269–83; Susan M. Roberts, "Small Place, Big Money: The Cayman Islands and the International Financial System," *Economic Geography* 71 (1995): 237–56.

10. Paul Sutton, "The Politics of Small State Security in the Caribbean," *Journal of Commonwealth and Comparative Politics* 31 (1993): 1–32; Andy W. Knight and Randolph B. Persaud, "Subsidiarity, Regional Governance, and Caribbean Security," *Latin American Politics and Society* 43 (2001): 29–55.

11. Anthony B. van Fossen, *The International Political Economy of Pacific Islands Flags of Convenience* (Nathan, Queensland: Centre for the Study of Australian-Asia Relations Griffith University, 1992); Anthony B. van Fossen, "Money Laundering, Global Financial Instability, and Tax Havens in the Pacific Islands," *Contemporary Pacific* 15 (2003): 237–75; Terry Dwyer, "'Harmful' Tax Competition and the Future of Offshore Financial Centres, Such as Vanuatu," *Pacific Economic Bulletin* 15 (2000): 48–69; Gregory Rawlings, "Laws, Liquidity, and Eurobonds: The Making of Vanuatu as a Tax Haven," *Journal of Pacific History* 39 (2004): 325–41; Sharman, "South Pacific Tax Havens."

12. Michael Handel, *Weak States in the International System* (London: Frank Cass, 1981); Colin Clarke and Tony Payne, eds., *Politics, Security, and Development in Small States* (London: Allen and Unwin, 1987); Anthony Payne, "The Politics of Small State Security in the Pacific," *Journal of Commonwealth and Comparative Politics* 31 (1993): 103–32; Sutton, "The Politics of Small State Security in the Caribbean"; World Bank/Commonwealth, *Report of the Joint Task Force on the Vulnerability of Small States* (1995); Efraim Inbar and Gabriel Sheffer, *The National Security of Small States in a Changing World* (London: Frank Cass, 1997); Alan K. Hendrikson, "Small States in World Politics: The International Political Position and Diplomatic Influence of the World's Growing Number of Small Countries," Conference on Small States (St. Lucia, February 1999); Rajiv Biswas, "Global Competition in Offshore Business Services: Prospects for Developing Services," *Commonwealth Heads of Government Reference Book* (2001), 104–13; Alan L. Winters and Pedro M. G. Martins, "Beautiful but Costly: An Analysis of the Operating Cost of Doing Business in Small Economies" (Commonwealth/UNCTAD, 2003).

13. Palan, "Trying to Have Your Cake and Eating It"; Ronen Palan, "Offshore and the Structural Enablement of Sovereignty," in *Offshore Finance Centres and Tax Havens,* ed. Mark P. Hampton and Jason P. Abbott (West Lafayette, Ind.: Ichor, 1999); Palan, "Tax Havens and the Commercialization of State Sovereignty"; Palan, *The Offshore World.*

14. For the example of Niue and the .nu domain name, see Philip E. Steinberg and Stephen D. McDowell, "Mutiny on the Bandwidth: The Semiotics of Statehood in the Internet Domain Name Registries of Pitcairn Island and Niue," *New Media and Society* 5 (2003): 47–67.

15. Biswas, "Global Competition in Offshore Business Services," 107.

16. Rawlings, "Laws, Liquidity, and Eurobonds."

17. Terry Dwyer, "'Harmful' Tax Competition and the Future of Offshore Financial Centres, Such as Vanuatu."

18. Biswas, "Global Competition in Offshore Business Services."

19. For the latest see 2002; see also *Tolleys Tax Havens*, 2nd ed.; *Tolleys Tax Havens*, 3rd ed.; Azzara, *Tax Havens of the World;* various issues of *Offshore Investment.*

20. Hampton, *The Offshore Interface;* Picciotto, "Offshore: The State as Legal Fiction"; Palan, *The Offshore World.*

21. *Trident Practical Guide to International Trusts*, 4th ed. (London: Chancellor 2004); Harvey M. Silets and Michael C. Drew, "Offshore Asset Protection Trusts: Tax Planning or Tax Fraud?" *Journal of Money Laundering Control* 5 (2001): 9–15; Reuben Tylor, "A New Twist on Private Trustee Companies," Cook Island Trust Corporation, available at: http://www.cookislandstrust .com/a%20new%20twist.htm.

22. Milton Grundy, *The World of International Tax Planning* (Cambridge: Cambridge University Press, 1984), 2.

23. U.S. Treasury, "Corporate Inversion Transactions: Tax Policy Implications," Office of Tax Policy, May (Washington, D.C., 2002); Thomas Bernaur and Vit Styrsky, "Adjustment or Voice? Corporate Responses to International Tax Competition," *European Journal of International Relations* 10 (2004): 61–97.

24. For an introduction to these and other corporate uses, see Doggart, *Tax Havens and Their Uses*, 9th ed. (London: Economist Intelligence Unit, 1997); Doggart, *Tax Havens and Their Uses*, 10th ed; OECD, *International Tax Avoidance and Tax Evasion: Four Related Studies* (Paris, 1987); Sol Picciotto, *International Business Taxation* (London: Quorum, 1992); Lorraine Eden, *Taxing Multinationals: Transfer Pricing and Corporate Income Tax in North America* (Toronto: University of Toronto Press, 1998); OECD, *Behind the Corporate Veil: Using Corporate Entities for Illicit Purposes* (Paris, 2001); Government Accounting Office, "Suspicious Banking Activities: Possible Money Laundering by U.S. Corporations Formed for Russian Entities," Permanent Subcommittee on Investigations, U.S. Senate (Washington, D.C., 2000); STEP/ITIO, *Towards a Level Playing Field* (London, 2002); on Enron, Senator Levin, "U.S. Tax Shelter Industry: The Role of Accountants, Lawyers, and Financial Professionals," Permanent Subcommittee on Investigations Report (Washington, D.C., 2003); Stephen L. Schwarcz, "Enron, and the Use and Abuse of Special Purpose Entities in Corporate Structures," Duke Law School Research Paper 28 (2002); various issues of *Offshore Investment.*

25. Edmund Bendelow, "A Vehicle for Multi-Asset Structures," *Offshore Investment* 143 (2004): 20–22.

26. Eric Helleiner, "State Power and the Regulation of Illicit Activity in Global Finance," in *The Illicit Global Economy and State Power*, ed. R. Friman and P. Andreas (New York: Rowman and Littlefield, 1999); Jack A. Blum, Michael Levi, R. Thomas Naylor, and Phil Williams, *Financial Havens, Banking Secrecy, and Money Laundering*, United Nations Office for Drug Control and Crime Prevention (Washington, D.C., 1998); Palan, *The Offshore World.*

27. Michael C. Webb, "Defining the Boundaries of Legitimate State Practice: Norms, Transnational Actors, and the OECD's Project on Harmful Tax Competition," *Review of International Political Economy* 11 (2004): 787–827.

28. Andreas Haufler, *Taxation in a Global Economy* (Cambridge: Cambridge University Press, 2001).

29. Claudio M. Radaelli, "Harmful Tax Competition in the EU: Policy Narratives and Advocacy Coalitions," *Journal of Common Market Studies* 37 (1999): 667.

30. Claudio M. Radaelli, "Game Theory and Institutional Entrepreneurship: Transfer Pricing and the Search for Co-ordination in International Tax Policy," *Policy Studies Journal* 26 (1998): 603–19; Radaelli, "Harmful Tax Competition in the EU: Policy Narratives and Advocacy Coalitions."

31. European Commission, "Taxation in the European Union," Ecofin Discussion Paper (Brussels, 1996). Author's interview, European Commission, Brussels, Belgium, 5 November 2003; author's interview, Centre for European Policy Studies, Brussels, Belgium, 4 November 2003.

32. "European Tax Disharmony," *The Economist*, 3 April 1997.

33. Haufler, *Taxation in a Global Economy*, 15.

34. Radaelli, "Harmful Tax Competition in the EU: Policy Narratives and Advocacy Coalitions," 678.

35. George P. Gilligan, "Whither or Wither the European Savings Tax Directive? A Case Study in the Political Economy of Taxation," *Journal of Financial Crime* 11 (2003): 56–72.

36. Ibid.; David E. Spencer, "OECD Proposals on Harmful Tax Practices: An Update," *Journal of International Taxation* 15 (2004) 8–23, 46–47. Author's interview, European Commission, Brussels, Belgium, 5 November 2003; author's interview, Centre for European Policy Studies, Brussels, Belgium, 4 November 2003.

37. Lowtax, *The Future of Offshore as a Business Location Following the EU/OECD/FATF/FSF Initiatives* (London, 2004); Gilligan, "Whither or Wither the European Savings Tax Directive?"; David E. Spencer, "EU Agrees at Last on Taxation of Savings," *Journal of International Taxation* 14 (2003): 4–18. Author's interview, European Commission, Brussels, Belgium, 5 November 2003.

38. Alan Lambert, "The Caribbean Anti-Money Laundering Programme," *Journal of Money Laundering Control* 5 (2001): 158–62.

39. John Braithwaite and Peter Drahos, *Global Business Regulation* (Cambridge: Cambridge University Press, 2000).

40. William F. Wechsler, "Follow the Money," *Foreign Affairs* 80 (2001): 40–57. Author's phone interview, United States Treasury, 26 September 2002.

41. Wechsler, "Follow the Money," 48–49.

42. Government Accounting Office, "Suspicious Banking Activities: Possible Money Laundering by U.S. Corporations Formed for Russian Entities," Permanent Subcommittee on Investigations, U.S. Senate (Washington, D.C., 2000); Senator Levin, "U.S. Tax Shelter Industry"; "Les Mains Sales," *Economist*, 11 October 2001; author's interview, United Nations Office on Drugs and Crime, Vienna, Austria, 17 September 2004.

43. Financial Action Task Force, *Review to Identify Non-Co-operative Countries or Territories: Increasing the Worldwide Effectiveness of Anti-Money Laundering Measures* (2000), 13.

44. Financial Action Task Force, *Review to Identify Non-Co-operative Countries or Territories* (2000); Financial Action Task Force, *Second Review to Identify Non-Co-operative Countries or Territories* (2001); Financial Action Task Force, *Third Annual Review to Identify Non-Co-operative Countries or Territories* (2002); Financial Action Task Force, *Fifth Annual Review of Non-Co-operative Countries or Territories* (2004).

45. The jurisdictions that have appeared on the FATF's Non-Co-operative Countries and Territories List are the Bahamas, the Cayman Islands, the Cook Islands, Dominica, Israel, Lebanon, Liechtenstein, the Marshall Islands, Nauru, Niue, Panama, the Philippines, Russia, St. Kitts and Nevis, St. Vincent and the Grenadines (2000); Egypt, Guatemala, Hungary, Indonesia, Myanmar, Nigeria (2001); Grenada, Ukraine (2002).

46. United Nations Office on Drugs and Crime, "Anti-Money Laundering Unit/Global Program against Money Laundering Publications 2004," Vienna (Compact Disc).

47. IMF, *Offshore Financial Centers: The Role of the IMF* (Washington, D.C., 2000); IMF, *Offshore Financial Centers: IMF Background Paper* (Washington, D.C., 2000); IMF, *Offshore Financial Center Program: A Progress Report* (Washington, D.C., 2003); IMF, *Offshore Financial Center Program: A Progress Report* (Washington, D.C, 2005).

48. OECD, *Access for Tax Authorities to Information Gathered by Anti-Money Laundering Authorities* (Paris, 2002); Bruce Zagaris, "Issues Low Tax Regimes Should Raise when Negotiating with the OECD," *Tax Notes International* (29 January 2001): 523–32; Bruce Zagaris, "Tax Havens Beware, Fiscal Transparency, and What Else? The Rules are Changing and It's Crazy Out There!" *Journal of International Banking Regulation* 3 (2001): 111–44; Benjamin R. Hartman, "Coercing Cooperation from Offshore Financial Centers: Identity and Coincidence of International Obligations against Money-Laundering and Harmful Tax Competition," *Boston College International and Comparative Law Review* 24 (2001): 253–90.

49. OECD, *Improving Access to Bank Information for Tax Purposes* (Paris, 2000), 9; see also

OECD, *Improving Access to Bank Information for Tax Purposes: The 2003 Progress Report* (Paris, 2003).

50. OECD, *Improving Access to Bank Information*, 13.

51. OECD, *Improving Access to Bank Information: Progress Report; Financial Times* (September 2003). Author's interview, OECD, Paris, France, 9 July 2004.

52. Jeffrey Owens, "Tax Administration in the New Millennium," *Intertax* 30 (2002): 125–30.

53. Author's interview, OECD, Paris, France, 9 July 2004.

54. Wechsler, "Follow the Money," 49.

55. FSF Press Release, 26 May 2000: Group 1: Dublin, Guernsey, Hong Kong, Isle of Man, Jersey, Luxembourg, Singapore, Switzerland. Group 2: Andorra, Bahrain, Barbados, Bermuda, Gibraltar, Labuan, Macau, Malta, Monaco. Group 3: Anguilla, Antigua and Barbuda, Aruba, Bahamas, Belize, British Virgin Islands, Cayman Islands, Cook Islands, Costa Rica, Cyprus, Lebanon, Liechtenstein, Marshall Islands, Nauru, Netherlands Antilles, Niue, Panama, Samoa, Seychelles, St. Kitts and Nevis, St. Lucia, St. Vincent and the Grenadines, Turks and Caicos, Vanuatu.

56. Zagaris, "Tax Havens Beware"; Gilbert N. M. O Gilbert, "A Preliminary Briefing on Recent International Financial Regulations," Paper Prepared for the Nassau Institute (Nassau, 2002). Author's interview, IMF, Washington, D.C., 28 June 2004.

57. Picciotto, *International Business Taxation;* Lorraine Eden and Robert T. Kudrle, "Tax Havens: Renegade States in the International Tax Regime," *Law and Policy* 27 (2005): 1.

58. OECD, *International Tax Avoidance and Tax Evasion: Four Related Studies.*

59. Marnin Michaels and Thomas A. O'Donnell, "The Death of Information Exchange Agreements," *Journal of International Taxation* 13 (2002): 8–45.

60. Gordon Report, "Tax Havens and Their Use by U.S. Taxpayers," prepared for the Internal Revenue Service (Washington, D.C., 1981), quoted in Eden and Kudrle, "Tax Havens: Renegade States in the International Tax Regime," 115.

61. Author's interview, United States Treasury, by phone, 26 September 2002.

62. Barry A. K. Rider, "Law: The War on Terror and Crime and the Offshore Centres: The "New" Perspective," in *Global Financial Crime: Terrorism, Money Laundering, and Offshore Centres,* edited by Donato Masciandaro (Aldershot: Ashgate, 2004), 61–95.

63. Council on Foreign Relations, "Terrorist Financing," Task Force Report (Washington, D.C.: Council on Foreign Relations Press, 2002), 47; see also Kern Alexander, "Extraterritorial U.S. Banking Regulation and International Terrorism: The Patriot Act and the International Response," *Journal of International Banking Regulation* 3 (2002): 307–26; Ethan Preston, "The USA PATRIOT Act: New Adventures in American Extraterritoriality," *Journal of Financial Crime* 10 (2002): 104–16.

64. Bob Reinalda and Bertjan Verbeek, eds., *Autonomous Decision Making by International Organizations* (London: Routledge, 1998); Bob Reinalda and Bertjan Verbeek, eds., *Decision Making within International Organizations* (London: Routledge, 2004).

65. Charles M. Tiebout, "A Pure Theory of Local Expenditures," *Journal of Political Economy* 64 (1956): 416–24.

66. Wallace E. Oates, *Fiscal Federalism* (New York: Harcourt Brace Jovanovich, 1972).

67. Timothy J. Goodspeed, "Tax Competition and Tax Structure in Open Federal Economies: Evidence from OECD Countries with Implications for the European Union," *European Economic Review* 46 (2002): 357–74.

68. Reuven S. Avi-Yonah, "Globalization, Tax Competition, and the Fiscal Crisis of the Welfare State," *Harvard Law Review* 113 (2000): 1575–676.

69. Geoffrey Brennan and James M.. Buchanan, *The Power to Tax* (Cambridge: Cambridge University Press, 1980).

70. John Douglas Wilson, "Theories of Tax Competition," *National Tax Journal* 52 (1999) 269–303.

71. John M. Hobson, "Disappearing Taxes or 'Race to the Middle?' Fiscal Policy in the OECD," in *Bringing Domestic Actors Back In,* ed. Linda Weiss (Cambridge: Cambridge University

Press), 37–57; Michael C. Webb and Kenneth G. Stewart, "Tax Competition and Corporate Tax Rates," paper presented at International Studies Association conference (Portland, 2003).

72. Geoffrey Garrett, "Global Market and National Politics: Collision Course or Virtuous Circle," *International Organization* 52 (1998): 787–825.

73. James R. Hines and Eric M. Rice, "Fiscal Paradise: Foreign Tax Havens and American Business," *Quarterly Journal of Economics* 109 (1994): 149–82; James R. Hines, "Lessons from Behavioural Responses to International Tax Competition," *National Tax Journal* 52 (1999): 305–22; Harry Grubert and John Mutti, "Do Taxes Influence Where U.S. Corporations Invest?" *National Tax Journal* 53 (2000): 825–39; OECD, *Corporate Tax Incentives and Foreign Direct Investment* (Paris, 2001).

74. Hines and Rice, "Fiscal Paradise," 151.

75. Grubert and Mutti, "Do Taxes Influence Where U.S. Corporations Invest?" 825.

76. Ibid., 309.

77. Webb and Stewart, "Tax Competition and Corporate Tax Rates."

78. Cited in OECD, *Harmful Tax Competition—An Emerging Global Issue* (Paris, 1998).

79. Martin Marcussen, "The OECD in Search of a Role: Playing the Ideas Game," paper presented at ECPR 29th Joint Session of Workshops, Grenoble (France, 2001); Martin Marcussen, "The Organization for Economic Co-operation and Development as Ideational Artist and Arbitrator: Dream or Reality?" in *Decision Making within International Organizations*, ed. B. Reinalda and B. Verbeek (London: Routledge, 2004), 90–106.

80. Marcussen, "The OECD in Search of a Role."

81. Paul Krugman, *Pop Internationalism* (Cambridge, Mass.: MIT Press, 1996), 3–24.

82. Author's interview, OECD, Canberra, Australia, 1 October 2002; author's interview, OECD, Paris, France, 9 July 2004; Webb, "Defining the Boundaries of Legitimate State Practice."

83. European Commission, "Taxation in the European Union," 6, 13.

84. Webb, "Defining the Boundaries of Legitimate State Practice."

85. OECD, *Harmful Tax Competition*, 25.

86. Author's interviews, OECD, Canberra, Australia, 1 October 2002; author's interview, OECD, Paris, France, 9 July 2004; Webb, "Defining the Boundaries of Legitimate State Practice."

87. OECD, *Harmful Tax Competition*, 20.

88. Ibid., 22–23.

89. Ibid., 16.

90. Gregory Rawlings and Valerie Braithwaite, eds., *Voices for Change: Australian Perspectives on Tax Administration*, special issue of *Australian Journal of Social Issues* 38 (August 2003): 261–430.

91. See also OECD, *Harmful Tax Practices: The 2004 Progress Report* (Paris, 2004), 14.

92. OECD, *Harmful Tax Competition*, 37.

93. Fabrazio Pagani, "Peer Review: A Tool for Cooperation and Change: An Analysis of the OECD Working Method." General Secretariat, Directorate for Legal Affairs (Paris, 2002), 4–5; see also Tony Porter and Michael Webb, "The Role of the OECD in the Orchestration of Global Knowledge Networks," paper presented at International Studies Association Conference (Montreal, 2004); David Henderson, "International Economic Competition Revisited," *Government and Opposition* 28 (1993); Marcussen, "The OECD in Search of a Role"; Marcussen, "The Organization for Economic Co-operation and Development as Ideational Artist and Arbitrator"; Dorte Salskov-Iversen, Hans Krause Hansen, and Sven Bislev, "Governmentality, Globalization, and Local Practice: Transformations of a Hegemonic Discourse," Department of Intercultural Communication and Management, Copenhagen Business School, October 1999; Kerstin Martens and Carolin Balzer, "Comparing Governance of International Organizations: The EU, the OECD, and Educational Policy," paper presented at the American Political Science Association Conference (Chicago, 2004).

94. Robert T. Kudrle and Lorraine Eden, "The Campaign against Tax Havens: Will It Last? Will It Work?" *Stanford Journal of Law Business and Finance* 9 (2003): 38.

95. OECD, *Harmful Tax Competition*, 38.
96. OECD, *Towards Global Tax Co-operation*, 25–26.
97. OECD, *Harmful Tax Competition*, 73–78.

2. Regulative Norms and Inappropriate Means

1. Peter J. Katzenstein, ed., *The Culture of National Security: Norms and Identity in World Politics* (New York: Columbia University Press, 1996); Martha Finnemore, *The Purpose of Intervention: Changing Beliefs about the Use of Force* (Ithaca: Cornell University Press, 2003); Martha Finnemore, *National Interests in International Society* (Ithaca: Cornell University Press, 1996).

2. James Cable, *Gunboat Diplomacy, 1919–79: Political Applications of Limited Naval Force*, 2nd ed. (Basingstoke: Macmillan, 1981).

3. Jon Elster, *Nuts and Bolts for the Social Sciences* (Cambridge: Cambridge University Press, 1989), 113.

4. Jon Elster, *The Cement of Society: A Study of Social Order* (Cambridge: Cambridge University Press, 1989).

5. James G. March and Johan P. Olsen, *Rediscovering Institutions: The Organizational Basis of Politics* (New York: Free Press, 1989); James G. March and Johan P. Olsen, "The Institutional Dynamics of International Political Order," *International Organization* 52 (1998): 943–70.

6. Paul Kowert and Jeffrey Legro, "Norms, Identity, and Their Limits: A Theoretical Reprise," in *The Culture of National Security: Norms and Identity in World Politics*, ed. Peter J. Katzenstein (New York: Columbia University Press, 1996), 463.

7. Regulative norms are distinguished from 'constitutive norms' that help define actors' identities by laying down basic "rules of the game," and provide the shared stock of meanings that makes possible communication and the social interaction in world politics. Some emphasize that this distinction is not water-tight in that rules can be both regulative and constitutive. John Gerard Ruggie, *Constructing the World Polity: Essays on International Institutionalization* (London: Routledge, 1998); Alexander Wendt, *Social Theory of International Politics* (Cambridge: Cambridge University Press, 1999); Martha Finnemore and Kathryn Sikkink, "International Norms Dynamics and Political Change," *International Organization* 52 (1998): 887–917; Friedrich V. Kratochwil, *Rules, Norms, and Decisions: On the Conditions of Practical and Legal Reasoning in International Relations and Domestic Affairs* (Cambridge: Cambridge University Press, 1989); Katzenstein, *The Culture of National Security;* Nicholas Onuf, "Constructivism: A User's Manual," in *International Relations in a Constructed World*, ed. K. Vendulka, N. Onuf, and P. Kowert (Armonk, N.Y: M. E. Sharpe, 1998), 68.

8. Elster, *The Cement of Society*, 110; Jeffrey W. Legro, "Which Norms Matter? Revisiting the "Failure' of Internationalism," *International Organization* 51 (1997): 33; Onuf, "Constructivism: A User's Manual," 70; Ronald B. Mitchell, "Norms as Regulative Rules: Inducing Compliance Through Logics of Appropriateness," paper presentation, APSA Conference, San Francisco, September 2001; James Fearon and Alexander Wendt, "Rationalism vs. Constructivism: A Skeptical View," in *Handbook of International Relations*, ed. Walter Carlesnaes, Thomas Risse, and Beth A. Simmons (London: Sage, 2002), 60; Kratochwil, *Rules, Norms, and Decisions*, 102, 125; Vaughn P. Shannon, "Norms Are What States Make of Them: The Political Psychology of Norm Violation," *International Studies Quarterly* 44 (2000): 294; March and Olsen, *Rediscovering Institutions*, 23–26; Finnemore, *National Interests in International Society*, 134–39; Finnemore, *The Purpose of Intervention*, 18; John Boli and George M. Thomas, "World Culture in the World Polity: A Century of International Non-Governmental Organizations," *American Sociological Review* 62 (1997): 173.

9. Elster, *The Cement of Society*, 130; Fearon and Wendt, "Rationalism vs. Constructivism," 60; Ole Jacob Sending, "Constitution, Choice, and Change: Problems with the 'Logic of Appropriateness' and Its Use in Constructivist Theory," *European Journal of International Relations* 8

(2002): 445–48; March and Olsen, *Rediscovering Institutions*, 24; Finnemore, *National Interests in International Society*, 29.

10. Finnemore and Sikkink, "International Norms Dynamics, and Political Change," 914; Thomas M. Franck, *Fairness in International Law and Institutions* (Oxford: Clarendon Press, 1995), 14, 477; Kratochwil, *Rules, Norms, and Decisions*, 30; Thomas Risse, "'Let's Argue!': Communicative Action in World Politics," *International Organization* 54 (2000): 2; Neta C. Crawford, *Argument and Change in World Politics: Ethics, Decolonization, and Humanitarian Intervention* (Cambridge: Cambridge University Press, 2002); Finnemore, *The Purpose of Intervention*, 2.

11. For those who have recognized the agency of norms, see Elster, *Nuts and Bolts for the Social Sciences*, 113; Kratochwil, *Rules, Norms, and Decisions;* March and Olsen, *Rediscovering Institutions;* Nicholas Onuf, *A World of Our Making* (Columbia: University of South Carolina Press, 1989). For an approach that downplays the agential component of norms, see Legro, "Which Norms Matter?" 31; Jeffrey T. Checkel, "Norms, Institutions, and National Identity in Contemporary Europe," *International Studies Quarterly* 43 (1999), 84; Shannon, "Norms Are What States Make of Them," 293.

12. For example, see John L. Campbell, "Ideas, Politics, and Public Policy," *Annual Review of Sociology* 28 (2002): 21–38; Judith Goldstein and Robert O. Keohane, eds., *Ideas and Foreign Policy: Beliefs, Institutions, and Political Change* (Ithaca: Cornell University Press, 1993), 6; Legro, "Which Norms Matter?" 31; Ian Hurd, "Legitimacy and Authority in International Politics," *International Organization* 53 (1999): 380; Emanuel Adler, "Constructivism and International Relations," in *Handbook of International Relations*, ed. Walter Carlesnaes, Thomas Risse, and Beth A. Simmons (London: Sage, 2002), 109; Katzenstein, *The Culture of National Security*, 29–30; Wendt, *Social Theory of International Politics*, 4; Shannon, "Norms Are What States Make of Them," 294; Richard Price and Christian Reus-Smit, "Dangerous Liaisons? Critical International Theory and Constructivism," *European Journal of International Relations* 4 (1998): 272; March and Olsen, *Rediscovering Institutions*, 48; Finnemore, *National Interests in International Society*, 32; Emanuel Adler, "Seizing the Middle Ground: Constructivism in World Politics," *European Journal of International Relations* 3 (1997): 320.

13. Audie Klotz and C. Lynch, *Constructivist Methods* (forthcoming); Finnemore and Sikkink, "International Norms Dynamics and Political Change"; Martha Finnemore and Kathryn Sikkink, "Taking Stock: The Constructivist Research Program in International Relations and Comparative Politics," *Annual Review of Political Science* 4 (2001): 391–416; Elster, *The Cement of Society*, 106, 150; Fearon and Wendt, "Rationalism vs. Constructivism," 61–62; Jeffery T. Checkel, "Why Comply? Social Learning and European Identity Change," *International Organization* 55 (2001): 581; Shannon, "Norms Are What States Make of Them," 310; Finnemore, *National Interests in International Society*, 29–31, and *The Purpose of Intervention*, 5, 16.

14. Finnemore and Sikkink, "International Norm Dynamics and Political Change"; Finnemore and Sikkink, "Taking Stock"; Elster, *The Cement of Society*, 106, 150; Fearon and Wendt, "Rationalism vs. Constructivism," 61–62; Checkel, "Why Comply?" 581; Shannon, "Norms Are What States Make of Them," 310; Finnemore, *National Interests in International Society*, 29–31, and *The Purpose of Intervention*, 5, 16.

15. "World Wide Web of Tax Dodgers," *Observer*, 24 February 2002.

16. Author's interview, OECD, Paris, France, 9 July 2004.

17. Stephen D. Krasner, *Sovereignty: Organized Hypocrisy* (Princeton: Princeton University Press, 1999).

18. Kenneth N. Waltz, *Theory of International Politics* (Reading: Addison, 1979); Markus Fischer, "Feudal Europe, 800–1300: Communal Discourse and Conflictual Practices," *International Organization* 46 (1992): 427–65; John J. Mearsheimer, "Back to the Future: Instability in Europe after the Cold War," *International Security* 15 (1990): 5–56; John J. Mearsheimer, "The False Promise of International Institutions," *International Security* 19 (1994–1995): 329–39; John J. Mearsheimer, *The Tragedy of Great Power Politics* (New York: W. W. Norton, 2001); see also Jeffrey W. Legro and Andrew Moravcsik, "Is Anyone Still a Realist?" *International Security* 24 (1999): 5–55.

172 Notes to Pages 53–60

19. Finnemore, *The Purpose of Intervention*, 17–18.

20. Ibid.

21. James Cable, *Gunboat Diplomacy, 1919–1997: Political Applications of Limited Naval Force*, 3rd ed. (Basingstoke: Macmillan, 1998), 199.

22. Cable, *Gunboat Diplomacy, 1919–1979.*

23. Anthony Cordesman and Abraham Wagner, *The Lessons of Modern War IV: The Gulf War* (Boulder, Colo.: Westview, 1996), 810–18.

24. Michael Handel, *Weak States in the International System* (London: Frank Cass, 1981), 242.

25. Robert H. Jackson, *Quasi-States: Sovereignty, International Relations, and the Third World* (Cambridge: Cambridge University Press, 1989); see also David Strang, "Anomaly and Commonplace in European Political Expansion: Realist and Institutional Accounts," *International Organization* 45 (1991): 143–62.

26. Wendt, *Social Theory of International Politics*, 289.

27. Ibid.

28. OECD, *Towards Global Tax Co-operation* (Paris, 2000).

29. For the effectiveness of sanctions, or lack thereof see Gary Clyde Hufbauer, Jeffrey Schott, and Kimberly Ann Elliott, *Economic Sanctions Reconsidered* (Washington, D.C.: Institute for International Economics, 1990); M. Miyagawa, *Do Economic Sanctions Work?* (New York: St. Martin's, 1992); David Cortright and George Lopez, *Economic Sanctions: Panacea or Peacebuilding in a Post-Cold War World* (Boulder, Colo.: Westview. 1995); Robert Pape, "Why Economic Sanctions Do Not Work," *International Security* 27 (1997): 90–136; Richard Haass, ed., *Economic Sanctions and American Diplomacy* (Washington, D.C.: Council on Foreign Relations, 1998).

30. Author's phone interview, OECD, 19 September 2003.

31. William Gilmore, "The OECD, Harmful Tax Competition, and Tax Havens: Towards an Understanding of the International Legal Context," Commonwealth Secretariat Paper, March 2001; Roman Grynberg and Bridget Chilala, "WTO Compatibility of the OECD 'Defensive Measures' against 'Harmful Tax Competition,'" *Journal of World Investment and Trade* 2 (2001): 507–36; see also Hartman, "Coercing Co-operation from Offshore Financial Centers."

32. Grynberg and Chilala, "WTO Compatibility of the OECD 'Defensive Measures,'" 8.

33. Ibid., 15.

34. Gilmore, "The OECD, Harmful Tax Competition, and Tax Havens," 23–24.

35. Richard J. Hay, "Offshore Financial Centers and the Supranationals: Collision or Cohabitation?" *Chase Journal* 5 (2001): 1–18.

36. March and Olsen, *Rediscovering Institutions*, 22–26; Finnemore, *National Interests in International Society*, 29.

37. Author's interview, OECD, Paris, France, 9 July 2004; author's interview, ITIO, Bridgetown, Barbados, 27 August 2002; author's interview, PIF, Suva, Fiji, 22 November 2004; author's interview, ITIO, London, UK, 4 September 2002; author's interview, CFP, Sydney, Australia, 19 November 2005.

38. Author's phone interview, PIF, 27 September 2002.

39. Author's interview, ITIO, London, UK, 4 September 2002; author's interview, ITIO, Bridgetown, Barbados, 5 September 2005.

40. Lowtax, *Offshore as a Business Location.*

41. Author's interview, OECD, Canberra, Australia, 1 October 2002.

42. Commonwealth Secretariat, paper by Legal and Constitutional Affairs Division and Economic Affairs Division for Finance Ministers Meeting Malta (London, 2000).

43. Author's interview, ITIO, Bridgetown, Barbados, 27 August 2002; author's interview, PIF, by phone, 27 September 2002.

44. Author's interview, OECD, Canberra, Australia, 1 October 2002.

45. Author's interviews, ITIO, Bridgetown, Barbados, 27 August 2002; author's interview, CFP, by phone, 28 November 2002.

46. Pacific Islands Forum Secretariat, "Offshore Financial Centre Issues," Economic Minis-

ters' Meeting Rarotonga (Cook Islands, 2001); Pacific Islands Forum Secretariat, "International Tax and Investment Issues," Economic Ministers' Meeting, Port Vila (Vanuatu, 2002).

47. Linda Peter-Szerenyi, "The OECD's Artificial Approach to Tax Havens: Part 2," *Journal of International Taxation* 14 (2003): 13; "Australia Calls for OECD Leniency for Pacific Tax Offenders," Agence France Press, 1 March 2002.

48. Author's phone interview, U.S. Treasury, 26 September 2002.

49. Author's interview, OECD, Canberra, Australia, 1 October 2002.

50. Robert Goulder, "OECD Updates Tax Haven Blacklist, Claims Progress in Curing Harmful Tax Competition," *Tax Notes International,* 29 April 2002.

51. "CFR Catches Up with one of the OECD's Senior Tax Experts," *Cayman Financial Review,* issue 6, 2004.

52. Bruce Zagaris, "OECD Issues Progress Report on Harmful Tax Practices with New Deadline," *International Enforcement Law Reporter* 18 (2002).

53. Keith Taylor, "Harmful Tax Practices," *Tax Specialist* 5 (2001): 53.

54. Zagaris, "Issues Low Tax Countries Should Raise."

55. Author's interview, OECD, by phone, 19 September 2003; author's interview, OECD, Paris, France, 9 July 2004; author's interview, OECD, Paris, France, 2 May 2005; author's interview, European Commission, Brussels, Belgium, 5 November 2003.

56. Author's phone interview, CFP, 28 November 2002.

57. Author's phone interview, CFP, 28 November 2002; author's interview, CFP, Sydney, Australia, 19 November 2005.

58. Author's interview, ITIO, London, UK, 4 September 2002.

59. *Tax Notes International,* 9 January 2001.

60. Robert Novak, *Chicago Sun-Times,* 19 April 2001; *National Review,* 23 April 2001.

61. Letter from Dick Armey available at: www.freedomandprosperity.org/armey.pdf

62. *New Republic,* 21 August 2001; author's phone interview, CFP, 28 November 2002.

63. *Washington Times,* 10 May 2001.

64. Thomas Risse-Kappen, "Ideas Do Not Float Freely," *International Organization* 48 (1994): 185–214; Checkel, "Norms, Institutions, and National Identity in Contemporary Europe"; Checkel, "Why Comply?"

65. David Henderson, *The MAI Affair: A Story and Its Lessons,* International Economic Program, Royal Institute of International Affairs, 1999; Salskov-Iversen, Hansen, and Bislev, "Governmentality, Globalization, and Local Practice"; Katia Tieleman, "The Failure of the Multilateral Agreement on Investment (MAI) and the Absence of a Global Public Policy Network," Case Study Project for the UN Vision Project on Global Public Policy Networks, 2000; Fabrazio Pagani, "Peer Review: A Tool for Co-operation and Change: An Analysis of the OECD Working Method," OECD Directorate for Legal Affairs, September 2002; Tony Porter and Michael Webb, "The Role of the OECD in the Orchestration of Global Knowledge Networks," paper presentation, International Studies Association conference, Montreal, March 2004; Martin Marcussen, "The Organisation for Economic Co-operation and Development as Ideational Artist and Arbitrator: Dream or Reality?" in *Decision Making within International Organizations,* ed. Bob Reinalda and Bertjan Verbeek (London: Routledge, 2004), 90–106; Kerstin Martens, "(Ab)using International Organizations? States, the OECD, and Educational Policy," paper presentation, International Studies Association conference, Hawai'i, March 2005.

66. March and Olsen, *Rediscovering Institutions,* 23–24.

67. Niels Thygesen, "Peer Pressure as Part of Surveillance by International Institutions," discussion led by Niels Thygesen, Chairman Economic Development Review Committee, OECD, 4 June 2002, 4.

68. March and Olsen, *Rediscovering Institutions,* 30.

69. Steven Lukes, *Power: A Radical View* (London: Macmillan, 1975).

70. Author's interview, OECD, Canberra, Australia, 1 October 2002.

71. OECD 2003: www.oecd.org/dataoecd/2/38/20655083.pdf (76).

72. Toshiaki Katsushima, "Harmful Tax Competition," *Intertax* 27 (1999): 396–97; Barry Bracewell-Milnes, "Tax Competition: Harmful or Beneficial?" *Intertax* 27 (1999): 86–88.

73. Zagaris, "Tax Havens Beware," 126.

74. Richard J. Hay, "Beyond a Level Playing Field: Free(r) Trade in Financial Services?" paper presentation, Society of Trust and Estate Practitioners Conference, London, September 2005, 34.

75. Author's phone interview, U.S. Treasury, 26 September 2002; author's interview, ITIO, Bridgetown, Barbados, 27 August 2002; author's interview, ITIO, London, UK, 4 September 2002; author's interview, OECD, Canberra, Australia, 1 October 2002.

76. Thomas Bernaur and Vit Styrsky, "Adjustment or Voice? Corporate Responses to International Tax Competition," *European Journal of International Relations* (2004): 61–97.

77. Author's interviews, George Town, Cayman Islands, 19–20 January 2004; author's interview, Bridgetown, Barbados, 27 August 2002.

78. Andrew Rich, *Think Tanks, Public Policy, and the Politics of Expertise* (Cambridge: Cambridge University Press, 2004), 1.

79. Ibid., 206.

80. *Tax Notes International,* 9 January 2001.

81. http://www.freerepublic.com/forum/a3ac157ae3e92.htm.

82. Author's interview, CFP, by phone, 28 November 2002.

83. Author's interview, ITIO, London, UK, 4 September 2002.

84. Lowtax, "The Future of Offshore as a Business Location."

85. Author's interview, U.S. Treasury, by phone, 26 September 2002; author's interview, ITIO, Bridgetown, Barbados, 27 August 2002; author's interview, ITIO London, UK, 4 September 2002; author's interview, OECD, Canberra, Australia, 1 October 2002; author's interview, Commonwealth Secretariat, Sydney, Australia, 30 October 2002; author's interview, CFP, Sydney Australia, 19 November 2005.

86. Palan, *The Offshore World,* 3, 8–11, 72, 182, 190–191.

87. Finnemore, *National Interests in International Society.*

3. Hearts and Minds in the Global Arena

1. Gilligan, "Overview: Markets, Offshore Sovereignty, and Onshore Legitimacy"; Hay, "Offshore Financial Centers and the Supranationals"; Robert T. Kudrle, "Are There Two Sides to the Tax Haven Issue?" paper presented at International Studies Association conference, Portland, 2003; Spencer, "OECD Proposals on Harmful Tax Practices"; Webb, "Defining the Boundaries of Legitimate State Practice."

2. Mikhail Bakhtin, *Problems of Dostoevsky's Poetics,* trans. R. W. Rotsel (Ann Arbor: Ardis, 1973).

3. Samuels and Kolb, "The OECD Initiative"; David E. Spencer, "OECD Model Information Exchange Agreement: Part 1," *Journal of International Taxation* 13 (2002): 32–41; Spencer, "OECD Proposals on Harmful Tax Practices: An Update"; David E. Spencer, "Tax Information Exchange: Part 1" *Journal of International Taxation* 16 (2005) 18–27; Hay, "Offshore Financial Centers and the Supranationals"; Richard J. Hay, "A Level Playing Field for Tax Information Exchange?" *Tax Planning International Review* (September 2003): 2–12; Webb, "Defining the Boundaries of Legitimate State Practice"; Zagaris, "Tax Havens Beware"; "Issues Low Tax Countries Should Raise"; and "The Gatekeepers Initiative: An Emerging Challenge for International Financial Advisers," *Institutional Investor* (Summer 2001): 28–32. Terence Dwyer and Deborah Dwyer, "Transparency versus Privacy: Reflections on OECD Concepts of Unfair Tax Competition," *International Capital Markets Quarterly Review* 21 (2001); Kudrle, "Are There Two Sides to the Tax Haven Issue?"; Eden and Kudrle, "Tax Havens"; Eden, *Taxing Multinationals;* Gilligan, "Overview: Markets, Offshore Sovereignty, and Onshore Legitimacy"; Lowtax, "The Future of Offshore as a Business Location."

4. Zagaris, "Tax Havens Beware."

5. Author's interview, OECD, Paris, France, 9 July 2004.

6. OECD, "Ottawa Report of the Global Forum on Harmful Tax Practices" (Paris, 2003).

7. Wechsler, "Follow the Money."

8. See especially Kudrle, "Are There Two Sides to the Tax Haven Issue?" Eden and Kudrle, "Tax Havens"; Eden, *Taxing Multinationals;* Hay, "Offshore Financial Centers and the Supranationals"; Gilligan, "Overview: Markets, Offshore Sovereignty, and Onshore Legitimacy"; Webb, "Defining the Boundaries of Legitimate State Practice."

9. Kratochwil, *Rules, Norms, and Decisions*, 13, 36.

10. Jeffrey Owens, "Towards World Tax Co-operation," *OECD Observer* (2000): 88.

11. Frances M. Horner, "The OECD, Tax Competition, and the Future of Tax Reform," OECD Committee on Fiscal Affairs (Paris, 2000); Frances M. Horner, "Fighting for Balance, Not for Harmony," *International Tax Review* 11 (2000): 11–14.

12. OECD, *Harmful Tax Competition*, 10.

13. Jeffrey Owens, "Curbing Harmful Tax Practices," *OECD Observer* (1999): 13.

14. *Japan Economic Newswire*, 9 May 1998.

15. *International Money Marketing* (August 2000): 10.

16. Commonwealth Law Ministers and Attorney Generals of Small Commonwealth Jurisdictions, May 2000.

17. *International Money Marketing* (August 2000): 10.

18. Blum, Levi, Naylor, and Williams, *Financial Havens, Banking Secrecy, and Money Laundering;* OECD, *Improving Access to Bank Information for Tax Purposes* (Paris, 2000); OECD, *Improving Access to Bank Information for Tax Purposes: Progress Report* (Paris, 2003); OECD, *Access for Tax Authorities to Information Gathered by Anti-Money Laundering Authorities* (Paris, 2002); OECD, *Behind the Corporate Veil: Using Corporate Entities for Illicit Purposes* (Paris, 2001); see also Prem Sikka, "The Role of Offshore Financial Centres in Globalization," *Accounting Forum* 27 (2004): 365–99.

19. "International Bodies Turn Up the Heat on Tax," *Private Banker International* (July 1998).

20. *Private Banker International* (July 1998): 1.

21. Anand Giriharadas, "The Treasury Coddles Tax Cheats: Saved Havens," *New Republic*, 27 August 2001, 23.

22. "Mr. Bush and Dirty Money," *Le Monde* [English edition], 17 May 2001.

23. "OECD Clamps Down on Drug and Terror Havens," *Edinburgh Evening News*, 19 April 2002.

24. Owens, "Tax Administration in the New Millennium," 129.

25. Blum, Levi, Naylor, and Williams, *Financial Havens, Banking Secrecy, and Money Laundering*, 23.

26. Helleiner, "State Power and the Regulation of Illicit Activity in Global Finance" and "The Politics of Global Financial Reregulation"; Sica, "Cleaning the Laundry"; Hay, "Offshore Financial Centers and the Supranationals"; Wechsler, "Follow the Money"; Cueller, "The Tenuous Relationship between the Fight against Money Laundering and the Disruption of Criminal Finance"; Gilligan, "Overview: Markets, Offshore Sovereignty, and Onshore Legitimacy"; Rider, "Law: The War on Terror and Crime and the Offshore Centers: The 'New' Perspective."

27. Lynette Eastmond, presentation at the Caribbean Financial Action Task Force meeting, Port of Spain, Trinidad and Tobago, 5 December 2000; author's interview, ITIO, Bridgetown, Barbados, 27 August 2002; author's interview, ITIO, London, UK, 4 September 2002; author's phone interview, PIF, 27 September 2002; author's interview, PIF, Suva, Fiji, 22 November 2004; author's interviews, public and private sectors, Vaduz, Liechtenstein, 29 January 2004.

28. Author's interview, FATF, Paris, France, 8 July 2004.

29. U.S. State Department, Bureau for International Narcotics and Law Enforcement Affairs, "International Narcotics Control Strategy Report 2003," (Washington, D.C, 2004); Cueller, "The Tenuous Relationship between the Fight against Money Laundering and the Disruption of Crim-

inal Finance"; Rider, "Law: The War on Terror and Crime and the Offshore Centers: The 'New' Perspective."

30. Congressional Black Caucus letter, 14 March 2001, available at http://www.freerepublic .com/forum/a3ac157ae3e92.htm.

31. Carlyle Rogers, "The Case for International Tax Competition: A Caribbean Perspective," *Prosperitas* Center for Freedom and Prosperity 2 (2002): 1–6.

32. Seiichi Kondo, "Little Cheats Will Have to Repent: 'Unco-operative Tax Havens,'" *International Herald Tribune,* 10 May 2002.

33. Bruce Zagaris, "OECD Issues Progress Report on Harmful Tax Practices with New Deadline," *International Enforcement Law Reporter,* January 2002; "OECD Says Will Ensure That Blacklisted Tax Havens Do Not Attract Funds," *AFX European Focus,* 18 April 2002.

34. "U.S. Takes Credit for Dubious Haven 'Success,'" *International Tax Review,* May 2002.

35. "Liechtenstein Regrets OECD's 'Unco-operative' Tag," Agence France Presse, 18 April 2002.

36. *9/11 Investigations* (New York: Public Affairs, 2004).

37. Author's interview, FATF, Paris, France, 8 July 2004; author's interview, APG, by phone, 30 September 2002.

38. Author's interviews, UNODC, Vienna, Austria, 17 September 2004.

39. Author's interview, ITIO, Bridgetown, Barbados, 27 August 2002.

40. Author's interview, Liechtenstein Bankers' Association, Vaduz, Liechtenstein, 29 January 2004.

41. Horner, "Fighting for Balance, Not Harmony," 12–13.

42. OECD, *Towards Global Tax Co-operation,* 5; OECD, *Harmful Tax Competition,* 15.

43. Robert Goulder, "OECD Updates Tax Haven Blacklist, Claims Progress in Curbing Harmful Tax Competition," *Tax Notes International,* 26 (2002): 375–87.

44. Horner, "Fighting for Balance, Not for Harmony."

45. Owens, "Tax Administration in the New Millennium," 129; OECD, *Towards Global Tax Co-operation,* 5; OECD, *Harmful Tax Practices: 2001 Progress Report,* 4.

46. Blum, Levi, Naylor, and Williams, *Financial Havens, Banking Secrecy and Money Laundering,* 65.

47. OECD, *Harmful Tax Practices: 2001 Progress Report,* 4.

48. OECD, *Harmful Tax Competition,* 15.

49. Ibid., 73–78.

50. "CARICOM Urges OECD to Delay Tax Havens List," *Financial Times,* 16 March 2000.

51. "Pacific Tax Havens Set to Defy Close-Down Orders from Rich Club," Agence France Press, 29 April 2001; "Pacific Nations to Lobby U.S. on Protocol," New Zealand Press Association, 20 August 2001.

52. Papali'i Scanlan, Governor, Central Bank of Samoa, "Globalization and Tax Related Issues: What Are the Concerns?" Tokyo, 14–15 February 2001.

53. "Liechtenstein Regrets OECD 'Unco-operative' Tag," Agence France Presse, 18 April 2002.

54. Ronald Sanders, presentation at PricewaterhouseCoopers conference, Nassau, Bahamas, 7 September 2001.

55. Prime Minister, Owen Arthur, opening statement, OECD-Commonwealth conference, Shelbourne, Barbados, 8 January 2001.

56. Commonwealth Secretariat, "Finance Ministers Meeting, Malta, 19–21 September 2000," paper by Legal and Constitutional Affairs Division and Economic Affairs Division (London, 2000), 1.

57. Spencer, "OECD Proposals on Harmful Tax Practices: An Update"; Frances M. Horner, "Do We Need an International Tax Organization?" paper presentation, UN Ad Hoc Group of Experts on International Co-operation in Tax Matters, Geneva, Switzerland, 15–19 December 2003.

58. CARICOM secretariat, "Developed Countries' Gain, Caribbean Pain," *OECD Observer* (1 June 2000): 96.

59. William Lee Andrews, "A Mighty Stone for Davis's Sling: The International Space Company," *Regent Journal of International Law* 1 (2003): 5–32.

60. Christopher Fildes, "Tax Haven in Paris Sets Out to Bully a Microdot in the South Seas," *Spectator* (1 July 2000): 26.

61. United Nations press release, 28 May 1999.

62. "Small States, Big Money," *Economist,* 21 September 2000.

63. *AFX News,* 26 January 2001.

64. "Attack of the Global Tax Police," *National Review,* 23 April 2001.

65. Daniel J. Mitchell, "An OECD Proposal to Eliminate Tax Competition Would Mean Higher Tax and Less Privacy," Heritage Foundation Backgrounder No. 1395, September 18 (Washington, D.C., 2000), 2, 5.

66. *Financial Times,* 22 February 2000; Alex Easson, "Harmful Tax Competition: An Evaluation of the OECD Initiative," *Tax Notes International* 34 (2004): 1037–77.

67. Elster, *Nuts and Bolts for the Social Sciences,* 128; Risse, "Let's Argue!" 17; Frank Schimmelfennig, "The Community Trap: Liberal Norms, Rhetorical Action, and the Eastern Enlargement of the European Union," *International Organization* 55 (2001): 64.

68. ITIO/STEP, "Towards a Level Playing Field."

69. OECD, "Berlin Report of the Global Forum on Harmful Tax Practices" (Paris, 2004), 2.

70. "Caribbean Tax Havens Seek Refuge in the Arms of the WTO," *Financial Times,* 3 October 2000.

71. Owen Arthur, Shelbourne, Barbados, 8 January 2001.

72. "Tax Havens Seek OECD Resolution," *Financial Times,* 24 March 2000.

73. "U.S. Rep. Rangel, Other Blacks Attack OECD Tax Initiative," *Dow Jones Newswire,* 27 March 2001.

74. "Tax Talks End," PIF Press statement 0901, 19 February 2001.

75. "Caribbean: Is Anyone Listening to the Small Countries?" Inter Press Service, 10 December 1999.

76. George A. McCarthy, "Promoting a More Inclusive Dialogue," presentation, OECD-Commonwealth conference, Shelbourne, Barbados, 8–9 January 2001.

77. Goulder, "OECD Updates Tax Haven Blacklist."

78. Comment quoted in Gilligan, "Overview: Markets, Offshore Sovereignty, and Onshore Legitimacy," 22.

79. BIAC, "A Business View on Tax Competition" (June 1999): 1.

80. Ibid., 3.

81. Australian Chamber of Commerce and Industry, "Harmful Tax Competition," November 2000.

82. Paul O'Neill, "Confronting the OECD's 'Harmful' Tax Approach," *Washington Times,* 11 May 2001.

83. Author's interview, OECD, Canberra, Australia, 1 October 2002; author's phone interview, OECD, 19 September 2003; author's interview, OECD, Paris, France, 9 July 2004; author's interview, OECD, Paris, France, 2 May 2005.

84. Webb, "Defining the Boundaries of Legitimate State Practice."

85. "Globalization and Tax," *Economist,* 27 January 2000.

86. Author's interview, OECD, Paris, France, 9 July 2004.

87. OECD, *Harmful Tax Practices: 2001 Progress Report,* 5; "UK Welcomes OECD Report on the Elimination of Harmful Tax Practices," Inland Revenue Press Release, 14 November 2001.

88. OECD, *Harmful Tax Competition,* 73.

89. Ibid., 76–77.

90. "Marshall Islands Says That OECD Tax Haven List Has Little Credibility," Agence France Presse, 19 April 2002.

91. Pacific Islands Forum Secretariat, "Offshore Financial Centre Issues," Forum, Economic Ministers' Meeting, Rarotonga, Cook Islands, 19–20 June 2001.

92. *Financial Times,* 7 June 2001.

93. Georgina Stanley, "Conditional Success for OECD Harmful Tax Project," *International Tax Review*, 2 April 2002.

94. "Is the OECD Preparing Sanctions against Switzerland and Luxembourg or Not?" ITIO Press release, 18 April 2002.

95. Bruce Zagaris, "Consultations in Barbados on OECD Harmful Tax Competition Initiative Yield Progress," *International Enforcement Law Reporter* 17 (February 2001).

96. "Tax Havens," *Financial Times*, 14 May 2001.

97. Hay, "Offshore Financial Centers and the Supranationals" and "A Level Playing Field for Tax Information Exchange?"

98. Seiicho Kondo, "Little Cheats Will Have to Repent"; Gabriel Makhlouf, "OECD Releases the List of Unco-operative Tax Havens," OECD Press release, 18 April 2002.

99. Goulder, "OECD Updates Tax Haven Blacklist."

100. Ibid.

101. Kudrle, "Are There Two Sides to the Tax Haven Issue?"

102. The letters are available at www.oecd.org/document/39/0,2340,en.

103. "Tax Axe Swings on Treasure Islands," *Australian Financial Review*, 28 May 2002.

104. "U.S. Takes Credit for Dubious Tax Haven 'Success.'"

105. Goulder, "OECD Updates Tax Haven Blacklist."

106. Dwyer, "'Harmful' Tax Competition and the Future of Offshore Financial Centres, Such as Vanuatu"; Rawlings, "Laws, Liquidity, and Eurobonds."

107. Courtney Blackman, "Removing Barriers to Trade—Benefits to Both Parties?" paper presented to Society of Trust and Estate Practitioners conference, London, UK, 19 September 2005.

108. *Financial Times*, 1 July 1999.

109. Author's interviews, UNODC, Vienna, Austria, 17 September 2004; author's phone interview, APG, 30 September 2002.

110. U.S. Treasury Department, "U.S. Money Laundering Threat Assessment," December 2005, 47–48, and Government Accounting Office, "Company Formations: Minimal Ownership Information Is Collected and Available," April 2006, 55; see also Government Accounting Office, "Suspicious Banking Activities: Possible Money Laundering by U.S. Corporations Formed for Russian Entities"; Senator Levin, "U.S. Tax Shelter Industry: The Role of Accountants, Lawyers, and Financial Professionals"; ITIO, "Towards a Level Playing Field."

111. Thomas M. Franck, *The Power of Legitimacy among Nations* (New York: Oxford University Press, 1990).

112. Kratochwil, *Rules, Norms, and Decisions*, 13.

113. Elster, *The Cement of Society*, 51.

114. Finnemore, *National Interests in International Society*, 30.

115. Risse, "Let's Argue!" 18; Schimmelfennig, "The Community Trap," 64–65; Elster, *The Cement of Society*, 128; Thomas M. Franck, *Fairness in International Law and Institutions* (Oxford: Clarendon, 1995), 51; Shannon, "Norms Are What States Make of Them," 294.

116. McCarthy, "Promoting a More Inclusive Dialogue."

117. Goulder, "OECD Updates Tax Haven Blacklist."

118. Owens, "Curbing Harmful Tax Practices," 14.

119. "IFAs Have Nothing to Fear," *International Money Marketing* (August 2000): 10.

120. Horner, "Fighting for Balance, Not Harmony," 12.

121. Ibid., 13.

122. Zagaris, "Consultations in Barbados on OECD Harmful Tax Competition Initiative."

123. *Tax Notes International*, 28 May 2001.

124. Scanlan, "Globalization and Tax Related Issues."

125. "OECD Compromise Fails to Satisfy Havens," *International Tax Review*, December 2001.

126. CARICOM, "Developed Countries' Gain, Caribbean Pain."

127. "Tax Havens Get the Shakes Over 'Anti-' Report," *International Money Marketing*, 5 January 2000.

128. "Buoyant Market Shrugs Off Outside Pressures," *International Money Marketing,* 3 July 2001.

129. "A Taxing Issue," *Guardian,* 1 February 2001.

130. "Offshore Bankers Continue to Resist OECD Pressure," Inter Press Service, 4 March 2001.

131. "OECD Tax Haven Summit Opens with Accusations of Bad Faith," *AFX News,* 26 January 2001.

132. "OECD Threatens Sanctions to Force 'Tax Havens' into Line," *AFX News,* 28 February 2001.

133. "OECD Threatens Sanctions."

134. *Tax Notes International,* 1 March 2001.

135. "Antiguan Diplomat Dismayed by OECD Inflexibility at Taxation Meeting," *BBC Monitoring,* 31 January 2001.

136. PIF, "Regional Position Statement," Suva, Fiji, 28 April 2001.

137. Oxfam, *Tax Havens: Releasing the Hidden Billions for Poverty Eradication* (London: Oxfam, 2000).

138. Lynette Eastmond, presentation at the Caribbean Financial Action Task Force meeting, Port of Spain, Trinidad and Tobago, 5 December 2000.

139. Horner, "The OECD, Tax Competition, and the Future of Tax Reform," 7.

4. Reputation, Blacklisting, and the Tax Havens

1. CFP Memo, 16 June 2001.

2. Author's phone interview, CFP, 28 November 2002; author's interview, CFP, Melbourne, Australia, 14 November 2005.

3. "Interview with Jeffrey Owens," *Caymans Financial Review,* no. 6 (2004).

4. Kudrle and Eden, "The Campaign against Tax Havens"; Gilligan, "Overview: Markets, Offshore Sovereignty, and Onshore Legitimacy"; Webb, "Defining the Boundaries of Legitimate State Practice"; Rawlings, "Mobile People, Mobile Capital, and Tax Neutrality."

5. OECD, press release, Berlin Global Forum Meeting, June 2004; OECD, press release, Melbourne Global Forum Meeting, 16 November 2005.

6. Barnett, "Historical Sociology and Constructivism"; Michael N. Barnett and Martha Finnemore, "Politics, Power, and Pathologies in International Organizations," *International Organization* 53 (1999): 699–732; Michael N. Barnett and Martha Finnemore, *Rules for the World: International Organizations in Global Politics* (Ithaca: Cornell University Press, 2004); Adler, "Seizing the Middle Ground," 336.

7. Mykola Orlov, "The Concept of Tax Haven: A Legal Analysis," *Intertax* 32 (2004): 96.

8. OECD, *International Tax Avoidance and Tax Evasion,* 20–21.

9. Ibid., 22.

10. OECD, *Harmful Tax Competition,* 20.

11. Ibid., 21.

12. Katsushima, "Harmful Tax Competition"; Doggart, *Tax Havens and Their Uses,* 2002.

13. "Uncle Sam Upsets the Tax Shelter Game," *Financial Times,* 11 April 2002.

14. Gordon Report, "Tax Havens and Their use by U.S. Taxpayers," 26.

15. Palan, "Tax Havens and the Commercialization of State Sovereignty," 155; see also Palan and Abbott, *State Strategies in the Global Political Economy,* 168.

16. Marshall J. Langer, *Tax Notes International,* 18 December 2000.

17. Hay, "Offshore Financial Centers and the Supranationals"; ITIO/STEP, *Towards a Level Playing Field;* Bruce Zagaris, "Caribbean Jurisdictions Must 'Get Up, Stand Up' against U.S. Discriminatory Sanctions," *Tax Notes International,* 19 August 2002, 923–39. David E. Spencer and J. C. Sharman, "The OECD Proposals on Harmful Tax Practices: Status Report (Part 1)," *Jour-*

nal of International Taxation 17 (forthcoming, August 2006); David E. Spencer and J. C. Sharman, "The OECD Proposals on Harmful Tax Practices: Status Report (Part 2)," *Journal of International Taxation* 17 (forthcoming, September 2006).

18. As detailed in "The UK—A Tax Haven for Some?" *International Tax News*, 28 March 2002, 1–4.

19. "Viking Investment Companies—Denmark versus Sweden," *Offshore Investment* (June 2004): 31–34.

20. See also "Sweden: A New Tax Haven?" *Offshore Investment* (November 2003).

21. Spencer, "OECD Proposals on Harmful Tax Practices: An Update," 14; Frances M. Horner, "Do We Need an International Tax Organization?" paper presentation, UN Ad Hoc Group of Experts on International Cooperation in Tax Matters, Geneva, Switzerland, December 2003.

22. B. Persaud, "OECD Curbs on International Financial Centres: A Major Issue for Small States," paper presentation, Commonwealth Finance Ministers' Meeting, September, Malta, 2000.

23. Joel J. Karp, "Effect of the OECD and Similar Initiatives on Multilateral Operations," *International Tax Journal* 27 (Summer 2001): 12.

24. Tim Bennett, *International Initiatives Affecting Financial Havens*, 2nd ed. (London: Tolley, 2002).

25. Caroline Doggart, *Tax Havens and Their Uses*, 10th ed., 1.

26. *Tax Haven Reporter* (November 2002): 1.

27. Terence MacDonald, "Harmful Tax Regimes: An Isle of Man Perspective (Does the Isle of Man have a Global Financial Future?)" manuscript, University of Lancashire, 2004.

28. Available at: www.gov.im/ipa/iom/reputation.xml

29. "Special Report—The Bahamas," *Lloyd's List*, 10 March 2000.

30. Available at: www.pwc.com/aw/nfr 10/1/05

31. Tax news.com, 6 August 2003.

32. Tax news.com, 18 December 2001.

33. Hudson, "Placing Trust, Trusting Place"; Alan Hudson, "Offshores Onshore: New Regulatory Spaces and Real Historical Spaces in the Landscape of Global Money," in *Money and the Space Economy*, ed. R. Martin (Chichester: Wiley, 1999), 139–54.

34. Blum, Levi, Naylor, and Williams, *Financial Havens, Banking Secrecy, and Money Laundering*, 36.

35. Gilligan, "Overview: Markets, Offshore Sovereignty, and Onshore Legitimacy," 44.

36. Author's interviews, public and private sector, George Town, Cayman Islands, 19–20 January 2004; author's interviews, St. Helliers, Jersey, 26 January 2004; author's interviews, Road Town, British Virgin Islands, 20–21 January 2005; 31 January–2 February, public and private sectors, Douglas, Isle of Man, 2005.

37. Hudson, "Placing Trust, Trusting Place," 928; see also Hudson, "Offshores Onshore."

38. Palan and Abbott, *State Strategies in the Global Political Economy*, 178; Kudrle and Eden "The Campaign against Tax Havens."

39. Hudson, "Placing Trust, Trusting Place," 930.

40. Ibid., 929.

41. Available at www.bviifc.gov.vg/home.php

42. "Nations Wiped Off Haven List," *Miami Herald*, 19 April 2002.

43. "Getting the Regulatory System On Track," *International Monetary Marketing*, 6 December 2001.

44. Author's interview, St. John's, Antigua, 24 January 2005.

45. Author's interviews, Port Louis, Mauritius, 1 June 2005.

46. IMF, "Caribbean Offshore Financial Centers: Past, Present, and Possibilities for the Future," Working Paper no. 88, Western Hemisphere Department (Washington, D.C., 2002), 18.

47. Author's interview, FATF, Paris, France, 8 July 2004.

48. Author's interviews, public and private sectors, Avarua, Cook Islands, 14 June 2004; au-

thor's interviews, public and private sectors, George Town, Cayman Islands, 19–20 January 2004; author's interview, Oranjestad, Aruba, 27 January 2005; author's interviews, public and private sectors, Port Louis, Mauritius, 25 May and 1–2 June 2005; author's interview, Montserrat, 25 January 2005.

49. Available at www.startrust.co.uk

50. Author's interview, Liechtenstein Bankers' Association, Vaduz, Liechtenstein, 29 January 2004.

51. Drew Fudenberg and Jean Tirole, *Game Theory* (Cambridge, Mass.: MIT Press, 1991), 9; Robert Axelrod, *Evolution of Cooperation* (New York: Basic Books, 1984); Robert O. Keohane, *After Hegemony* (Princeton: Princeton University Press, 1984); Paul R. Milgrom, Douglass C. North, and Barry R. Weingast, "The Role of Institutions in the Revival of Trade: The Medieval Law Merchant, Private Judges, and Champagne Fairs," *Economics and Politics* 2 (1990): 1–23; Kenneth W. Abbott and Duncan Snidal, "Hard and Soft Law in International Governance," *International Organization* 54 (2000): 421–56; Anne Sartori, "The Might of the Pen: A Reputational Theory of Communication in International Disputes," *International Organization* 56 (2002): 129–50.

52. George Downs and M. Jones, "Reputation, Compliance, and International Law," *Journal of Legal Studies* 31 (2002): 96, 100.

53. Jonathan Mercer, *Reputation and International Politics* (Ithaca: Cornell University Press, 1996), 34.

54. Downs and Jones, "Reputation, Compliance, and International Law," 96.

55. Mercer, *Reputation and International Politics*, 6–26.

56. Abbott and Snidal, "Hard and Soft Law in International Governance"; Sartori, "The Might of the Pen"; Beth Simmons, "International Law and State Behavior: Commitment and Compliance in International Monetary Affairs," *American Political Science Review* 94 (2000): 819–36; Beth Simmons, "Capacity, Commitment, and Compliance: International Institutions and Territorial Disputes," *Journal of Conflict Resolution* 46 (2002): 829–56; Andrew T. Guzman, "A Compliance-Based Theory of International Law," *California Law Review* 90 (2002): 1823–88; Downs and Jones, "Reputation, Compliance, and International Law."

57. Kenneth A. Schultz, "The Politics of the Business Cycle," *British Journal of Political Science* 25 (1995): 79–100.

58. Joel Sobel, "A Theory of Credibility," *Review of Economic Studies*, 52 (1985): 557–74; Simmons, "International Law and State Behavior."

59. Downs and Jones, "Reputation, Compliance, and International Law," 95–96.

60. David M. Kreps, "Corporate Culture and Economic Theory," in *Perspectives on Positive Political Economy*, ed. James E. Alt and Kenneth A. Shepsle (Cambridge: Cambridge University Press, 1990), 116; see also Oliver Williamson, *The Economic Institutions of Capitalism* (New York: Free Press, 1985); Douglass C. North, *Institutions, Institutional Change, and Economic Performance* (Cambridge: Cambridge University Press, 1990).

61. Kreps, "Corporate Culture," 94.

62. Mercer, *Reputation and International Politics*.

63. *St. Kitts and Nevis Visitors' Guide, 2003–2004*.

64. *Frommer's Guide to the Caribbean 2004*, 539.

65. Adler, "Seizing the Middle Ground"; Adler, "Constructivism and International Relations"; Katzenstein, ed., *The Culture of National Security;* Kratochwil, *Rules, Norms, and Decisions;* Onuf, *A World of Our Making;* Price and Reus-Smit, "Dangerous Liaisons?"; John Gerard Ruggie, *Constructing the World Polity: Essays on International Institutionalization* (London: Routledge, 1998); Wendt, *Social Theory of International Politics*.

66. Wendt, *Social Theory of International Politics*, 160.

67. Ibid., 161–62.

68. Keohane, *After Hegemony*.

69. Author's interview, Australian Transaction Reports and Analysis Centre, Sydney, Australia, 1 November 2004.

70. Alice M. Tybout and Tim Calkins, eds., *Kellogg on Branding* (New York: John Wiley, 2005).

71. Cited in Peter van Ham, "Branding Territory: Inside the Wonderful Worlds of PR and IR Theory," *Millennium* 31 (2002): 253; see also Peter van Ham, "The Rise of the Brand State," *Foreign Affairs* 80 (2001).

72. van Ham, "Branding Territory," 263.

73. "The Future Is Aubergine for Former Shady Haven," *Guardian,* 2 July 2004.

74. Author's interview, Liechtenstein Bankers' Association, Vaduz, Liechtenstein, 29 January 2004.

75. *Cayman Financial Review* (2001; 2003).

76. Author's interviews, public and private sectors, George Town, Cayman Islands, 19–20 January 2004.

77. "Perception vs. Perception," *Cayman Financial Review,* Issue 6 (2004).

78. Author's interview, IMF, Washington, D.C., 28 June 2004.

79. Doggart, *A Study for the Implications of the HTI, FATF, and FSF for the Independent Caribbean,* 18.

80. Author's interviews, public and private sectors, Port Vila, Vanuatu, 4–5 March 2004.

81. Author's interviews, Pacific Financial Technical Assistance Center, Sydney, Australia, 10 November 2004; author's interview, PIF, Suva, Fiji, 22 November 2004; author's interview, Montserrat, 25 January 2005.

82. For example, www.bviifc.gov.vg/home.php; www.samoaofc.ws; www.nevisfinance.com

83. J. L. Austin, *How to Do Things with Words* (Oxford: Clarendon, 1975).

84. Kratochwil, *Rules, Norms, and Decisions;* Onuf, *A World of Our Making.*

85. Austin, *How to Do Things with Words,* 5.

86. See also Quentin Skinner, *Meaning in Context: Quentin Skinner and His Critics* (Cambridge: Cambridge University Press, 1988).

87. Austin, *How to Do Things with Words,* 151–63.

88. John Searle, *Expression and the Meaning: Studies in the Theory of Speech Acts* (Cambridge: Cambridge University Press, 1979), 17.

89. Ibid., 19.

90. Zagaris, "Issues Low Tax Countries Should Raise," 524.

91. K. G. Anthony Hill, "Tax Competition and International Cooperation," paper presentation, the Commonwealth Finance Ministers' Meeting, Malta, 19–21 September 2000.

92. McCarthy, "Promoting a More Inclusive Dialogue," 4–5.

93. Sharman and Rawlings, *Deconstructing National Tax Blacklists.*

94. Pacific Islands Forum Secretariat, "International Tax and Banking Issues," report, Economic Ministers' Meeting, Majuro, Marshall Islands, June 2003.

95. Author's interview, Basseterre, St. Kitts and Nevis, 22 January 2004; author's phone interview, ITIO, 1 March 2004.

96. Australian Tax Office, *Tax Havens and Tax Administration* (Canberra, 2004), 2.

97. Author's interview, Basseterre, St. Kitts and Nevis, 22 January 2004; author's interview, Oranjestad, Aruba, 27 January 2005; authors interviews, public and private sector, Douglas, Isle of Man, 31 January–2 February 2005; author's interviews, St. Hellier, Jersey, 26 January 2004; author's interview, PIF, Suva, Fiji, 22 November 2004. Richard J. Hay, "OECD Harmful Tax Practices Project—Where to from Here?" paper presentation, Society of Trust and Estate Practitioners Conference, London, UK 20 September 2005.

98. Jeffrey Owens, press conference, OECD Global Forum Meeting, Melbourne, Australia, 16 November 2005.

99. Marshall J. Langer, "Blacklists," paper presentation, International Tax Planners' Association, Cannes, France, 2002; Doggart, *Tax Havens and Their Uses,* 12–16; Sharman and Rawlings, *Deconstructing National Tax Blacklists.*

100. Langer, "Blacklists"; author's interviews, Road Town, British Virgin Islands, 20–21 January 2005; author's interview, public and private sectors, Bridgetown Barbados, 8 September 2005.

101. Author's interview, ITIO, London, 3 November 2003; author's interview, ITIO, Bridgetown, Barbados, 5 September 2005.

102. Zagaris, "Issues Low Tax Countries Should Raise."

103. "Liechtenstein Girds for Clash over Money Laundering," Reuters, 9 June 2000.

104. van Fossen, "Money Laundering, Global Financial Instability, and Tax Havens in the Pacific Islands."

105. Author's interviews, public and private sectors, George Town, Cayman Islands, 19–20 January 2004; author's interviews, public and private sectors, Douglas, Isle of Man, 31 January-2 February 2005; author's interviews, St. Hellier, Jersey, 26 January 2004. Kudrle and Eden, "The Campaign against Tax Havens."

106. Author's interviews, public and private sectors, George Town, Cayman Islands, 19–20 January 2004; author's interviews, public and private sectors, Port Louis, Mauritius, 25 May and 1–2 June 2005; author's interviews, public and private sectors, Douglas Isle of Man, 31 January-2 February 2005; author's interviews, St. Hellier, Jersey, 26 January 2004; Roberts, "Small Place, Big Money."

107. Author's interviews, St. Hellier, Jersey, 26 January 2004; author's interview, Avarua, Cook Islands, 14 June 2004; Zagaris, "Issues Low Tax Countries Should Raise."

108. Author's interviews, UNODC, Vienna, Austria, 17 September 2004.

109. Author's interviews, public and private sectors, George Town, Cayman Islands, 19–20 January 2004; author's interviews, public and private sectors, Douglas, Isle of Man, 31 January-2 February 2005; author's interviews, St. Hellier, Jersey, 26 January 2004; author's interview, ITIO, Bridgetown, Barbados, 27 August 2002.

110. Author's interviews, public and private sectors, Port Vila, Vanuatu, 4–5 March 2004; author's interviews, public and private sectors, Avarua, Cook Islands, 14–15 June 2004; author's phone interview, PIF, 27 September 2002; author's interview, PIF, Suva, Fiji 22 November 2004; author's interview, Pacific Islands Financial Technical Assistance Center, Sydney, Australia, 10 November 2004; author's interview, OECD, Paris, France, 9 July 2004.

111. Author's interviews, public and private sectors, Avarua, Cook Islands, 14–15 June 2004.

112. Author's interview, OECD, Paris, France, 9 July 2004.

113. Doggart, *Tax Havens and Their Uses.*

114. Author's interview, Basseterre, St. Kitts and Nevis, 22 January 2004; author's interviews, St. Hellier, Jersey, 26 January 2004; author's interviews, public and private sector, Vaduz, Liechtenstein, 29 January 2004; author's interviews, Road Town, British Virgin Islands, 20–21 January 2005; author's interview, public and private sectors, Port Vila, Vanuatu, 4–5 March 2004; author's interviews, public and private sectors, Avarua, Cook Islands, 14–15 June 2004; author's phone interview, PIF, 27 September 2002; author's interview, PIF, Suva, Fiji, 22 November 2004; author's interview, ITIO, Bridgetown, Barbados, 27 August 2002.

115. "Tax Havens Get the Shakes Over 'Anti-' Report," *International Money Marketing,* 5 January 2000.

116. Author's interview, Commonwealth, Sydney, Australia, 30 October 2002; author's interview, PIF, by phone, 27 September 2002.

117. Blum, Levi, Naylor, and Williams, *Financial Havens, Banking Secrecy, and Money Laundering.*

118. Author's interview, St. John's, Antigua, and Barbuda, 24 January 2005.

119. Wrenford Ferrance, "Case Study: Antigua and Barbuda," paper presentation, the Caribbean Financial Action Task Force Conference, Port of Spain, Trinidad and Tobago, 5 December 2000.

120. Ferrance, "Case Study: Antigua and Barbuda"; author's interview, St. John's, Antigua and Barbuda, 24 January 2005.

121. Author's interviews, public and private sector, George Town, Cayman Islands, 19–20 January 2004.

122. Author's interview, ITIO, Bridgetown, Barbados, 27 August 2002.

123. Author's interview, Oranjestad, Aruba, 27 January 2005; "EU Rules Rile Member State Territories," *International Tax Review,* 31 October 2004.

124. Author's interviews, public and private sectors, Douglas, Isle of Man, 31 January–2 February 2005.

125. Author's interview, Basseterre, St. Kitts and Nevis, 22 January 2004; author's interviews, Avarua, Cooks Islands, 14–15 June 2004; author's interviews, public and private sectors, Port Louis, Mauritius, 25 May and 1–2 June 2005; author's interview, Brades, Montserrat, 25 January 2005; author's interview, St. John's, Antigua and Barbuda, 24 January 2004; author's interview, ITIO, Bridgetown, Barbados, 27 August 2002.

126. Author's interview, former Cook Islands official.

127. Author's phone interview, PIF, 27 September 2002; author's interviews, public and private sector, Port Vila, Vanuatu, 4–5 March 2004; "Globalization and Tax," *Economist.*

128. Author's interviews, public and private sector, Port Vila, Vanuatu, 4–5 March 2004.

129. Reserve Bank of Vanuatu, Quarterly Economic Report (2004).

130. IMF, *Vanuatu: Selected Issues and Statistical Appendix* (Washington, D.C., 2005).

131. Reserve Bank of Vanuatu, Quarterly Economic Report (2004).

132. Author's interview, PIF, Suva, Fiji, 22 November 2004; Van Fossen, "Offshore Financial Centers and Internal Developments in the Pacific Islands."

133. *Liechtenstein Bankers' Association Annual Report 2003* (Vaduz), 4.

134. Author's interviews, public and private sectors, Vaduz, Liechtenstein, 29 January 2004.

135. Author's interview, Vaduz, Liechtenstein, 29 January 2004.

5. The OECD Rhetorically Entrapped

1. Risse, "Let's Argue!" 16.

2. Kowert and Legro, "Norms, Identity, and Their Limits," 491.

3. March and Olsen, *Rediscovering Institutions;* Onuf, *A World of Our Making;* Onuf, "Constructivism"; Ted Hopf, "The Promise of Constructivism in International Relations Theory," *International Security* 23 (1998): 171–200.

4. Timothy J. Sinclair, "The Infrastructure of Global Governance: Quasi-Regulatory Mechanisms, and the New Global Finance," *Global Governance* 7 (2001): 441–51.

5. Finnemore, *National Interests in International Society,* 16.

6. Wendt, *Social Theory of International Politics,* 170; see also Katzenstein, ed., *The Culture of National Security.*

7. Hopf, "The Promise of Constructivism in International Relations Theory," 190.

8. Barnett and Finnemore, *Rules for the World;* John M. Hobson and J. C. Sharman, "The Enduring Place of Hierarchy in World Politics: Tracing the Social Logics of Hierarchy and Political Change," *European Journal of International Relations* 11 (2005): 63–99.

9. Finnemore, *National Interests in International Society;* Martha Finnemore, "Norms Culture and World Politics: Insight from Sociology's Institutionalism," *International Organization* 50 (1996): 325–47; Barnett and Finnemore, "Politics, Power, and Pathologies in International Organizations"; Barnett and Finnemore, *Rules for the World;* Michael N. Barnett, "Historical Sociology and Constructivism: An Estranged Past, a Federated Future?" in *Historical Sociology of International Relations,* ed. Stephen Hobden and John M. Hobson (Cambridge: Cambridge University Press, 2002), 99–119; Michael N. Barnett, *Eyewitness To Genocide* (Ithaca: Cornell University Press, 2002); Boli and Thomas, "World Culture in the World Polity"; J. M. Meyer et al., "World Society and the Nation-State," *American Journal of Sociology* 103 (1997): 144–81; W. Richard Scott and John W. Meyer, eds., *Institutional Environment and Organizations: Structural Complexity and Individualism* (Thousand Oaks, Calif.: Sage, 1994); Jens Steffek, "The Legitimation of International Governance: A Discourse Approach," *European Journal of International Relations* 9 (2003): 249–75.

10. Steffek, "The Legitimation of International Governance," 262.

11. David Beetham, *Bureaucracy,* 2nd ed. (Buckingham: Open University Press, 1996), 53.

12. Max Weber, *Selections in Translation,* trans. Eric Matthews (Cambridge: Cambridge University Press, 1978); Beetham, *Bureaucracy,* 2nd ed.

13. Boli and Thomas, "World Culture in the World Polity."

14. Steffek, "The Legitimation of International Governance," 261.

15. Barnett and Finnemore, *Rules for the World,* 5, 23; Finnemore, *National Interests in International Society,* 125.

16. Craig N. Murphy, "Global Governance: Poorly Done and Poorly Understood," *International Affairs* 76 (2000): 799.

17. Salskov-Iversen, Hansen, and Bislev, "Governmentality, Globalization, and Local Practice," 19.

18. Marcussen, "The OECD in Search of a Role," 1.

19. Peter M. Haas, *Saving the Mediterranean: The Politics of International Environmental Cooperation* (New York: Columbia University Press, 1990); Haas, "Introduction"; Emanuel Adler and Peter M. Haas, "Conclusion: Epistemic Communities, World Order, and the Creation of a Reflective Research Program," *International Organization* 46 (1992): 367–91.

20. Braithwaite and Drahos, *Global Business Regulation,* 29.

21. Eden, *Taxing Multinationals;* Eden and Kudrle, "Tax Havens."

22. Marcussen, "The OECD in Search of a Role," 4–5.

23. Henderson, "The MAI Affair," 37.

24. Tieleman, "The Failure of the Multilateral Agreement on Investment," 17.

25. Quoted in Steffek, "The Legitimation of International Governance," 250.

26. Marcussen, "The OECD in Search of a Role," 4; see also Tieleman, "The Failure of the Multilateral Agreement on Investment," 6; Henderson, "The MAI Affair," 46.

27. Authors' interview, ITIO, Bridgetown, Barbados, 27 August 2002; author's interview, PIF, by phone, 27 September 2002.

28. March and Olsen, *Rediscovering Institutions.*

29. Braithwaite and Drahos, *Global Business Regulation;* Porter and Webb, "The Role of the OECD in the Orchestration of Global Knowledge Networks."

30. Eden, *Taxing Multinationals;* Kudrle and Eden, "The Campaign against Tax Havens"; Eden and Kudrle, "Tax Havens."

31. Kerstin Martens and Carolin Balzer, "Comparing Governance of International Organisations: The EU, the OECD and Educational Policy," paper presentation American Political Science Association Conference, September 2004.

32. "Bad Marks All Round," *Economist,* 11 December 2004.

33. Emanuel Adler, "The Seeds of Peaceful Change: The OSCE's Security-Community Building Model," in *Security Communities,* eds. Michael N. Barnett and Emanuel Adler (Cambridge: Cambridge University Press, 1998), 119–60.

34. Marcussen, "The OECD in Search of a Role," 20.

35. Marcussen, "The OECD in Search of a Role"; Marcussen, "The Organisation for Economic Co-operation and Development as Ideational Artist and Arbitrator"; Porter and Webb, "The Role of the OECD in the Orchestration of Global Knowledge Networks."

36. Pagani, "Peer Review," 7.

37. Helen Wallace, "The Institutional Setting: Five Variations on a Theme," in *Policy Making in the European Union,* ed. Helen Wallace and William Wallace, 4th ed. (Oxford: Oxford University Press, 2000), 32.

38. Pagani, "Peer Review," 5–6.

39. Ibid., 6.

40. Ibid., 10.

41. Porter and Webb, "The Role of the OECD in the Orchestration of Global Knowledge Networks," 19.

42. Barnett and Finnemore, "Politics, Power, and Pathologies in International Organizations," 708.

43. Barnett, "Historical Sociology and Constructivism," 113.

44. Finnemore, *National Interests in International Society,* 84.

45. Barnett, *Eyewitness to Genocide.*

46. Richard M. Price, "Transnational Civil Society and Advocacy in World Politics," *World Politics* 55 (2003): 588.

47. Sinclair, "The Infrastructure of Global Governance."

48. Porter and Webb, "The Role of the OECD in the Orchestration of Global Knowledge Networks," 7.

49. OECD, *Review of Agricultural Policy in Bulgaria* (Paris, 2000).

50. J. C. Sharman, "Agrarian Politics in Eastern Europe in the Shadow of EU Accession," *European Union Politics* 4 (2003): 447–72.

51. Author's interview, European Commission Delegation in Bulgaria, Sofia, Bulgaria, 24 March 2001; author's interview, Ministry of Agriculture, Blagoevgrad, Bulgaria, 23 April 2000; author's interview, European Commission Delegation in Romania, Bucharest, Romania, 27 October 2000; author's interview, European Commission Directorate General Enlargement, Brussels, Belgium, 4 April 2002.

52. Author's interviews, UNODC, Vienna, Austria, 17 September 2004.

53. J. C. Sharman, "The Effective Participation of Small States in International Financial Fora," Commonwealth Economic Papers 60 (London, 2004), 59–77.

54. Meyer et al., "World Society and the Nation-State," 157.

55. Ian Hurd, "Legitimacy and Authority in International Politics"; Ian Hurd, "Legitimacy, Power, and the Symbolic Life of the UN Security Council," *Global Governance* 8 (2002): 35–51; Tony Porter, "The Democratic Deficit in the Institutional Arrangements for Regulating Government Finance," *Global Governance* 7 (2001): 427–39.

56. Franck, *The Power of Legitimacy Among Nations;* Franck, *Fairness in International Law and Institutions.*

57. Quoted in Randall D. Germain, "Global Financial Governance and the Problem of Inclusion," *Global Governance* 7 (2001): 411–26.

58. Author's interview, IMF, Washington, D.C., 28 June 2004; author's interview, World Bank, Washington, D.C., 7 September 2004; author's interview, FATF, Paris, France, 8 July 2004; author's interviews, UNODC, Vienna, Austria, 17 September 2004; author's interview, UN Ad Hoc Committee of Tax Experts, New York, USA, 25 June 2004; author's phone interview, APG, 30 September 2002.

59. Horner, "Do We Need an International Tax Organization?"

60. *Observer,* 21 December 2003.

61. Author's interviews, Commonwealth, Sydney, Australia, 30 October 2002; author's interviews, public and private sector, Douglas, Isle of Man, 31 January–2 February 2005; author's interview, Road Town, British Virgin Islands, 20–21 January 2005; author's interviews, public and private sectors, George Town, Caymans Islands, 19–20 January 2004; author's interview, ITIO, Bridgetown, Barbados, 27 August 2002; author's interview, ITIO, London, UK, 4 September 2002.

62. See Gruber, *Ruling the World.*

63. Author's interview, UN Ad Hoc Committee of Tax Experts, New York, USA, 25 June 2004; Eden and Kudrle, "Tax Havens."

64. Spencer, "OECD Proposals on Harmful Tax Practices: An Update," 20; Zedillo Report 2001; Monterrey, Financing for Development, 2002.

65. Author's interviews, public and private sector, Douglas, Isle of Man, 31 January–2 February 2005; author's interview, OECD, Paris, France, 9 July 2004; Rawlings, "Mobile People, Mobile Capital, and Tax Neutrality"; IMF, *Offshore Financial Centers: The Role of the IMF;* IMF, *Offshore Financial Center Program: A Progress Report,* 2003; IMF, *Offshore Financial Center Program: A Progress Report,* 2005.

66. IMF, *Offshore Financial Centers: The Role of the IMF.*

67. Author's interview, IMF, Washington, D.C., 28 June 2004; IMF, Offshore Financial Center Program, 2003.

68. IMF, *Offshore Financial Centers: The Role of the IMF.*

69. Such as ITIO/STEP, *Towards a Level Playing Field*, 2002.

70. Author's interview, CFP, by phone, 28 November 2002.

71. CFP press release, 21 October 2004.

72. Jeffrey Owens, press conference, OECD Global Tax Forum Melbourne, Australia, 16 November 2005; author's interview, OECD, Paris, France, 9 July 2004.

73. Risse, "Let's Argue!"

74. Ibid., 22–23.

75. Schimmelfennig, "The Community Trap"; Frank Schimmelfennig, *The EU, NATO, and the Integration of Europe: Rules and Rhetoric* (Cambridge: Cambridge University Press, 2003).

76. Schimmelfennig, "The Community Trap," 48.

77. Ibid.

78. Braithwaite and Drahos, *Global Business Regulation*, 34.

79. Schimmelfennig, "The Community Trap," 62–63.

80. Marc W. Steinberg, "Tilting the Frame: Considerations on Collective Action Framing from a Discursive Turn," *Theory and Society* 27 (1998): 845–72; Marc W. Steinberg, "The Talk and Back Talk of Collective Action: A Dialogic Analysis of Repertoires of Discourse among Nineteenth-Century English Cotton Spinners," *American Journal of Sociology* 105 (1999): 736–80.

81. See James C. Scott, *Domination and the Arts of Resistance: Hidden Transcripts* (New Haven: Yale University Press, 1990).

82. James C. Scott, *Weapons of the Weak: Everyday Forms of Peasant Resistance* (New Haven: Yale University Press, 1985); Scott, *Domination and the Arts of Resistance.*

83. Scott, *Domination and the Arts of Resistance*, 98.

84. Ibid., 105–6.

85. Ibid., 103.

86. Author's interview, PIF, Suva, Fiji, 22 November 2004.

87. "Globalization and Tax," *Economist*, 27 January 2000.

88. Elster, *The Cement of Society;* Jon Elster, *Nuts and Bolts for the Social Sciences* (Cambridge: Cambridge University Press, 1989); Kratochwil, *Rules, Norms, and Decisions;* Franck, *The Power of Legitimacy Among Nations;* Franck, *Fairness in International Law and Institutions.*

89. Mlada Bukovansky, "Hypocrisy and Legitimacy: Agricultural Trade in the World Trade Organization," paper presentation, International Studies Association Conference, Hawaii. March 2005.

90. Author's interview, OECD, Canberra, Australia, 1 October 2002.

6. Implications for Policy and Theory

1. OECD, *The OECD's Project on Harmful Tax Practices: 2004 Progress Report* (Paris, 2004), 6–7.

2. Ibid., 10.

3. Getha Somasundaran, "New Zealand: Pearl of the Pacific," *Offshore Investment* (December 2004/January 2005): 28–29.

4. Richard J. Hay, "A Level Playing Field for Information Exchange?" *Tax Planning International Review* (September 2003); Hay, "The OECD Harmful Tax Practices Initiative—Where to Now?"; GAO, "Company Formations"; U.S. Treasury, "U.S. Money Laundering Threat Assessment."

5. Alex Easson, "Harmful Tax Competition: An Evaluation of the OECD Initiative," *Tax Notes International* 34 (2004): 1037–77.

6. Tim Bennet, *International Initiatives Affecting Financial Havens* (London: Tolley, 2002), 98.

7. Ibid.

8. Author's interview, Treasury Department, Canberra, Australia, 16 March 2005.

9. OECD, *2004 Progress Report,* 14.

10. Easson, "Harmful Tax Competition."

11. OECD, press release, Global Tax Forum, Melbourne, Australia, 16 November 2005; author's interview, OECD, Paris, France, 9 July 2004; author's interview, Paris, France, OECD, 2 May 2005.

12. Spencer and Sharman, "OECD Harmful Tax Practices Status Report (Part 1)"; Spencer and Sharman, "OECD Harmful Tax Practices Status Report (Part 2)."

13. See http://www.taxjustice.net/cms/front_content.php?idcat=15&lang=1&client=1.

14. See http://www.iosco.org/news/pdf/IOSCONEWS86.pdf.

15. Author's interviews, Road Town, British Virgin Islands, 20–21 January 2005; author's interviews, St. Hellier, Jersey, 26 January 2004; author's interview, public and private sectors, Avarua, Cook Islands, 14–15 June 2004; author's interview, Basseterre, St. Kitts and Nevis, 22 January 2004; author's interviews, public and private sectors, George Town, Cayman Islands, 19–20 January 2004; author's interviews, public and private sector, Vaduz, Liechtenstein, 29 January 2004; author's interviews, public and private sectors, Victoria, Seychelles, 30 May 2005.

16. Author's interview, FATF, Paris, France, 8 July 2004.

17. Author's phone interview, APG, 30 September 2002.

18. Author's interview, UNODC, Vienna, Austria, 17 September 2004.

19. Author's interview, IMF, Washington, D.C., 28 June 2004.

20. Author's interview, World Bank, Washington, D.C., 17 September 2004.

21. J. C. Sharman, "The Effective Participation of Small States in International Financial Fora," *Commonwealth Economic Papers* 60 (London, 2004): 59–77.

22. It must be emphasized, however, that interviewees almost always claimed to be optimistic about their own jurisdiction as an exception to the prevailing decline (author's interviews, public and private sectors, George Town, Cayman Islands, 19–20 January 2004; author's interviews, public and private sectors, Douglas, Isle of Man, 31 January–2 February 2005; author's interview, Brades, Montserrat, 25 January 2005; author's interviews, St. Hellier, Jersey, 26 January 2004; author's interviews, public and private sector, Port Louis, Mauritius, 25 May and 1–2 June 2005; author's interviews, Road Town, British Virgin Islands, 20–21 January 2005.

23. *Observer,* 27 March 2005.

24. Commonwealth/ITIO Workshop on Small States, London, UK, 5–6 June 2003.

25. Lloyd Gruber, *Ruling the World: World Politics and the Rise of Supranational Institutions* (Princeton: Princeton University Press, 2000).

26. Richard H. Steinberg, "In the Shadow of Law or Power? Consensus-Based Bargaining and Outcomes in the GATT/WTO," *International Organization* 56 (2002): 339–74.

27. John Braithwaite and Peter Drahos, *Global Business Regulation* (Cambridge: Cambridge University Press, 2000).

28. J. C. Sharman, "South Pacific Tax Havens: Leaders in the Race to the Bottom or Laggards in the Race to the Top?" *Accounting Forum* 29 (2005): 311–23.

29. William Vlcek, "Offshore Finance, Harmful Tax Competition, and Global Financial Flows," paper presentation, University of Sussex, 26 May 2005.

30. Akiko Hishikawa, "The Death of Tax Havens?" *Boston College International and Comparative Law Review* 25 (2002): 389–418.

31. Author's interviews, Road Town, British Virgin Islands, 20–21 January 2005; author's interviews, public and private sectors, Victoria, Seychelles, 30 May 2005; Sharman "South Pacific Tax Havens."

32. Charles A. Cain, "Old Man River, He Just Keeps Rolling," *Offshore Investment;* http://www.bifc.finance.gov.bn; http://www.botswanaifsc.com.

33. Author's interviews, Road Town, British Virgin Islands, 20–21 January 2005.

34. Lowtax, *The Future of Offshore as a Business Location.*

35. Reuven S. Avi-Yonah, "Globalization, Tax Competition, and the Fiscal Crisis of the Welfare State," *Harvard Law Review* 113 (2000): 1573.

36. Paul Krugman, *Pop Internationalism* (Cambridge, Mass.: MIT Press, 1996); Garrett, "Global Market and National Politics"; Linda Weiss, *The Myth of the Powerless State* (Ithaca: Cornell University Press, 1997); Radaelli, "Harmful Tax Competition in the EU"; Drezner, "Who Rules?"; Hobson, "Disappearing Taxes or 'Race to the Middle'?"

37. Gruber, *Ruling the World.*

38. Webb, "Defining the Boundaries of Legitimate State Practice."

39. Stephen D. Krasner, "State Power and the Structure of International Trade," *World Politics* 28 (1976).

40. March and Olsen, *Rediscovering Institutions,* 5.

41. For example, Elster, *The Cement of Society.*

42. Mikhail Bakhtin, *Problems of Dostoevsky's Poetics;* Mikhail Bakhtin, *The Dialogic Imagination: Four Essays,* trans. Caryl Emerson and Michael Holquist (Austin: University of Texas Press, 1981).

43. R. Adcock and David Collier, "Measurement Validity: A Shared Standard for Qualitative and Quantitative Research," *American Political Science Review* 95 (2000): 529–46.

44. BBC News monitoring, South Asia, 31 March 2005.

BIBLIOGRAPHY

9/11 Investigations. New York: Public Affairs, 2004.

Abbott, Kenneth W., and Duncan Snidal. "Hard and Soft Law in International Governance." *International Organization* 54 (2000): 421–56.

Abbott, Kenneth W., Robert O. Keohane, Andrew Moravcsik, Anne-Marie Slaughter, and Duncan Snidal. "The Concept of Legalization." *International Organization* 54 (2000): 401–19.

Adams, Charles. *For Good or Evil: The Impact of Taxes on the Course of Civilization.* Lanham, Md.: Madison, 1993.

Adcock, Robert, and David Collier. "Measurement Validity: A Shared Standard for Qualitative and Quantitative Research." *American Political Science Review* 95 (2001): 529–46.

Adler, Emanuel. "Seizing the Middle Ground: Constructivism in World Politics." *European Journal of International Relations* 3 (1997): 319–63.

———. "The Seeds of Peaceful Change: The OSCE's Security-Community Building Model." In *Security Communities,* edited by Michael N. Barnett and Emanuel Adler, 119–60. Cambridge: Cambridge University Press, 1998.

———. "Constructivism and International Relations." In *Handbook of International Relations,* edited by Walter Carlesnaes, Thomas Risse, and Beth A. Simmons, 95–118. London: Sage, 2002.

Adler, Emanuel, and Peter M. Haas. "Conclusion: Epistemic Communities, World Order, and the Creation of a Reflective Research Program." *International Organization* 46 (1992): 367–91.

Adorno, Theodor W., and Max Horkheimer. *Dialectic of Enlightenment.* London: Allen Lane, 1972.

Alexander, Kern. "Extraterritorial U.S. Banking Regulation and International Terrorism: The Patriot Act and the International Response." *Journal of International Banking Regulation* 3 (2002): 307–26.

191

Andrews, William Lee. "A Mighty Stone for Davis's Sling: The International Space Company." *Regent Journal of International Law* 1 (2003): 5–32.

Austin, J. L. *How to Do Things with Words.* Oxford: Clarendon, 1975.

Australian Tax Office. *Tax Havens and Tax Administration.* Canberra, 2004.

Avi-Yonah, Reuven S. "Globalization, Tax Competition, and the Fiscal Crisis of the Welfare State." *Harvard Law Review* 113 (2000): 1575–1676.

———. "Globalization and Tax Competition: Implications for Developing Countries." Paper presented at the UN Ad Hoc Group of Experts on International Co-operation in Tax Matters, Geneva, Switzerland. December 2003.

Axelrod, Robert. *Evolution of Co-operation.* New York: Basic Books, 1984.

Azzara, Thomas P. *Tax Havens of the World.* Nassau: New Providence, 2003.

Bachrach, Peter, and Morton S. Baratz. "The Two Faces of Power." *American Political Science Review* 56 (1962): 947–52.

Bakhtin, Mikhail. *Problems of Dostoevsky's Poetics.* Translated by R. W. Rotsel. Ann Arbor: Ardis, 1973.

———. *The Dialogic Imagination: Four Essays.* Translated by Caryl Emerson and Michael Holquist. Austin: University of Texas Press, 1981.

Barnett, Michael N. "Historical Sociology and Constructivism: An Estranged Past, A Federated Future?" In *Historical Sociology of International Relations,* edited by Stephen Hobden and John M. Hobson, 99–119. Cambridge: Cambridge University Press, 2002.

———. *Eyewitness To Genocide.* Ithaca: Cornell University Press, 2002.

Barnett, Michael N., and Martha Finnemore. "Politics, Power, and Pathologies in International Organizations." *International Organization* 53 (1999): 699–732.

———. *Rules for the World: International Organizations in Global Politics.* Ithaca: Cornell University Press, 2004.

Beetham, David. *Bureaucracy.* 2nd ed. Buckingham: Open University Press, 1996.

Bendelow, Edmund. "A Vehicle for Multi-Asset Structures." *Offshore Investment* 143 (2004): 20–22.

Bennett, Tim. *International Initiatives Affecting Financial Havens.* 2nd ed. London: Tolley, 2002.

Bernaur, Thomas, and Vit Styrsky. "Adjustment or Voice? Corporate Responses to International Tax Competition." *European Journal of International Relations* 10 (2004): 61–97.

Best, Jacqueline. *The Limits of Transparency.* Ithaca: Cornell University Press, 2005.

Biswas, Rajiv. "Global Competition in Offshore Business Services: Prospects for Developing Services." In *Commonwealth Heads of Government Reference Book,* 104–13. London: Commonwealth, 2001.

Blum, Jack A., Michael Levi, R. Thomas Naylor, and Phil Williams. *Financial Havens, Banking Secrecy, and Money Laundering.* Prepared for the United Nations Office for Drug Control and Crime Prevention, Washington, D.C., 1998.

Blyth, Mark. *Great Transformations.* Cambridge: Cambridge University Press, 2002.

Boli, John, and George M. Thomas. "World Culture in the World Polity: A Century of International Non-Governmental Organizations." *American Sociological Review* 62 (1997): 171–90.

Bracewell-Milnes, Barry. "Tax Competition: Harmful or Beneficial?" *Intertax* 27 (1999): 86–88.

Brady, Henry E., and David Collier, eds. *Rethinking Social Inquiry: Diverse Tools, Shared Standards.* New York: Rowman and Littlefield, 2004.

Braillard, Phillipe, Oleg Guy Betcher, and Graziano Lusenti. *Switzerland as a Financial Centre: Structures and Policies: A Comparison at the International Level.* Dordrecht: Kluwer, 1988.

Braithwaite, John, and Peter Drahos. *Global Business Regulation.* Cambridge: Cambridge University Press, 2000.

Brennan, Geoffrey, and James M. Buchanan. *The Power to Tax.* Cambridge: Cambridge University Press, 1990.

Bukovansky, Mlada. "Hypocrisy and Legitimacy: Agricultural Trade in the World Trade Organization." Paper presented at the International Studies Association Conference, Hawaii. March 2005.

Cable, James. *Gunboat Diplomacy, 1919–79: Political Applications of Limited Naval Force.* 2nd ed. Basingstoke: Macmillan, 1981.

———. *Gunboat Diplomacy, 1919–1991: Political Applications of Limited Naval Force.* 3rd ed. Basingstoke: Macmillan, 1998.

Campbell, John L. "Ideas, Politics, and Public Policy." *Annual Review of Sociology* 28 (2002): 21–38.

Checkel, Jeffrey T. "Norms, Institutions, and National Identity in Contemporary Europe." *International Studies Quarterly* 43 (1999): 83–114.

———. "Why Comply? Social Learning and European Identity Change." *International Organization* 55 (2001): 553–88.

Clarke, Colin, and Tony Payne, eds. *Politics, Security, and Development in Small States.* London: Allen and Unwin, 1987.

Cohen, Benjamin J. "International Finance." In *Handbook of International Relations,* edited by Walter Carlsnaes, Thomas Risse, and Beth A. Simmons, 429–47. London: Sage, 2002.

Commonwealth. "Finance Ministers Meeting Malta 19–21 September." Paper by the Legal and Constitutional Affairs Division and Economic Affairs Division, Commonwealth Secretariat. London, 2000.

Cordesman, Anthony, and Abraham Wagner. *The Lessons of Modern War IV: The Gulf War.* Boulder: Westview, 1996.

Cortright, David, and George Lopez. *Economic Sanctions: Panacea or Peacebuilding in a Post-Cold War World.* Boulder: Westview, 1995.

Council on Foreign Relations. "Terrorist Financing." October, Washington, D.C., 2002.

Crawford, Neta C. *Argument and Change in World Politics: Ethics, Decolonization, and Humanitarian Intervention.* Cambridge: Cambridge University Press, 2002.

Cueller, Mariano-Florentino. "The Tenuous Relationship between the Fight against Money Laundering and the Disruption of Criminal Finance." Research paper 64, Stanford Law School, 2003.

Diamond, Walter, and Dorothy Diamond. *Tax Havens of the World.* New York: Matthew Bender, 1998.

Doggart, Caroline. *Tax Havens and Their Uses.* 9th ed. London: Economist Intelligence Unit, 1997.

———. *A Study for the Implications of the HTI, FATF, and FSF for the Independent Caribbean.* Prepared for the UK Department for International Development (Caribbean), 2001.

———. *Tax Havens and Their Uses.* 10th ed. London: Economist Intelligence Unit, 2002.

Downs, George, and M. Jones. "Reputation, Compliance, and International Law." *Journal of Legal Studies* 31 (2002): 95–114.

Drezner, Daniel W. "Who Rules? The Regulation of Globalization." Paper presented at the American Political Science Association Conference, Boston, September 2002.

———. "The Hidden Hand of Economic Coercion." *International Organization* 57 (2003): 643–59.

Duusma, Jorri. *Fragmentation and the International Relations of Micro-States.* Cambridge: Cambridge University Press, 1996.

Dwyer, Terry. "'Harmful' Tax Competition and the Future of Offshore Financial Centres, Such as Vanuatu." *Pacific Economic Bulletin* 15 (2000): 48–69.

Dwyer, Terence, and Deborah Dwyer. "Transparency versus Privacy: Reflections on OECD Concepts of Unfair Tax Competition." Center for Freedom and Prosperity, November 2001.

Eden, Lorraine. *Taxing Multinationals: Transfer Pricing and Corporate Income Tax in North America.* Toronto: University of Toronto Press, 1998.

Eden, Lorraine, and Robert T. Kudrle. "Tax Havens: Renegade States in the International Tax Regime." *Law and Policy* 27 (2005): 100–127.

Eden, Lorraine, and Jun Li. "Tax Competition between Tax Havens and the OECD: Myth or Reality?" Paper presented at the International Studies Association conference, New Orleans, March 2002.

Elster, Jon. *Nuts and Bolts for the Social Sciences.* Cambridge: Cambridge University Press, 1989.

———. *The Cement of Society: A Study of Social Order.* Cambridge: Cambridge University Press, 1989.

English, William B. "Understanding the Costs of Sovereign Default: American States' Debts in the 1840s." *American Economic Review* 86 (1996): 259–75.

European Commission. "Taxation in the European Union." Discussion paper, ECOFIN, Brussels, 1996.

Fearon, James D. "Domestic Political Audiences and the Escalation of International Disputes." *American Political Science Review* 88 (1994): 577–92.

Fearon, James, and Alexander Wendt. "Rationalism vs. Constructivism: A Skeptical View." In *Handbook of International Relations,* edited by Walter Carlesnaes, Thomas Risse, and Beth A. Simmons, 52–72. London: Sage, 2002.

Financial Action Task Force. *Review to Identify Non-Co-operative Countries or Territories: Increasing the Worldwide Effectiveness of Anti–Money Laundering Measures.* 22 June 2000, Paris.

———. *Second Review to Identify Non-Co-operative Countries or Territories: Increasing the Worldwide Effectiveness of Anti–Money Laundering Measures.* 22 June 2001, Paris.

———. *Third Annual Review to Identify Non-Co-operative Countries or Territories.* Paris, 2002.

———. *Fifth Annual Review of Non-Co-operative Countries or Territories.* Paris, 2004.

Financial Stability Forum. "Financial Stability Forum Releases Grouping of Offshore Financial Centres to Assist in Setting Priorities for Assessment." Press release, Basel, 26 May 2000.

Finnemore, Martha. "Norms Culture and World Politics: Insight from Sociology's Institutionalism." *International Organization* 50 (1996): 325–47.

———. *National Interests in International Society.* Ithaca: Cornell University Press, 1996.

———. *The Purpose of Intervention: Changing Beliefs about the Use of Force.* Ithaca: Cornell University Press, 2003.

Finnemore, Martha, and Kathryn Sikkink. "International Norms Dynamics and Political Change." *International Organization* 52 (1998): 887–917.

———. "Taking Stock: The Constructivist Research Program in International Relations and Comparative Politics." *Annual Review of Political Science* 4 (2001): 391–416.

Finnemore, Martha, and Stephen J. Toope. "Alternatives to 'Legalization': Richer Views of Law and Politics." *International Organization* 3 (2001): 743–59.

Fischer, Markus. "Feudal Europe, 800–1300: Communal Discourse and Conflictual Practices." *International Organization* 46 (1992): 427–65.

Franck, Thomas M. *The Power of Legitimacy among Nations.* New York: Oxford University Press, 1990.

———. *Fairness in International Law and Institutions.* Oxford: Clarendon Press, 1995.

Friman, H. Richard, and Peter Andreas, eds. *The Illicit Global Economy and State Power.* Lanham, Md.: Rowman and Littlefield, 1999.

Fudenberg, Drew, and Jean Tirole. *Game Theory.* Cambridge MA: MIT Press, 1991.

Garrett, Geoffrey. "Global Market and National Politics: Collision Course or Virtuous Circle." *International Organization* 52 (1998): 787–825.

Germain, Randall D. "Global Financial Governance and the Problem of Inclusion." *Global Governance* 7 (2001): 411–26.

Gilligan, George P. "Whither or Wither the European Savings Tax Directive? A Case Study in the Political Economy of Taxation." *Journal of Financial Crime* 11 (2003): 56–72.

———. "Overview: Markets, Offshore Sovereignty, and Onshore Legitimacy." In *Global Financial Crime: Terrorism, Money Laundering, and Offshore Centres,* edited by Donato Masciandaro, 7–59. Aldershot: Ashgate, 2004.

Gilmore, William. "The OECD, Harmful Tax Competition, and Tax Havens: Towards an Understanding of the International Legal Context." Paper prepared for the Commonwealth Secretariat, March 2001.

Goldstein, Judith, and Robert O. Keohane, eds. *Ideas and Foreign Policy: Beliefs, Institutions, and Political Change.* Ithaca: Cornell University Press, 1993.

Goodspeed, Timothy J. "Tax Competition and Tax Structure in Open Federal Economies: Evidence from OECD Countries with Implications for the European Union." *European Economic Review* 46 (2002): 357–74.

Gordon Report. *Tax Havens and Their Use by U.S. Taxpayers.* Washington, D.C.: Internal Revenue Service, 1981.

Government Accounting Office. "Suspicious Banking Activities: Possible Money Laundering by U.S. Corporations formed for Russian Entities." Report for Permanent Subcommittee on Investigations, U.S. Senate, Washington, D.C., 2000.

———. "Company Formations: Minimal Ownership Information Is Collected and Available." Report for Permanent Subcommittee on Investigations., U.S. Senate, Washington, D.C., 2006.

Gruber, Lloyd. *Ruling the World: Power Politics and the Rise of Supranational Institutions.* Princeton: Princeton University Press, 2000.

Grubert, Harry, and John Mutti. "Do Taxes Influence Where U.S. Corporations Invest?" *National Tax Journal* 53 (2000): 825–39.

Grundy, Milton. *The World of International Tax Planning.* Cambridge: Cambridge University Press, 1984.

Grynberg, Roman, and Bridget Chilala. "WTO Compatibility of the OECD 'Defensive Measures' against 'Harmful Tax Competition.'" *Journal of World Investment and Trade* 2 (2001): 507–36.

Guzman, Andrew T. "A Compliance-Based Theory of International Law." *California Law Review* 90 (2002): 1823–88.

Haas, Peter M. *Saving the Mediterranean: The Politics of International Environmental Cooperation.* New York: Columbia University Press, 1990.

——. "Introduction: Epistemic Communities and International Policy Co-ordination." *International Organization* 46 (1992): 1–35.

Haass, Richard, ed. *Economic Sanctions and American Diplomacy.* Washington, D.C.: Council on Foreign Relations, 1998.

Hammer, Richard M., and Jeffrey Owens. "Promoting Tax Competition." Paper prepared for the Business Industry Advisory Council, Paris, 2000.

Hampton, Mark P. *The Offshore Interface: Tax Havens in the Global Economy.* Basingstoke: Macmillan, 1996.

Hampton, Mark P., and Jason P. Abbott, eds. *Offshore Finance Centers and Tax Havens: The Rise of Global Capital.* West Lafayette, Ind.: Purdue University Press, 1999.

Hampton, Mark P., and John Christensen. "Offshore Pariahs? Small Island Economies, Tax Havens, and the Re-configuration of Global Finance." *World Development* 30 (2002): 1657–73.

Handel, Michael. *Weak States in the International System.* London: Frank Cass, 1981.

Hartman, Benjamin R. "Coercing Co-operation from Offshore Financial Centers: Identity Co-incidence of International Obligations against Money-Laundering and Harmful Tax Competition." *Boston College International and Comparative Law Review* 24 (2001): 253–90.

Haufler, Andreas. *Taxation in a Global Economy.* Cambridge: Cambridge University Press, 2001.

Hay, Richard J. "Offshore Financial Centers and the Supranationals: Collision or Cohabitation?" *Chase Journal* 5 (2001): 1–18.

——. "A Level Playing Field for Tax Information Exchange?" *Tax Planning International Review* (September 2003): 1–12.

——. "Beyond a Level Playing Field: Free(r) Trade in Financial Services?" Paper presented at the Society of Trust and Estate Practitioners Conference, London, September 2005.

——. "OECD Harmful Tax Practices Project—Where to from Here?" Paper presented at the Society of Trust and Estate Practitioners Conference, London, September 2005.

Helleiner, Eric. "State Power and the Regulation of Illicit Activity in Global Finance." In *The Illicit Global Economy and State Power,* edited by R. Friman and P. Andreas, 53–90. New York: Rowman and Littlefield, 1999.

——. "The Politics of Global Financial Reregulation: Lessons from the Fight against Money Laundering." Working paper no. 15, Center for Economic Policy Analysis, New School, April 2000.

Henderson, David. "International Economic Competition Revisited." *Government and Opposition* 28, no. 1 (1993).

——. "The Role of the OECD in Liberalizing Trade and Capital Flows." *World Economy* 19 (1996): 11–27.

——. "The MAI Affair: A Story and Its Lessons." Working paper, International Economic Program, Royal Institute of International Affairs, 1999.

Hendrikson, Alan K. "Small States in World Politics: The International Political Position and Diplomatic Influence of the World's Growing Number of Small Countries." Paper presented at Conference on Small States, 17–19 February 1999, St. Lucia.

Hill, K. G. A. "Tax Competition and International Co-operation." Paper presented at the Commonwealth Finance Ministers' Meeting, 19–21 September 2000, Malta.

Hines, James R. "Lessons from Behavioral Responses to International Tax Competition." *National Tax Journal* 52 (1999): 305–22.

Hines, James R., and Eric M. Rice. "Fiscal Paradise: Foreign Tax Havens and American Business." *Quarterly Journal of Economics* 109 (1994): 149–82.

Hishikawa, Akiko. 2002. "The Death of Tax Havens?" *Boston College International and Comparative Law Review* 25 (2002): 389–418.

Hobson, John M. "Disappearing Taxes or 'Race to the Middle'? Fiscal Policy in the OECD." In *Bringing Domestic Actors Back In,* edited by Linda Weiss, 37–57. Cambridge: Cambridge University Press, 2003.

Hobson, John M., and J. C. Sharman. "The Enduring Place of Hierarchy in World Politics: Tracing the Social Logics of Hierarchy and Political Change." *European Journal of International Relations* 11 (2005): 63–99.

Holquist, Michael. *Dialogism: Bakhtin and His World.* London: Routledge, 1990.

Hopf, Ted. "The Promise of Constructivism in International Relations Theory." *International Security* 23 (1998): 171–200.

Horner, Frances M. "The OECD, Tax Competition, and the Future of Tax Reform." Paper prepared for the OECD Committee on Fiscal Affairs, Paris, 2000.

——. "Fighting for Balance, Not Harmony." *International Tax Review* 11 (2000): 11–14.

——. "Do We Need an International Tax Organization?" Paper presented at the UN Ad Hoc Group of Experts on International Co-operation in Tax Matters, 15–19 December 2003, Geneva, Switzerland.

Hudson, Alan C. "Placing Trust, Trusting Place: On the Social Construction of Offshore Financial Centres." *Political Geography* 17 (1998): 915–37.

——. "Offshores Onshore: New Regulatory Spaces and Real Historical Spaces in the Landscape of Global Money." In *Money and the Space Economy,* edited by R. Martin, 139–54. Chichester: Wiley. 1999.

——. "Offshoreness, Globalisation, and Sovereignty: A Post-Modern Geo-Political Sovereignty?" *Transactions of the Institute of British Geographers* 15 (2000): 269–83.

Hufbauer, Gary Clyde, Jeffrey Schott, and Kimberly Ann Elliott. *Economic Sanctions Reconsidered.* Washington, D.C.: Institute for International Economics, 1990.

Hurd, Ian. "Legitimacy and Authority in International Politics." *International Organization* 53 (1999): 379–408

——. "Legitimacy, Power, and the Symbolic Life of the UN Security Council." *Global Governance* 8 (2002): 35–51.

IMF. *Offshore Financial Centers: The Role of the IMF.* Washington, D.C., 2000.

——. *Offshore Financial Centers: IMF Background Paper.* Washington, D.C., 2000.

——. "Financial Sector Regulation: The Case of Small Pacific Island Countries." Policy Discussion Paper, Riechel Klaus-Walter, Asia Pacific Department, November 2001, Washington, D.C.

——. *Offshore Financial Center Program: A Progress Report.* Washington, D.C., 2002.

——. "Caribbean Offshore Financial Centers: Past, Present, and Possibilities for the Future." Working Paper 88, Western Hemisphere Department, Washington, D.C., 2002.

——. *Vanuatu: Assessment of the Supervision and Regulation of the Financial Sector.* Washington, D.C., 2003.

——. *Jersey: Assessment of the Supervision and Regulation of the Financial Sector.* Washington, D.C., 2003.

——. *Offshore Financial Center Program: A Progress Report.* Washington, D.C., 2003.

——. *Offshore Financial Center Program: A Progress Report.* Washington, D.C., 2005.

——. *Vanuatu: Selected Issues and Statistical Appendix.* Washington, D.C., 2005.

Inbar, Efraim, and Gabriel Sheffer. *The National Security of Small States in a Changing World.* London: Frank Cass, 1997.

ITIO. "Towards a Level Playing Field: Regulating Corporate Vehicles in Cross-Border Transactions." Report for the Society of Trust and Estate Practitioners and the ITIO conducted by Stikeman Elliott, London, 2002.

Jackson, Robert H. *Quasi-States: Sovereignty, International Relations, and the Third World.* Cambridge: Cambridge University Press, 1989.

Joachim, Jutta, and Bertjan Verbeek. "International Organisations and Policy Implementation: Pieces of the Puzzle." Paper presented at the ECPR Joint Sessions Workshop, Uppsala, Sweden, April 2004.

Johnson, James. "Is Talk Really Cheap? Prompting Conversation between Critical Theory and Rational Choice." *American Political Science Review.* 87 (1993): 74–86.

Karp, Joel J. "Effect of the OECD and Similar Initiatives on Multilateral Operations." *International Tax Journal* (2001): 12–22.

Katsushima, Toshiaki. "Harmful Tax Competition." *Intertax* 27 (1999): 396–97.

Katzenstein, Peter J., ed. *The Culture of National Security: Norms and Identity in World Politics.* New York: Columbia University Press, 1996.

Keohane, Robert O. *After Hegemony: Cooperation and Discord in the World Political Economy.* Princeton: Princeton University Press, 1984.

King, Gary, Robert O. Keohane, and Sidney Verba. 1994. *Designing Social Inquiry: Scientific Inference in Qualitative Research.* Princeton: Princeton University Press, 1994.

Klotz, Audie, and Cecilia Lynch. *Constructing Global Politics: Strategies for Research.* Ithaca: Cornell University Press, forthcoming.

Knight, W. Andy, and Randolph B. Persaud. "Subsidiarity, Regional Governance, and Caribbean Security." *Latin American Politics and Society* 43 (2001): 29–55.

Kowert, Paul, and Jeffrey Legro. "Norms, Identity, and Their Limits: A Theoretical Reprise." In *The Culture of National Security: Norms and Identity in World Politics,* edited by Peter J. Katzenstein, 451–97. New York: Columbia University Press, 1996.

Krasner, Stephan D. "State Power and the Structure of International Trade." *World Politics* 28 (1976): 317–47.

———. "Global Communications and National Power: Life on the Pareto Frontier." *World Politics* 43 (1991): 336–66.

———. *Sovereignty: Organized Hypocrisy.* Princeton: Princeton University Press, 1999.

Kratochwil, Friedrich V. *Rules, Norms, and Decisions: On the Conditions of Practical and Legal Reasoning in International Relations and Domestic Affairs.* Cambridge: Cambridge University Press, 1989.

———. "Constructing a New Orthodoxy? Wendt's 'Social Theory of International Politics' and the Constructivist Challenge." *Millennium* 29 (2000): 73–101.

Kreps, David. "Corporate Culture and Economy Theory." In *Perspectives on Positive Political Economy,* edited by James E. Alt and Kenneth A. Shepsle, 90–143. Cambridge: Cambridge University Press, 1990.

Krugman, Paul. *Pop Internationalism.* Cambridge, Mass.: MIT Press, 1996.

Kudrle, Robert T. "Are There Two Sides to the Tax Haven Issue?" Paper presented at the annual conference of the International Studies Association, Portland, 2003.

Kudrle, Robert T., and Lorraine Eden. "The Campaign against the Tax Havens: Will It Last? Will It Work?" *Stanford Journal of Law, Business, and Finance* 9 (2003): 37–68.

Lambert, Alan. "The Caribbean Anti-Money Laundering Programme." *Journal of Money Laundering Control* 5 (2001): 158–62.

Legro, Jeffrey W. "Which Norms Matter? Revisiting the 'Failure' of Internationalism." *International Organization* 51 (1997): 31–63.

Legro, Jeffrey W., and Andrew Moravcsik. "Is Anyone Still a Realist?" *International Security* 24 (1999): 5–55.

Levin, Carl. "U.S. Tax Shelter Industry: The Role of Accountants, Lawyers, and Financial Professionals." Report by Permanent Subcommittee on Investigations, U.S. Senate, Washington, D.C., 2003.

Levin, Mattias. "The Prospects for Offshore Financial Centres in Europe." Research report, Centre for European Policy Studies, August 2002.

Link, Bruce G., and Jo C. Phelan. "Conceptualizing Stigma." *Annual Review of Sociology* 27 (2001): 363–85.

Low-tax.com. *The Future of Offshore as a Business Location Following the EU/OECD/FATF/FSF Initiatives.* London: Lowtax, 2004.

Lukes, Steven. *Power: A Radical View.* London: Macmillan, 1975.

MacDonald, Terence. "Harmful Tax Regimes: An Isle of Man Perspective (Does the Isle of Man have a Global Financial Future?)." Master's thesis, University of Lancashire, 2004.

March, James G., and Johan P. Olsen. *Rediscovering Institutions: The Organizational Basis of Politics.* New York: Free Press, 1989.

———. "The Institutional Dynamics of International Political Order." *International Organization* 52 (1998): 943–70.

Marcuse, Herbert. *One-Dimensional Man.* Boston: Beacon, 1964.

Marcussen, Martin. "The OECD in Search of a Role: Playing the Ideas Game." Paper presented at ECPR 29th Joint Session of Workshops, April 2001, Grenoble, France.

———. "The Organisation for Economic Co-operation and Development as Ideational Artist and Arbitrator: Dream or Reality?" In *Decision Making within International Organizations,* edited by Bob Reinalda and Bertjan Verbeek, 90–106. London: Routledge, 2004.

Martens, Kerstin. "(Ab)using International Organisations? States, the OECD, and Educational Policy." Paper presented at the International Studies Association Conference, Hawaii, March 2005.

Martens, Kerstin, and Carolin Balzer. "Comparing Governance of International Organisations: The EU, the OECD, and Educational Policy." Paper presented at the American Political Science Association Conference, Chicago, September 2004.

Maurer, Bill. "Complex Subjects: Offshore Finance, Complexity Theory, and the Dispersal of the Modern." *Socialist Theory* 25 (1995): 113–45.

———. "Cyberspacial Sovereignties: Offshore Finance, Digital Cash, and the Limits of Liberalism." *Indiana Journal of Global Legal Studies* 5 (1998): 493–519.

Mearsheimer, John J. 1990. "Back to the Future: Instability in Europe after the Cold War." *International Security* (1990): 5–56.

———. "The False Promise of International Institutions." *International Security* 19 (1994/95): 329–39.

———. 2001. *The Tragedy of Great Power Politics.* New York: W. W. Norton.

Mercer, Jonathan. *Reputation and International Politics.* Ithaca: Cornell University Press, 1996.

Meyer, J. M., J. Boli, G. M. Thomas, and F. O. Ramirez. 1997. "World Society and the Nation-State." *American Journal of Sociology* 103 (1997): 144–81.

Michaels, Marnin, and Thomas A. O'Donnell. "The Death of Information Exchange Agreements." *Journal of International Taxation* 13 (2002): 8–45.

Milgrom Paul R., Douglass C. North, and Barry R. Weingast. "The Role of Institutions in the Revival of Trade: The Medieval Law Merchant, Private Judges, and Champagne Fairs." *Economics and Politics* 2 (1990): 1–23.

Milliken, Jennifer. "The Study of Discourse in International Relations: A Critique of Research Methods." *European Journal of International Relations* 5 (1999): 225–54.

Mitchell, Daniel J. "An OECD Proposal to Eliminate Tax Competition Would Mean Higher Tax and Less Privacy." Heritage Foundation Backgrounder No. 1395, 18 September 2000, Washington, D.C.

Mitchell, Ronald B. "Norms as Regulative Rules: Inducing Compliance through Logics of Appropriateness." Paper presented at American Political Science Association Conference, 30 August–2 September 2001, San Francisco.

Miyagawa, Makio. 1992. *Do Economic Sanctions Work?* New York: St. Martin's, 1992.

Morris, Gilbert N. M. O. "A Preliminary Briefing on Recent International Financial Regulations." Paper prepared for The Nassau Institute, Nassau, Bahamas, 2002.

Murphy, Craig N. "Global Governance: Poorly Done and Poorly Understood." *International Affairs* 76 (2000): 789–803.

Naylor, R. T. *Hot Money and the Politics of Debt.* New York: Simon and Schuster, 1987.

North, Douglass C. *Institutions, Institutional Change, and Economic Performance.* Cambridge: Cambridge University Press, 1990.

Oates, Wallace E. *Fiscal Federalism.* New York: Harcourt Brace Jovanovich, 1972.

OECD. *International Tax Avoidance and Tax Evasion: Four Related Studies.* Paris, 1987.

——. *Harmful Tax Competition—An Emerging Global Issue.* Paris, 1998.

——. *Review of Agricultural Policy in Bulgaria.* Paris, 2000.

——. *Towards Global Tax Co-operation.* Paris, 2000.

——. *Improving Access to Bank Information for Tax Purposes.* Paris, 2000.

——. *Corporate Tax Incentives and Foreign Direct Investment.* Paris, 2001.

——. *Harmful Tax Practices Progress Report.* Paris, 2001.

——. *Behind the Corporate Veil: Using Corporate Entities for Illicit Purposes.* Paris, 2001.

——. *Access for Tax Authorities to Information Gathered by Anti-Money Laundering Authorities.* Paris, 2002.

——. *Ottawa Report of the Global Forum on Harmful Tax Practices.* Paris, 2003.

——. *Improving Access to Bank Information for Tax Purposes: Progress Report.* Paris, 2003.

——. *The 2004 Progress Report: The OECD's Project on Harmful Tax Practices.* Paris, 2004.

——. *Report of the Level Playing Field Sub-Committee of the Global Forum on Harmful Tax Practices.* Paris, 2004.

——. *Berlin Report of the Global Forum on Harmful Tax Practices.* Paris, 2004.

Onuf, Nicholas. *A World of Our Making.* Columbia: University of South Carolina Press. 1989.

——. "Constructivism: A User's Manual." In *International Relations in a Constructed World,* edited by Vendulka Kulbakova, Nicholas Onuf, and Paul Kowert, 58–78. Armonk, N.Y.: M. E. Sharpe, 1998.

Orlov, Mykola. "The Concept of Tax Haven: A Legal Analysis." *Intertax* 32 (2004): 95–111.

Owens, Jeffrey. "Curbing Harmful Tax Practices." *OECD Observer* 215 (1999): 13–17.

——. "Towards World Tax Co-operation." *OECD Observer* 221 (2000): 88–91.

——. "Tax Administration in the New Millennium." *Intertax* 30 (2002): 125–30.

——. "OECD Updates Tax Haven Blacklist, Claims Progress in Curbing Harmful Tax Competition." *Tax Notes International* 29 (2002): 375–87.

Oxfam. *Tax Havens: Releasing the Hidden Billions for Poverty Eradication.* London, 2000.

Pacific Islands Forum Secretariat. "Offshore Financial Centre Issues." Paper presented at Economic Ministers' Meeting, Rarotonga, Cook Islands, 19–20 June 2001.

———. "International Tax and Investment Issues." Paper presented at Economic Ministers' Meeting, Port Vila, Vanuatu, 3–4 July 2002.

———. "International Tax and Banking Issues." Paper presented at Economic Ministers' Meeting, Majuro, Marshall Islands, 11–12 June 2003.

Pagani, Fabrazio. "Peer Review: A Tool for Co-operation and Change: An Analysis of the OECD Working Method." Paper prepared by Directorate for Legal Affairs for General Secretariat, 11 September 2002.

Palan, Ronen. "Trying to Have Your Cake and Eating It: How and Why the State System Has Created Offshore." *International Studies Quarterly* 42 (1998): 625–44.

———. "Offshore and the Structural Enablement of Sovereignty." In *Offshore Finance Centers and Tax Havens*, edited by Mark P. Hampton and Jason P. Abbott, 18–42. West Lafayette, Ind.: Ichor, 1999.

———. "Tax Havens and the Commercialization of State Sovereignty." *International Organization* 56 (2002): 151–76.

———. *The Offshore World: Sovereign Markets, Virtual Places, and Nomad Millionaires*. Ithaca: Cornell University Press, 2003.

Palan, Ronen, and Jason Abbott. *State Strategies in the Global Political Economy*. London: Pinter, 1996.

Pape, Robert. "Why Economic Sanctions Do Not Work." *International Security* 27 (1997): 90–136.

Parsons, Craig. *A Certain Idea of Europe*. Ithaca: Cornell University Press, 2003.

Payne, Anthony. "The Politics of Small State Security in the Pacific." *Journal of Commonwealth and Comparative Politics* 31 (1993): 103–32.

Persaud, B. "OECD Curbs on International Financial Centres: A Major Issue for Small States." Paper presented at the Commonwealth Finance Ministers' Meeting, Malta, 19–21 September 2000.

Picciotto, Sol. *International Business Taxation*. London: Quorum, 1992.

———. "Offshore: The State as Legal Fiction." In *Offshore Finance Centers and Tax Havens*, edited by Mark P. Hampton and Jason P. Abbott, 43–79. West Lafayette, Ind.: Ichor, 1999.

Porter, Tony. "The Democratic Deficit in the Institutional Arrangements for Regulating Government Finance." *Global Governance* 7 (2001): 427–39.

Porter, Tony, and Michael Webb. "The Role of the OECD in the Orchestration of Global Knowledge Networks." Paper presented at the International Studies Association Conference, Montreal, March 2004.

Preston, Ethan. "The USA PATRIOT Act: New Adventures in American Extraterritoriality." *Journal of Financial Crime* 10 (2002): 104–16.

Price, Richard M. "Transnational Civil Society and Advocacy in World Politics." *World Politics* 55 (2003): 578–605.

Price, Richard, and Christian Reus-Smit. "Dangerous Liaisons? Critical International Theory and Constructivism." *European Journal of International Relations* 4 (1998): 259–94.

Radaelli, Claudio M. "Game Theory and Institutional Entrepreneurship: Transfer Pricing and the Search for Co-ordination in International Tax Policy." *Policy Studies Journal* 26 (1998): 603–19.

———. "Harmful Tax Competition in the EU: Policy Narratives and Advocacy Coalitions." *Journal of Common Market Studies* 37 (1999): 661–82.

Ragin, Charles C., and Howard S. Becker, eds. *What Is a Case? Exploring the Foundations of Social Inquiry*. Cambridge: Cambridge University Press, 1992.

Rawlings, Gregory. "Laws, Liquidity, and Eurobonds: The Making of Vanuatu as a Tax Haven." *Journal of Pacific History* 39 (2004): 325–41.

———. "Mobile People, Mobile Capital, and Tax Neutrality: Sustaining a Market for Offshore Financial Centres." *Accounting Forum* 29 (2005): 289–310.

Rawlings, Gregory, and Valerie Braithwaite, eds. *Voices for Change: Australian Perspectives on Tax Administration.* Special issue of *Australian Journal of Social Issues* 38 (2003): 261–430.

Reinalda, Bob, and Bertjan Verbeek, eds. *Autonomous Decision Making by International Organisations.* London: Routledge, 1998.

———. *Decision Making within International Organizations.* London: Routledge, 2004.

Reserve Bank of Vanuatu. *Quarterly Economic Report.* Port Vila, 2004.

Reus-Smit, Christian, ed. *The Politics of International Law.* Cambridge: Cambridge University Press, 2004.

Rich, Andrew. *Think Tanks, Public Policy, and the Politics of Expertise.* Cambridge: Cambridge University Press, 2004.

Rider, Barry A. K. "Law: The War on Terror and Crime and the Offshore Centres: The "New" Perspective." In *Global Financial Crime: Terrorism, Money Laundering, and Offshore Centres,* edited by Donato Masciandaro, 61–95. Aldershot: Ashgate, 2004.

Risse-Kappen, Thomas. "Ideas Do Not Float Freely." *International Organization* 48 (1994): 185–214.

Risse, Thomas. "'Let's Argue!': Communicative Action in World Politics." *International Organization* 54 (2000): 1–39.

Roberts, Susan M. "Small Place, Big Money: The Cayman Islands and the International Financial System." *Economic Geography* 71 (1995): 237–56.

Rogers, Carlyle. "The Case for Tax Competition: A Caribbean Perspective." *Prosperitas* Centre for Freedom and Prosperity 2, no. 2 (2002): 1–6.

Ruggie, John Gerard. *Constructing the World Polity: Essays on International Institutionalization.* London: Routledge, 1998.

Salskov-Iversen, Dorte, Hans Krause Hansen, and Sven Bislev. "Governmentality, Globalization, and Local Practice: Transformations of a Hegemonic Discourse." Working paper, Department of Intercultural Communication and Management, Copenhagen Business School, Copenhagen, 1999.

Samuels, Leslie B., and Daniel C. Kolb. "The OECD Initiative: Harmful Tax Practices and Tax Havens." *Taxes* 79 (2001): 231–60.

Sartori, Anne. "The Might of the Pen: A Reputational Theory of Communication in International Disputes." *International Organization* 56 (2002): 129–50.

Schimmelfennig, Frank. "The Community Trap: Liberal Norms, Rhetorical Action, and the Eastern Enlargement of the European Union." *International Organization* 55 (2001): 47–80.

———. *The EU, NATO, and the Integration of Europe: Rules and Rhetoric.* Cambridge: Cambridge University Press, 2003.

Schultz, Kenneth A. "The Politics of the Business Cycle." *British Journal of Political Science* 25 (1995): 79–100.

Schwarcz, Stephen L. "Enron, and the Use and Abuse of Special Purpose Entities in Corporate Structures." Research Paper 28, Duke Law School, Durham. N.C., 2002.

Scott, James C. *Weapons of the Weak: Everyday Forms of Peasant Resistance.* New Haven: Yale University Press, 1985.

———. *Domination and the Arts of Resistance: Hidden Transcripts.* New Haven: Yale University Press, 1990.

Scott, W. Richard, and John W. Meyer, eds. *Institutional Environment and Organizations: Structural Complexity and Individualism.* Thousand Oaks, Calif.: Sage, 1994.

Seabrooke, Leonard. *The Social Sources of Financial Power.* Ithaca: Cornell University Press, 2006.

Searle, John. *Speech Acts: An Essay in the Philosophy of Language.* Cambridge: Cambridge University Press, 1969.

———. *Expression and Meaning: Studies in the Theory of Speech Acts.* Cambridge: Cambridge University Press, 1979.

Sending, Ole Jacob. "Constitution, Choice, and Change: Problems with the 'Logic of Appropriateness' and Its Use in Constructivist Theory." *European Journal of International Relations* 8 (2002): 443–70.

Shannon, Vaughn. P. "Norms Are What States Make of Them: The Political Psychology of Norm Violation." *International Studies Quarterly* 44 (2000): 293–316.

Sharman, J. C. "Agrarian Politics in Eastern Europe in the Shadow of EU Accession." *European Union Politics* 4 (2003): 447–72.

———. "The Effective Participation of Small States in International Financial Fora." *Commonwealth Economic Papers* (London) 60 (2004): 59–77.

———. "South Pacific Tax Havens: Leaders in the Race to the Bottom or Laggards in the Race to the Top?" *Accounting Forum* 29 (2005): 311–23.

Sharman, J. C., and Gregory Rawlings. "Deconstructing National Tax Blacklists." Report prepared for the Society of Trust and Estate Practitioners, 19 September 2005, London.

Sica, Vincent. "Cleaning the Laundry: States and the Monitoring of the Financial System." *Millennium* 29 (2000): 47–72.

Sikka, Prem. "The Role of Offshore Financial Centres in Globalization." *Accounting Forum* 27 (2003): 365–99.

Silets, Harvey M., and Michael C. Drew. "Offshore Asset Protection Trusts: Tax Planning or Tax Fraud?" *Journal of Money Laundering Control* 5 (2001): 9–15.

Simmons, Beth. "International Law and State Behavior: Commitment and Compliance in International Monetary Affairs." *American Political Science Review* 94 (2000): 819–36.

———. "Capacity, Commitment, and Compliance: International Institutions and Territorial Disputes." *Journal of Conflict Resolution* 46 (2002): 829–56.

Sinclair, Timothy J. "The Infrastructure of Global Governance: Quasi-Regulatory Mechanisms and the New Global Finance." *Global Governance* 7 (2001): 441–51.

Skinner, Quentin. *Meaning in Context: Quentin Skinner and His Critics.* Cambridge: Cambridge University Press, 1988.

Smith, Steve. "Historical Sociology and International Relations." In *Historical Sociology of International Relations,* edited by Stephen Hobden and John M. Hobson, 223–43. Cambridge: Cambridge University Press, 2002.

Sobel, Joel. "A Theory of Credibility." *Review of Economic Studies* 52 (1985): 557–74.

Spencer, David E. "OECD Model Information Exchange Agreement: Part 1." *Journal of International Taxation* 13 (2002): 32–41.

———. "OECD Model Information Exchange Agreement: Part 2." *Journal of International Taxation* 13 (2002): 1–19.

———. "EU Agrees at Last on Taxation of Savings." *Journal of International Taxation* 14 (2003): 4–18.

———. "OECD Proposals on Harmful Tax Practices: An Update." *Journal of International Taxation* 15 (2004): 8–23, 46–47.

———. "Tax Information Exchange: Part 1." *Journal of International Taxation* 16 (2005): 18–23.

———. "Tax Information Exchange: Part 2." *Journal of International Taxation* 16 (2005): 24–29, 57–58.

Spencer, David E., and J. C. Sharman. "The OECD Proposals on Harmful Tax Practices: Status Report (Part 1)." *Journal of International Taxation* 17 (forthcoming, August 2006).

———. "The OECD Proposals on Harmful Tax Practices: Status Report (Part 2)." *Journal of International Taxation* 17 (forthcoming, September 2006).

Steffek, Jens. "The Legitimation of International Governance: A Discourse Approach." *European Journal of International Relations* 9 (2003): 249–75.

Steinberg, Marc W. "Tilting the Frame: Considerations on Collective Action Framing from a Discursive Turn." *Theory and Society* 27 (1998): 845–72.

———. "The Talk and Back Talk of Collective Action: A Dialogic Analysis of Repertoires of Discourse among Nineteenth-Century English Cotton Spinners." *American Journal of Sociology* 105 (1999): 736–80.

Steinberg, Philip E., and Stephen D. McDowell. "Mutiny on the Bandwidth: The Semiotics of Statehood in the Internet Domain Name Registries of Pitcairn Island and Niue." *New Media and Society* 5 (2003): 47–67.

Steinberg, Richard H. "In the Shadow of Law or Power? Consensus-Based Bargaining and Outcomes in the GATT/WTO." *International Organization* 56 (2002): 339–74.

Stewart, Kenneth G., and Micheal C. Webb. "Tax Competition and Corporate Tax Rates." Working Paper 0301, Department of Economics, University of Victoria, 2003.

Stone, Diane. "Private Authority, Scholarly Legitimacy and Political Credibility." In *Non-State Actors and Authority in the State System*, edited by Richard A. Higgott, Geoffrey R. D. Underhill, and Andreas Bieler, 211–25. London: Routledge, 2000.

Stone, Diane, and Mark Garnett. "Introduction: Think Tanks, Policy Advice, and Governance." In *Think Tanks across Nations: A Comparative Approach*, edited by Diane Stone, Andrew Denham, and Mark Garnett, 1–21. Manchester: Manchester University Press, 1998.

Strang, David. "Anomaly and Commonplace in European Political Expansion: Realist and Institutional Accounts." *International Organization* 45 (1991): 143–62.

Sutton, Paul. "The Politics of Small State Security in the Caribbean." *Journal of Commonwealth and Comparative Politics* 31 (1993): 1–32.

Taylor, Keith. "Harmful Tax Practices." *Tax Specialist* 5 (2001): 50–53.

Thygesen, Niels. "Peer Pressure as Part of Surveillance by International Institutions." Discussion led by Niels Thygesen, Chairman Economic Development Review Committee, OECD, 4 June 2002.

Tiebout, Charles M. "A Pure Theory of Local Expenditures." *Journal of Political Economy* 64 (1956): 416–24.

Tieleman, Katia. "The Failure of the Multilateral Agreement on Investment (MAI) and the Absence of a Global Public Policy Network." Case Study for the UN Vision Project on Global Public Policy Networks, Washington, D.C., 2000.

Tierney, Michael, and Catherine Weaver, 2004. "Principals and Principles? The Possibilities for Theoretical Synthesis and Scientific Progress in the Study of International Organizations." Paper presented at the Conference on Theoretical Synthesis in the Study of International Organizations, Washington, D.C., 6–7 February 2004.

Tilly, Charles. *Coercion, Capital, and European States, AD 990–1992*. Oxford: Blackwell, 1992.

Tolley's Tax Havens. 2nd ed. London: Tolley's, 1990.

Tolley's Tax Havens. 3rd ed. London: Tolley's, 2000.

Trident Practical Guide to International Trusts. 4th ed. London: Chancellor, 2004.

Tybout, Alice M., and Tim Calkins, eds. *Kellogg on Branding.* New York: John Wiley, 2005.

United Nations Office on Drugs and Crime Prevention. "UN Offshore Forum: A United Nations Global Initiative to Prevent the Misuse of the Offshore Financial Sector for the Purpose of Laundering Criminal Proceeds." Paper presented at George Town, Cayman Islands, 30–31 March 2000.

——. Anti-Money Laundering Unit. Global Program against Money Laundering Publications, Vienna, 2004. Compact Disc.

U.S. Treasury. "Corporate Inversion Transactions: Tax Policy Implications." Office of Tax Policy, Washington, D.C., May 2002.

——. "U.S. Money Laundering Threat Assessment." Washington, D.C., December 2005.

van Fossen, Anthony B. *The International Political Economy of Pacific Islands Flags of Convenience.* Centre for the Study of Australia-Asia Relations, Griffith University, 1992.

——. "Norfolk Island and Its Tax Haven." *Australian Journal of Politics and History* 48 (2002): 209–26.

——. "Risk Havens: Offshore Financial Centres, Insurance Cycles, the 'Litigation Explosion' and a Social Democratic Alternative." *Social and Legal Studies* 11 (2002): 503–21.

——. "Offshore Financial Centres and Internal Developments in the Pacific Islands." *Pacific Economic Bulletin* 17 (2002): 38–62.

——. "Money Laundering, Global Financial Instability, and Tax Havens in the Pacific Islands." *Contemporary Pacific* 15 (2003): 237–75.

van Ham, Peter. "The Rise of the Brand State." *Foreign Affairs* 80 (2001): 2–7.

——. "Branding Territory: Inside the Wonderful Worlds of PR and IR Theory." *Millennium* 31 (2002): 249–69.

Vlcek, William. "Offshore Finance, Harmful Tax Competition, and Global Capital Flows." Paper presented at the University of Sussex Center for Global Political Economy, 26 May 2005.

Waltz, Kenneth N. *Theory of International Politics.* Reading: Addison, 1979.

Webb, Michael C. 2004. "Defining the Boundaries of Legitimate State Practice: Norms, Transnational Actors, and the OECD's Project on Harmful Tax Competition." *Review of International Political Economy* 11 (2004): 787–827.

Weber, Max. *Selections in Translation.* Translated by Eric Matthews. Cambridge: Cambridge University Press, 1978.

Wechsler, William F. "Follow the Money." *Foreign Affairs* 80 (2001): 40–57.

Weiss, Linda. *The Myth of the Powerless State.* Ithaca: Cornell University Press, 1997.

Wendt, Alexander. *Social Theory of International Politics.* Cambridge: Cambridge University Press, 1999.

Williamson, Oliver. *The Economic Institutions of Capitalism.* New York: Free Press, 1985.

Wilson, John Douglas. "Theories of Tax Competition." *National Tax Journal* (June 1999): 269–303.

Winters, Alan L., and Pedro M. G. Martins. "Beautiful but Costly: An Analysis of the Operating Cost of Doing Business in Small Economies." Commonwealth Secretariat and UNCTAD, New York and Geneva, 2003.

World Bank/Commonwealth. "Report of the Joint Task Force on the Vulnerability of Small States." Washington, D.C. 1995.

Zagaris, Bruce. 2001. "Issues Low Tax Regimes Should Raise When Negotiating with the OECD." *Tax Notes International* 29 (2001): 523–32.

——. "Exchange of Tax Information Policies at the Millennium: Balancing Enforcement with Due Process and International Human Rights." Paper presented at the International Platform Association Annual Convention, Washington, D.C., 8–12 August 2001.

——. "Tax Havens Beware, Fiscal Transparency, and What Else? The Rules Are Changing, and It's Crazy Out There!" *Journal of International Banking Regulation* 3 (2001): 111–44.

——. "The Gatekeepers Initiative: An Emerging Challenge for International Financial Advisors." *Institutional Investor* (Summer 2001): 28–32.

INDEX

Alaska, 25
American Enterprise Institute, 61, 67, 141
Andorra, 22, 31, 75, 78, 120
Anguilla, 18, 23
Anjouan, 158
anti-money laundering. *See* money laundering
Antigua and Barbuda, 23, 60–61, 84–85, 109, 114, 121, 124, 154. *See also* Sanders, Sir Ronald
Armey, Dick, 61
Aruba, 18, 31, 107, 123, 153, 158
Asia-Pacific Group on Money Laundering, 33, 81, 156
asset protection trust. *See* trusts
Austin, J. L., 13, 102, 115
Australia, 10, 16, 59–61, 88–89, 117, 152
Austria, 17–18, 29–31, 34, 66, 78, 90

Bahamas, 22, 55, 59, 74, 107–9, 124, 153
Bahrain, 22
bank secrecy, 22, 25, 30–32, 34, 47, 77–79, 81, 90, 93, 120, 154. *See also* tax information exchange
Barbados, 16, 26, 59–60, 66, 72, 74, 93, 98, 124, 139, 141; January 2001 meeting in, 16, 59–62, 73, 96, 98; Prime Minister Owen Arthur,16, 58–59, 74, 84, 87
Basel 2 banking accords, 157
bearer shares, 25

Belgium, 17–18, 29, 31, 34, 66, 90, 92
Belize, 21
Bermuda, 18, 22–23, 26, 66, 72–73, 85, 123, 158
Black Caucus, Congressional, 62, 67–68, 80, 87
blacklist, 9–10, 13, 35–36, 74–75, 96, 102, 114, 116–17, 148; Financial Action Task Force Non-Co-operative Countries and Territories, 33–34, 113, 116, 122, 125, 155–56; and Financial Stability Forum, 35, 116, 122, 140; International Organization of Securities Commissions, 155; national lists, 117–18, 121, 123; OECD tax haven, 15–16, 45–46, 58, 103, 113, 117–26; OECD uncooperative tax haven, 15, 17, 46, 73, 103, 113, 117, 120–26. *See also* top-down regulation
Botswana, 158
British Virgin Islands, 18, 23, 59, 85, 108–9, 113, 154, 158
Brunei, 22, 158
Bush, George W., administration, 10, 12, 17, 51, 60–62, 67–69. *See also* United States
Business Industry Advisory Council, 41, 65, 72–73, 88

Canada, 10, 16, 58, 60–61, 152
captive insurance. *See* insurance
Caribbean Association of Regulators of International Business, 58

207